S0-EKM-038

LAN Times Guide to Building
High-Speed Networks

Robert Lin
447-0393
OSSD, SNSL,
LAN LINKS,
Hewlett-Packard

LAN Times Guide to Building High-Speed Networks

Terè Parnell

Osborne **McGraw-Hill**

Berkeley New York St. Louis San Francisco
Auckland Bogotá Hamburg London Madrid
Mexico City Milan Montreal New Delhi Panama City
Paris São Paulo Singapore Sydney
Tokyo Toronto

Osborne **McGraw-Hill**
2600 Tenth Street
Berkeley, California 94710
U.S.A.

For information on translations or book distributors outside the U.S.A., or to arrange bulk purchase discounts for sales promotions, premiums, or fundraisers, please contact Osborne **McGraw-Hill** at the above address.

LAN Times Guide to Building High-Speed Networks

Copyright © 1996 by McGraw-Hill, Inc. All rights reserved. Printed in the United States of America. Except as permitted under the Copyright Act of 1976, no part of this publication may be reproduced or distributed in any form or by any means, or stored in a database or retrieval system, without the prior written permission of the publisher, with the exception that the program listings may be entered, stored, and executed in a computer system, but they may not be reproduced for publication.

234567890 DOC 99876

ISBN 0-07-882200-9

Acquisitions Editor	**Computer Designer**
Wendy Rinaldi	Richard Whitaker
Technical Reviewer	**Illustrators**
Eric Bowden	Leslee Bassin
	Loretta Au
Project Editor	
Mark Karmendy	**Series Design**
	Jani Beckwith
Copy Editor	
Dennis Weaver	**Quality Control Specialist**
	Joe Scuderi
Proofreader	
Stefany Otis	**Cover Design**
	Em Design

Information has been obtained by Osborne **McGraw-Hill** from sources believed to be reliable. However, because of the possibility of human or mechanical error by our sources, Osborne **McGraw-Hill**, or others, Osborne **McGraw-Hill** does not guarantee the accuracy, adequacy, or completeness of any information and is not responsible for any errors or omissions or the results obtained from use of such information.

To Ken Freo, a model of ability, dedication, and integrity

About the Author...

Terè Parnell is the Testing Center manager for *LAN Times* magazine. She has over 15 years of experience in information services as a programmer/analyst, network engineer, and manager. Terè holds an MSEE from George Washington University and an MBA from Southern Methodist University.

Contents at a Glance

Part III   How to Speed Up: Wide Area Solutions

Part IV   Caution: Network Construction Ahead

Part V   Appendixes

Contents

Part III

How to Speed Up: Wide Area Solutions

Part IV

Caution: Network Construction Ahead

Part V
Appendixes

Acknowledgments

Writing this book involved a lot more than I imagined it would. I suppose most authors feel this way, which explains why most books contain an "Acknowledgments" section thanking the people who helped the authors survive the project. I certainly have a lot of people to whom I owe a great deal.

First, I'd like to thank my good friends, Eric Bowden and Bradley Shimmin, for encouraging me to write this book and literally making it happen. Without them, I never would have begun the project. Eric also acted as my technical editor, and I want to thank him for his insight, guidance, and meticulous work.

Wendy Rinaldi of Osborne/McGraw-Hill should receive some sort of award for dealing with me while I was writing this book. She remained serene during my worst temper tantrums, and perfectly organized no matter how chaotic things became. Actually, I owe a debt of gratitude to the entire team at Osborne—especially Heidi Poulin and Mark Karmendy, who took a few direct hits on particularly stressful days.

Jody Balfour, Ken Freo, David Harmon, Linda Manson, Alicia North, Travis Peebles, Diana Price, Cathy Reese, Ralph Spears, Debi Tate, and Wanda Watson, my friends and former colleagues in the Information Services department at Thompson & Knight in Dallas, along with John Ozols of Computer Language Research, Inc., in Carollton, Texas, deserve a great deal of credit for "reality-checking" this book. When it comes to networking technology, they are experts in practical implementation, as well as in anticipating the unforeseeable. I have benefited immeasurably from their expertise and honest criticism.

If there are any useful management insights in this book, they are the result of my association with John Beebe, Executive Director of Thompson & Knight in Dallas. John has a very inclusive managerial style, characterized by prudence, impartiality, and communication. Following his advice and example has made many formidable networking projects go smoothly for me, and I hope I have imparted enough of the essence of his managerial perspective to help you craft successful implementations.

I want to give many thanks—and all my love—to my children, Claire and Elliot, for dealing with a stressed-out mother with grace and charm—and for not burning or detonating anything of significant value while I was distracted by working on this book.

A note of appreciation to Claude and Schatzy for alerting me to the DHL carrier's arrival well before the truck had pulled into the driveway.

Finally, I want to thank Susie Koehn and Anna Boehs, without whom this book could not have been written.

Introduction

Every network manager I know has asked me whether they should install a high-speed network, and if so, which one. Most of them have well-designed and well-managed networks that have been optimized to make the most of their network resources, yet nearly all of them are receiving performance complaints from users and pressure from managers to "speed up the network." As well, nearly all of them have at least one "project from hell" haunting their pasts and making them wake up in a cold sweat after nightmares about implementing a high-speed network protocol. This book is for them—and for you.

Truth is, it probably *is* time for you to begin building a high-speed network. Trick is, you need to know precisely what to build, where to begin building it, how to integrate it into your existing network, and what kind of performance boost you can realistically expect from it.

To that end, I've organized this book not only by type of high-speed protocol, but also by its appropriate *location*. Furthermore, each chapter discusses not only how the protocol works, but also the specific implementation issues surrounding it, along with its strengths and weaknesses, and my recommendations for where it should—and should not—be used.

Chapter 1, "Do You Really Need a High-Speed Network," discusses the general issues surrounding the implementation of a high-speed network.

Chapter 2, "The Backbone is Connected to the...," explains how backbones work and why they are usually the first place a high-speed network is needed. It describes how to diagnose some of the major problems of insufficient bandwidth. In this chapter we also discuss some of the issues involved in selecting a network protocol for the backbone.

Chapter 3, "Down on the Farm," defines that elusive entity, the server farm, and explains why and how they have come to be. It also gives hints on how to identify throughput problems in a server farm, as well as what you need to alleviate them.

Chapter 4, "Closer to Home," deals with power workgroups—those clusters of tough customers who use every PC and network resource within login distance, and still demand more. It describes the causes and cures of a bandwidth shortage within the workgroup.

Chapter 5, "The Wide Area," takes on just that. Although this area is technically beyond the boundaries of the local area network, it is becoming increasingly integrated with it. As a result, a shortage of bandwidth on the wide area becomes a problem for the *local* area network manager.

Chapter 6, "The Cost of Converting to High Speed," is devoted to building a framework for planning your protocol selection and implementation. It provides worksheets and procedures for determining exactly how much building a high-speed network or segment will cost in terms of both money and time.

In Part Two, "How to Speed Up: Local Area Solutions," Chapters 7 through 12 deal with high-speed local area protocols. Respectively, these are Fiber Distributed Data Interface, 100VG-AnyLAN, 100Base-T, Thomas-Conrad Networking System, Fibre Channel, and isoEthernet. Each protocol is discussed in technical detail, including frame composition and operation, access method, manageability, scalability, media support, cabling considerations, and fault tolerance. Each of these chapters ends with a summary of the strengths and weaknesses of the protocol in question, along with my recommendations for its best deployment.

Chapters 13 through 15 discuss the high-speed wide area protocol choices available today. These are, again respectively, Integrated Services Digital Network, Switched Multimegabit Data Services, and Frame Relay. Again, the technical details of the operation of the protocols are explained, along with implementation issues, strengths, weaknesses, and my recommendations.

Chapter 16 is devoted to Asynchronous Transfer Mode, that local- and/or wide-area-protocol-miracle that everyone has been hearing about—and waiting for—for so long. The technical issues surrounding implementing ATM are covered in detail, as well as the issues of standardization and integration that have kept people waiting for all these many years.

If, after careful scrutiny, none of the protocols described sound appropriate for your network, Chapter 17, "Alternatives to High-Speed Networking," may be just for you. This chapter talks about some alternatives, including segmentation with bridges and/or routers, switching, and virtual LANs (another popular term that is defined at length).

Finally, for the brave of heart who are ready to set forth building a high-speed network Chapter 18, "Speed Kills: Avoiding a Crash," gives some guidance in preparing for the great undertaking. It also includes, as the title suggests, some words of warning to heed before beginning a high-speed networking project.

Most technical books begin with a rather lengthy—and by now repetitive—chapter on the International Standards Organization's Open Systems Interconnectivity Reference Model. I decided not to. Because most network managers can recite the OSI Model's layers by heart, and generally only need to refer to the Model occasionally, I've put a concise explanation and discussion of the model, compliments of Tom Sheldon's wonderful *LAN Times Encyclopedia of Networking* (if you don't have a copy, get one), in Appendix A.

For those of you who may wonder exactly who and what all the standards organizations are and how they fit together in the Pantheon of Networking Standards, I've included a brief explanation in Appendix B.

Appendix C gives you the names, addresses, telephone numbers, and e-mail addresses of the supporting organizations for the protocols described in this book. It's a shame that not all of the protocols have such a fan club, because they provide valuable, up-to-date technical and marketing information to prospective purchasers.

Most people don't have the good fortune that I do to have a job that lets them spend hours talking to developers, vendors, analysts, and end users about a new and emerging technology, then spend days on end testing products based on that technology (I can't believe I get paid to do this). I can't give you transcripts of my reams of lab notes and countless interviews, but I can give you Appendix D, a bibliography of those reference works that I have found most helpful in building a foundation knowledge of high-speed networking.

I hope that you find this book not only useful, but fun to read. I certainly had fun writing it—most of the time.

PART ONE

Identifying the Bottlenecks

CHAPTER 1

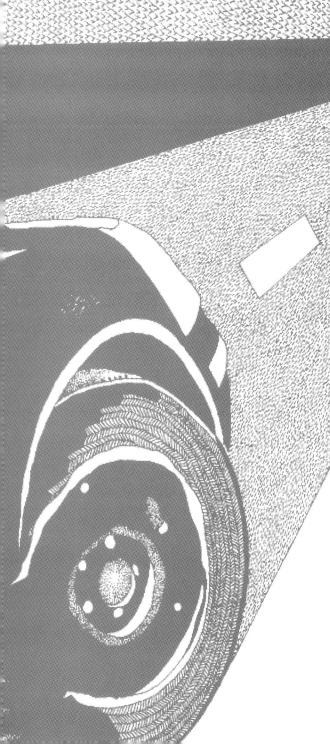

Do You Really Need a High-Speed Network?

Most network managers need more of everything. They need more time, more money, more equipment, more people, more patience, and more performance. Most of them have been doing the high tech equivalent of making a silk purse out of a sow's ear for so long that they work under the automatic assumption that they won't have the resources they need, so they have made improvisation a way of life. They spend hours kludging together network patches and fixes, dreaming of a world in which they could have the latest hot products they read about in glossy networking trade magazines. Under these circumstances, it's often easy to assume that nearly every network problem is the result of not having the latest, newest, and/or fastest technology.

And so it is with network performance. When your network slows to a crawl, your users are wailing, and your boss is threatening, your first thought might be to convert your network—or at least the slow segments of your network—to one of the new 100Mbps-and-faster protocols. After all, you figure that increasing the throughput ten times or greater *has* to improve your network's performance, even if excessive network traffic isn't the sole culprit.

Until recently, of course, high-speed networking was so expensive that it was really just a dream for most network managers. That's because if you wanted a fast network, you had one choice: FDDI. Originally, choosing FDDI also meant changing your cabling media to optical fiber. And that meant *major* bucks, which effectively priced most buyers out of the high-speed network market.

A lot has changed, however. Not only are fast transport protocols popping up like mushrooms, their components are competing in price with standard 10Mbps equipment. As well, some of them can use existing Category 3 cabling (like 100VG AnyLAN and 100Base-T), although some of them still require fiber-optic cabling (such as FDDI and 100Base-FX). Therefore, it seems only natural that the performance-starved network manager would think that now is the time to implement a high-speed network.

Read This First

This book is for you, the network manager poised to jump into the world of high-speed networking. The first thing we want to do is urge you not to leap just yet.

You have probably read a great deal about high-speed networks. You may have begun talking with vendors of high-speed networking products. You may have even begun the task of selecting a high-speed protocol for your network. We applaud your diligence. And we sympathize; of all the challenges that high-speed networking presents, the selection of the transport protocol is probably the most daunting.

Unfortunately, it's not the challenge you have to meet first.

Ask Yourself Why

Before taking the plunge, be sure you really need to.

As we mentioned, it's easy to attribute slow network performance to a shortage of bandwidth. It's also easy to assume that "more is better" and forge ahead into high-speed networking because it can't hurt. Neither assumption is true, and both are dangerous. The time to learn that high-speed networking cures your network's ills is *before* you invest the time and money to implement it.

Before you continue with your high-speed networking plans, ask yourself why you are considering high-speed networking. Is it because you are currently experiencing slow network performance? Or is it because your networking plans for the near future involve such bandwidth hungry application as multimedia and videoconferencing? In either case, why do you think more bandwidth will improve the situation?

It May Be Bandwidth

If your current problem is slow network performance, you *may* be on the right track. Often enough, poor network performance is indeed the result of excessive network traffic. There are a lot of factors that could be contributing to increasing network traffic. Too many workstations on one segment can generate more traffic than the available bandwidth can handle. There is also a trend in applications to use more bandwidth, due largely to the increasing popularity of multimedia applications. Finally, the average packet size for all applications is growing. Although the current average packet size ranges between 256 bytes and 512 bytes, it may soon grow to 1500 bytes and larger.

To determine whether excessive traffic is causing your network problems, you should put a *protocol analyzer* on each affected network segment. A protocol analyzer can be configured to monitor packets for the specific topology and protocol of the segment, letting you monitor the traffic on the segment to which it's connected. A protocol analyzer will help you determine not only the average bandwidth utilization on the segment, but also the average packet size and composition. As well, a protocol analyzer can assist in spotting trends in traffic, peak traffic periods, and devices that are generating bad packets or acting as network bottlenecks.

For your initial network evaluation, we recommend that you use a sophisticated protocol analyzer that offers packet-level decoding and analysis. If you don't have your own such protocol analyzer, you can rent one or even hire someone to bring in a protocol analyzer and do the traffic monitoring and protocol analysis for you. Most network integration firms offer protocol analysis equipment and services.

Don't feel you have to rush out to purchase a high-end protocol analyzer. After you complete your initial network evaluation and have established a "baseline" traffic pattern, you can monitor your network adequately with one of the software-only protocol analyzers, such as Etherpeek from AG Group. These software-only protocol analyzers are relatively inexpensive ($500 or less), and while they don't offer the packet-level analysis that more sophisticated protocol analyzers do, they enable you to spot trends and potential problems on your network.

In any event, *don't proceed with plans for implementing a high-speed network until you have monitored your network with a protocol analyzer and are satisfied that insufficient bandwidth is the problem.* This is the only way to be sure that a high-speed network will improve your network's performance.

And Then Again, It May Not Be Bandwidth

All the benefits of higher network bandwidth notwithstanding, a high-speed network isn't a panacea. There are many network problems that will slow performance that have nothing to do with insufficient bandwidth. If the real problem in your network is, for example, disk I/O on your servers, no amount of bandwidth is going to speed performance. Here are some problems that will slow your network that can't be fixed with a high-speed protocol.

Server-Related Performance Problems

There are several server components that affect network performance. Before contemplating a high-speed network, be sure to check out the following potential server bottlenecks.

Processor Speed

The actual speed of the processor is obviously a big factor in server performance. A heavily used server with an inadequate processor simply can't keep up with the requests for data it receives. Make sure that your servers have adequate processing power. Some network operating systems, such as NetWare 4.X, have server utilities that perform server speed tests. The results of such a speed test can give you a good idea of your server's overall performance, and indicate whether it has sufficient processing power for its job.

Even if you confirm that your servers have adequate processing power right now, you still may need to replace or enhance them when (and if) you implement a high-speed network. High-speed network interfaces place more demand on the server's CPU—after all, they *are* requiring the server to process incoming packets that are arriving many times faster than on a 10Base-T or Token Ring/16 network. Therefore, before you install your high-speed network adapter, make sure your server has processing power to spare.

Disk Subsystem

By definition, a file server provides file services: access to the data and application files stored on the file server's *disk subsystem*. The disk subsystem is the hard disk itself and the disk controller that manages the transfer of data between the disk and the server's processor. If the disk subsystem cannot provide fast enough access to the files stored on it, your network users will spend a lot of time waiting for the data they have sent to or requested from the file server to be processed. The *data transfer rate,* or speed with which a server can transfer files between its processor and disk subsystem, is a function of the disk itself, the disk controller, and the bus interfaces between the disk and the disk controller and between the disk controller and the processor. The faster these components are, the faster the network response time.

The first clue that the disk subsystem is slowing performance is when server requests to read and/or write data are waiting on disk input/output. Most network operating systems have integrated utilities that will show the percentage of time requests are waiting on disk input/output. If you find that requests are waiting excessively on disk input/output (and this will vary from server to server and network to network, so "excessive" will have to be defined in terms of your particular network), it's probably time to consider installing a faster disk subsystem.

Random Access Memory

Too little or poorly configured random access memory (RAM) can slow server performance. A network server *caches,* or holds, its most recently accessed data in memory as long as it can. When the server fills all of its memory allocated for caching, it writes the least recently accessed back to its disk. If your server has too little RAM, it will spend an excessive amount of time going to disk to retrieve data. Reading data from the disk drive is substantially slower than reading the information from RAM. Your network operating system will have an integrated utility that will tell you the percentage of *cache hits,* or times when requested data was retrieved from RAM. When cache hits drop below about 85 percent, you should consider adding more memory or readjusting memory caches.

The speed of your server's RAM also affects its overall performance. You should therefore check to see that your servers' memory speed fits their usage.

Network-Related Performance Problems

Some performance problems *are* related to the connection between the host device and the network media, but aren't the result of insufficient bandwidth. Here are some of the more common performance-sapping problems that occur at the network connection.

Network Interface Card Selection

Your choice of network interface cards, both in the server and in the workstation, can dramatically affect network performance. Network interface cards vary widely in both performance and cost, so you will have to weigh the benefits of faster performance against the relative cost of the cards. When choosing a network interface card, be sure to evaluate the following:

- **Data throughput.** This is the speed at which the network interface card transfers data between the host computer's memory to the network. The data throughput depends upon both the width of the bus interface to the host processor and the method the network interface card uses to transfer data.

   Currently, host bus widths are 8, 16, or 32 bits. The wider the data bus to the host processor, the faster the network interface card can transfer data. Different network interface card bus architectures offer different bus widths, with *Industry Standard Architecture (ISA)* network interface cards offering 8- and 16-bit buses, and *Extended Industry Standard Architecture (EISA)* and *Peripheral Component Interface (PCI)* network interface cards offering 32-bit buses. Servers, with their heavy traffic over their network interface cards, should really be computers designed with one of the 32-bit architecture buses and outfitted with corresponding network interface cards.

Network interface cards transfer data to and from host memory using one of three methods: direct memory mapping, input/output ports, or direct memory addressing (DMA). Direct memory mapping is usually the fastest data transfer method, so for highest performance, choose a network interface card that employs the direct memory mapping data transfer method.

■ **Onboard processor.** Network interface cards that employ an efficient onboard processor can improve the performance of the card and therefore of the network as a whole. Therefore, to improve performance, use network interface cards with high-performance onboard processors.

Chattering Cards

If you have a card *chattering*, or sending out streams of bad packets, no amount of bandwidth will improve network function. This is because the malfunctioning card may very well fill all available bandwidth with errant packets, meaning that increasing bandwidth to 100Mbps will only give you ten times the network garbage you now have.

Poor Network Interface Card Driver Support

If the *drivers*, those lines of code that translate network redirector program calls into instructions for your network interface cards, are poorly written, your users will experience all kinds of network difficulties, including slow performance. The poor performance comes from the retransmissions necessary to send a packet successfully from the network interface card to its addressee. Other problems associated with poorly-written drivers are network time-outs, lost connections, and "hung" servers.

Workstation-Related Performance Problems

Another aspect of network performance that is often overlooked is the workstation performance. Workstations with slower processors, slow hard disks, and/or insufficient memory won't be able to process quickly all the data it sends and receives from the server. This will give your users the impression of a slow network, although the problem is really much closer to home.

How to Determine that High-Speed Networking Will Help

Now that you have some idea of the scope of the many problems that high-speed networking *won't* solve, you're probably wondering how to go about determining if it *will* solve your particular network difficulties. Using the following worksheets and flowchart will help you determine whether high-speed networking will really help your network.

Step One: Evaluate Your Server Usage

Use the following form to determine whether your server is experiencing performance problems.

Server utilization:

The average server utilization should probably be below 60 percent. However, this will vary from operating system to operating system and network to network. Consult your network vendor to determine the appropriate server utilization for your network. If server utilization averages over 60 percent, consider upgrading the server's processor or moving some applications to another server.

Cache utilization:

Cache hits should average around 85 percent. If not, check the amount of memory and allocated cache buffers. The rule for most network operating systems is the more memory, the better. However, there are exceptions, especially when you are working with older versions of these network operating systems.

Disk utilization and swapping:

If server requests are waiting on disk input/output, or if the server is *disk swapping* (using disk storage to augment Random Access Memory), consider adding memory or increasing cache buffers.

If the server disk itself is more than 80 percent full, you'll need to increase disk capacity or remove some data from the existing disks.

Component device utilization:

With component device technologies such as *Small Computer Systems Interface (SCSI)*, the throughput is always reduced to the lowest common denominator. So if you have a bunch of devices attached to a single SCSI host adapter, the signaling throughput for the entire chain will match that of the slowest device in the chain.

Step Two: Evaluate Your Server Configuration

Using the following form, describe your server hardware and configuration. Make copies of the form as needed.

Server 1:

Processor:

Type:

Clock speed:

Random Access Memory:

Amount:

Speed:

Total cache buffers:

Disk Subsystem:

Controller type:

Disk access speed:

Disk capacity:

RAID level (if applicable):

Network Interface Card:

Manufacturer:

Model:

Host bus width:

Memory access method:

Onboard processor type:

Driver name:

Step Three: Evaluate Workstations

It's important to evaluate the processing power of the workstations on network segments that are experiencing poor performance. Even when the server and network are operating well, an underpowered workstation can give users the impression of a slow network.

Workstation 1:

   Processor:

      Type:

      Clock speed:

   Random Access Memory:

      Amount:

      Speed:

      Total cache buffers:

   Disk Subsystem:

      Controller type:

      Disk access speed:

      Disk capacity:

   Network Interface Card:

      Manufacturer:

      Model:

      Host bus width:

      Memory access method:

      Onboard processor type:

      Driver name:

Step Four: Evaluate Current Application Requirements

List in the next form the names and types of applications resident on each server. Database, statistical modeling, and CAD/CAM applications put a strain on server resources. If you see a server—or disk within a server—that has a disproportionate number of these types of applications, try to move them to another server or disk to try to balance the load. Imaging and multimedia applications, on the other hand, generate a lot of network traffic, and therefore indicate a need for a high-speed network protocol.

Also, make a note of the number of users for each application and the location of these users. The more users, obviously, the more load on the server—but also the more network traffic. Furthermore, users that must cross bridges to access servers are generating traffic on networks other than their local segment.

Server 1:

Disk 1

Operating system:

    Number of users:

    Location of users:

Word processing applications:

    Number of users:

Spreadsheet applications:

    Number of users:

Database applications:

    Number of users:

CAD/CAM applications:

    Number of users:

Imaging applications:

Number of users:

Multimedia applications:

Number of users:

Groupware applications:

Number of users:

Disk 2

Operating system:

Number of users:

Location of users:

Word processing applications:

Number of users:

Spreadsheet applications:

Number of users:

Database applications:

Number of users:

CAD/CAM applications:

Number of users:

Imaging applications:

Number of users:

Multimedia applications:

Number of users:

Groupware applications:

Number of users:

Disk 3

Operating system:

    Number of users:

    Location of users:

Word processing applications:

    Number of users:

Spreadsheet applications:

    Number of users:

Database applications:

    Number of users:

CAD/CAM applications:

    Number of users:

Imaging applications:

    Number of users:

Multimedia applications:

    Number of users:

Groupware applications:

    Number of users:

Disk 4

Operating system:

    Number of users:

Location of users:

Word processing applications:

Number of users:

Spreadsheet applications:

Number of users:

Database applications:

Number of users:

CAD/CAM applications:

Number of users:

Imaging applications:

Number of users:

Multimedia applications:

Number of users:

Groupware applications:

Number of users:

Step Five: Evaluate Future Application Requirements

Looking at your network's strategic and budget plans, list the names and types of applications you plan to add in the next 18 months. Beside each, list the number and location of the users of these applications.

Step Six: Evaluate Network Usage

If, however, after making the suggested changes to your network, summarized in Figure 1-1, you *still* have a performance problem, it's time to put a protocol analyzer on your network. This will tell you the amount and type of traffic being generated.

It will also tell you that you have network-related problems, such as chattering cards, that will cause slow network performance.

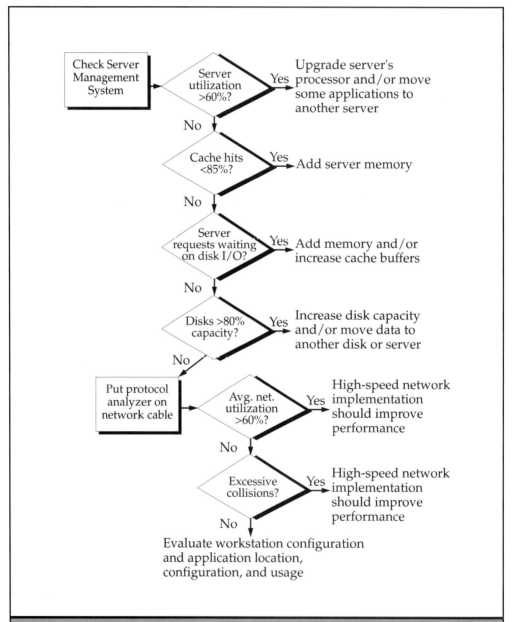

Figure 1-1. *Flowchart summarizing how to troubleshoot poor network performance*

Step Seven: Read On

If traffic monitoring with a protocol analyzer reveals exceedingly heavy network utilization, often characterized by an abundance of collisions, it's time to start planning your high-speed network. The following chapters show you how and why to implement high-speed protocols on different segments of your network.

CHAPTER 2

The Backbone Is Connected to the . . .

Probably the first place you will start feeling the bandwidth pinch is on your network's *backbone*. By its very nature, a network backbone is prone to congestion and slow network response. As a result, it is usually the first place high-speed networking is indicated—and implemented—in a network. However, before you conclude that a high-speed backbone is the answer to your performance problems, be sure that you understand the function of the network backbone, as well as your options for improving the handling of high traffic volume.

How It All Began

Back in the early days of networking, all networks were *linear networks*. This meant that a network consisted of a number of workstations connected by a single cable. At the time, this was fine, because networks tended to be small, and so cable problems were fairly easy to isolate. On larger networks, however, locating a loose connection or cable break could be a difficult and time-consuming process, often requiring special—and expensive—equipment to determine the type and location of the cable problem.

To solve the problem caused by a single network cable, wiring centers, or *hubs* were developed. The first hubs were nothing more than signal repeaters. They took a data signal from one cable segment and repeated it over another, extending the length of the network, as shown in Figure 2-1. However, these simple repeaters made it easy to divide networks into *segments*, meaning physical and/or logical groups of network users and resources. Dividing networks into segments enabled network managers to keep network users as close as possible to the network resources they used the most. This allowed the network administrator to control and isolate network traffic to a certain extent.

The potential usefulness of hubs went well beyond that of the first simple network repeaters. Soon after the appearance of the first basic hubs, a second generation of hubs appeared that offered management features. These hubs could collect management information from each network connection, then convert that

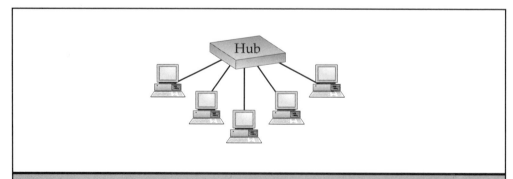

Figure 2-1. *A basic hub configuration. The hub regenerates, or repeats the transmission signals coming from the workstations.*

information into a standardized format (for example, Simple Network Management Protocol), then export that information to a number of management reporting systems. Often these hubs also had buses which allowed them to support multiple transport protocols on the same high-performance backplane. Then, thanks to the high performance backplane, hubs appeared that could support multiple logical network segments *within the hub*, meaning that a hub could now contain more than one segment, and that each of those segments could be managed separately. This enabled network managers to reconfigure network segments, making moves, adds, and changes on the fly and even from a remote console.

With these sophisticated new features came new roles for network hubs. Soon network managers were using hubs to concentrate, or *collapse*, network nodes into increasingly complex hierarchies of networks, often within a single chassis. Simple, unmanaged wiring center hubs were used to connect end user nodes to their login servers. These simple hubs were in turn connected to one another by more sophisticated hubs. These intermediate level hubs were then connected by extremely feature-rich and highly manageable chassis-based hubs, some employing bridging or routing modules. (See Figure 2-2.)

With this, the concept of structured wiring was born, and network managers began to realize its many benefits, including:

- easier moves, adds, and changes
- centralized management
- improved scalability
- better monitoring of network events and statistics
- improved reporting
- easier troubleshooting
- improved fault tolerance
- support for multiple transport protocols
- support for multiple communications protocols

Types of Backbones

The term *backbone*, although it is tossed around rather loosely, really means a network that connects multiple local area network segments. In this sense, a backbone is a "network of networks" that handles *internetwork traffic*—that is, traffic that originates in one LAN segment and is transmitted to another. Network segments, on the other hand, handle local network traffic. Because the backbone provides both a physical and logical data path among all the nodes connected to it, the network segments and subnetworks must be connected to the backbone by devices capable of performing the necessary bridging and routing of data packets being transmitted. These devices may be bridges (Figure 2-3), routers (Figure 2-4), and/or file servers (Figure 2-5) performing the bridging and routing functions among the network segments.

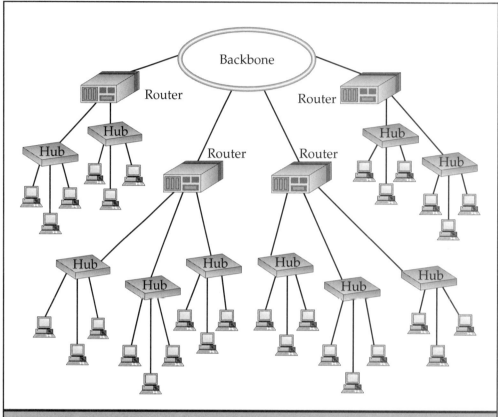

Figure 2-2. *A hierarchical network with hubs and routers concentrating network nodes at discreet levels*

Why Build a Backbone?

A well-designed backbone can bring order, ease of management, and the potential for improved performance to your network. Backbones enable network managers to centralize their network structures by providing a single point of monitoring, management, and control. Because all network servers are attached to a common cable, they can be moved to a central location. This centralization makes the network easier to configure, secure, and manage because:

- Repairs and maintenance are easier to schedule and perform
- All backups and archiving can be handled simultaneously

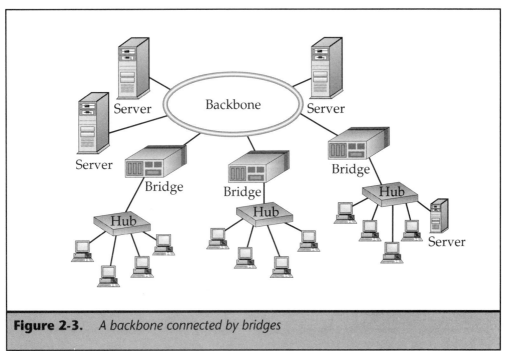

Figure 2-3. *A backbone connected by bridges*

■   Telecommunications connections can be pulled to one central location

What's more, network backbone designs have given rise to two related network designs which we touched on earlier: *structured wiring* and *collapsed backbones*. These two techniques further increase ease of network management.

Structured Wiring

Although any cable plant which involved a little forethought could be called a *structured wiring* system, the term is usually reserved for those standards-based wiring schemes that are hierarchically designed for easy management and expansion. Structured wiring systems generally incorporate a network design in which a central hub controls the flow of information between departments and also serves as a connection point for enterprise resources such as communications and applications servers. See Figure 2-6.

There are two keys to a good structured wiring system. The first is to keep network users as close as possible—both physically and logically—to the network resources they use the most. In Figure 2-6, for example, the members of the

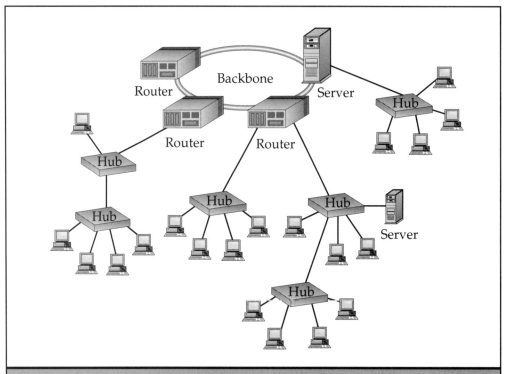

Figure 2-4. *A backbone connected by routers*

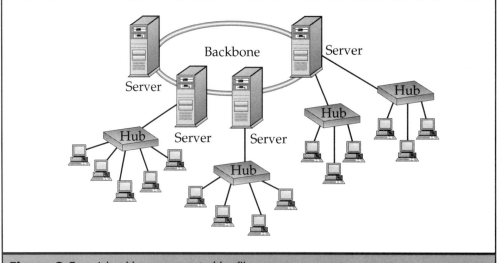

Figure 2-5. *A backbone connected by file servers*

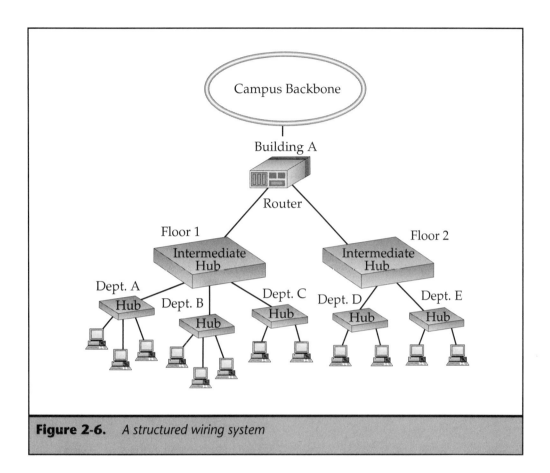

Figure 2-6. *A structured wiring system*

Accounting Department are directly attached to the server they use most frequently, ACCTG1. This eliminates unnecessary internetwork traffic that can slow down the performance of the whole network. The second key is to design the system so that adding, moving, and changing users (which you will occasionally have to do to keep them as close as possible to their preferred network resources) are as easy as possible.

Collapsed Backbones

A *collapsed backbone* is essentially a "backbone in a box." That is, an entire physical and logical data internetwork contained within a single device. (See Figure 2-7.)

Instead of running backbone media throughout the walls, ceilings, and floors of the building, each network segment is attached to a single hub or stack of hubs that connects all the segments and subnetworks to form the enterprise internetwork. The collapsed backbone design was a logical outgrowth of the centralized backbone network design. After all, if all the servers are in a central location for management

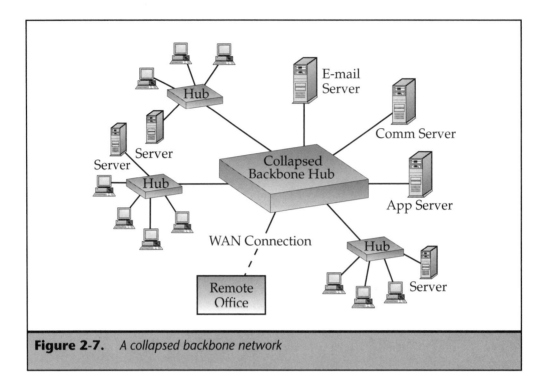

Figure 2-7.   *A collapsed backbone network*

purposes, the next step is to connect them to a single hub, replacing the backbone cable with the backplane of the hub. The advantages to this are many:

- hubs are modular and easily scaleable
- hubs are built on a chassis with high-speed backplanes that provide a high-speed bus for expansion boards
- most chassis-based hubs can simultaneously support multiple transport protocols, such as Ethernet, Token Ring, FDDI, and WAN
- most hubs offer optional integrated diagnostic and management tools

Furthermore, a collapsed backbone extends the manageability of the centralized backbone by:

- providing a central point for management of the entire network
- providing better management of and security for network resources

A collapsed backbone design provides better management because it offers a single point of network monitoring and control, which also makes troubleshooting easier. It improves security because all servers are moved to a central management area. Most important of all, a collapsed backbone design makes it easy to implement a high-speed network.

How Do You Build a Backbone?

You can configure backbones physically to accommodate your segmenting scheme. For example, local area network segments on each floor of an office building are connected to a backbone that runs through the conduit from one floor to the next.

Regardless of the physical configuration of your backbone, the network segments and subnetworks must be connected to the backbone by devices capable of performing the necessary bridging and routing of data packets being transmitted.

Building a Backbone with Bridges

This is one of the simplest and most straightforward ways to build a backbone. (See Figure 2-8.) The segments are connected to bridges, and the bridges in turn are connected to one another on the backbone cable. Building a backbone with bridges can quickly lead to excessive backbone traffic, however, because bridges don't filter traffic. They simply pass it from one ring to the next.

Building a Backbone with Routers

In a router-based backbone, a router or routers connect the segments to the backbone cable, as shown in Figure 2-9. A router functions as the connection point to the backbone for each segment. Using routers as the backbone can provide a level of fault tolerance that bridges can't. When the backbone is constructed of a dual-ring medium,

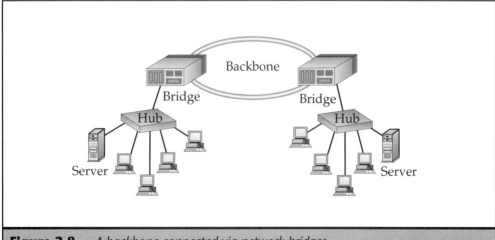

Figure 2-8.   *A backbone connected via network bridges*

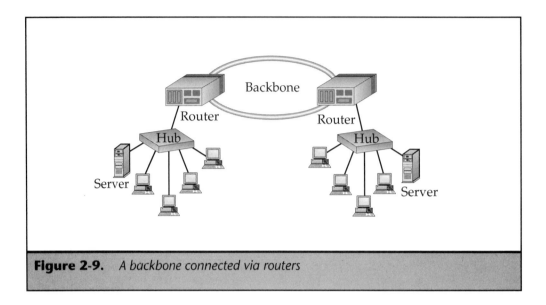

Figure 2-9. *A backbone connected via routers*

such as fiber-optic cable, the ring will loop back on itself, the routers will adjust the paths, and the data will continue uninterrupted across the backbone.

Building a Backbone with Network File Servers

In a server-based backbone, like the one shown in Figure 2-10, each server forming the backbone contains two or more network adapters. One of the adapters connects the

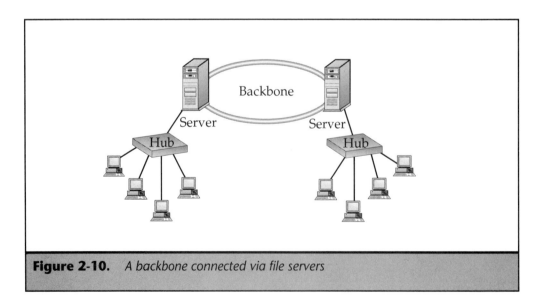

Figure 2-10. *A backbone connected via file servers*

server to the backbone. This provides backbone access for the server and for all the network segments attached to the server. The other network adapter(s) provides the connection between the server and its network segment(s).

The backbone is by nature a high-traffic area, so it will be one of the first places to experience slow performance caused by high traffic. This is especially true in server-based backbones, in which the network file server or servers connects the network segments to the backbone cable. Most network operating systems have integrated bridging and routing functions that enable them to connect the segments, although requiring the server to perform these functions steals processing cycles from other vital server activities such as file management. Therefore, managers of large networks and/or networks with heavy traffic should dedicate file servers either to file management or bridging and routing functions, *or* consider building a backbone using bridges or routers. In small-to-medium-sized networks that have relatively low traffic, however, the servers may be able to provide backbone connectivity without seriously affecting server performance.

The Effects of Excessive Internetwork Traffic

As we mentioned earlier, the backbone is probably the area of your network where you will first feel the effects of excessive traffic. If you are experiencing slow network performance, therefore, the backbone is probably your first suspect. A fairly reliable indicator of a clogged backbone is slow network response when handling internetwork traffic (packets that originate on one network segment and are then transmitted to another), despite the fact that all the servers and workstations are not overworked.

Causes and Cures for a Clogged Backbone

To be sure that the problem is indeed excessive *backbone* traffic, however, you will need to conduct a few tests. First, check to make sure that the slow performance you experience is occurring only during internetwork transmissions. If slow performance is characteristic of all network transmissions, the problem may not be your backbone—or at least not the backbone alone. Determine the physical location of the network applications you are using when the network response slows. If these applications are on another network segment, you may indeed be suffering from excessive traffic on the network backbone.

Location of Applications

Before you conclude that more backbone bandwidth is what you need, however, ask yourself whether it's possible to move the applications onto the same segment as the user without slowing down performance for users on other segments. Be sure all users are as close as possible—both physically and logically—to the network resources they use most frequently. This eliminates unnecessary internetwork traffic.

TIP: Balancing the location of your applications is much more efficient—and much less expensive—than implementing a high-speed protocol on your backbone.

Inadequate Hardware

Next, check your workstations and servers. Ensure that your workstations have sufficient memory and processing power for the job. Also, check servers to make sure that they are not the bottleneck. If your servers are waiting on disk input/output, that's probably the cause of the network slowdown, and it can be alleviated by installing a faster disk subsystem. Likewise, insufficient memory (often indicated by memory swapping to disk), low throughput to and from the network adapter (resulting in dropped packets and retransmissions), and inadequate processors can all slow your servers and cause them to be a bottleneck on your backbone.

"Chatty" Communication Protocols

Another cause of congested backbones is the *communication protocol* used by your network operating system. Among the functions of the communications protocol are creating service connections, getting network station addresses, and other tasks associated with transferring data from a station on one network to a station on another network. The communication protocol operates at the network layer as described on the International Standards Organization's Open Systems Interconnection model. (See Appendix A.) Communications protocols include Internet Protocol (IP) and NetWare's Internetwork Packet Exchange protocol (IPX).

Some communications protocols generate a lot of traffic because for every request for service they send, they require a response from the station that is granting the services. Because of this constant "conversation" between the requester and grantor of services, these protocols are called "chatty" protocols. IPX, for example, is the classic example of a "chatty" protocol—request then response, request then response. Often these requests and responses are larger than one packet. Therefore, a chatty protocol significantly increases the number of packets being transmitted. Consequently, chatty protocols are not a good choice for backbone deployment.

Transmission Control Protocol/Internet Protocol (TCP/IP), on the other hand, is not a chatty protocol. Rather than sending a request for service, waiting for a reply, then sending the next request for service, TCP/IP sends all requests for service in a single burst, sometimes called a "packet burst." It then receives multiple responses from the grantor of those services. This makes it a better choice for a backbone protocol than IPX.

To ease the congestion that IPX can cause, Novell has introduced PBURST NLM, a NetWare Loadable Module that enables the server and workstations to function in Packet Burst Mode, sending all service requests in a single burst. However, PBURST is not turned on by default. You will have to load PBURST manually or add the LOAD PBURST command to your STARTUP.NCF file.

Small Packet Size

Also, bigger is better when it comes to packet size on the backbone. That's because one large packet obviously represents less traffic than a lot of little ones. This has a couple of indications. First, you should select a backbone protocol with the largest packet size available. Second, if you're running NetWare, you may have to make some adjustments.

Your NetWare servers could be needlessly creating more backbone traffic because they are limiting packet size to a 512KB maximum. By default, NetWare servers route a default packet size of 512KB. This is because 512KB used to be the largest packet that all routers could route. However, most routers these days will route at the maximum packet size for each protocol. Therefore, if you have a NetWare 4.X network, check to make sure your routers can handle a larger packet size. If they can, you may want to consider enabling the Large Internet Packet support.

The Final Analysis

Of course, the true and indisputable determination of where your backbone's bottleneck lies comes from in-depth analysis of your network traffic with a protocol analyzer (see Chapter 1). A protocol analyzer will help you determine whether packets are being dropped, resulting in retransmissions, and pinpoint where those packets are being dropped. It will also help you confirm whether your network has heavy internetwork traffic (data packets addressed to a node not on the same segment it originated). You can also use the protocol analyzer to determine *bandwidth utilization*, or the average percentage of bandwidth being used, on your network's backbone. If you are experiencing slow network performance, dropped packets, and if your network's bandwidth utilization over the backbone consistently averages over 50 percent, it's fairly safe to say that the problem is too much backbone traffic, and your network is a good candidate for implementing high-speed networking protocols.

What You Gain

Putting a high-speed protocol on the backbone will result in higher network throughput, and will eliminate any bottleneck caused by insufficient internetwork bandwidth. However, please be aware that a high-speed backbone usually gives subtle network improvements: faster internetwork transmissions and better server-to-server communication. The dramatic improvements in network response time—the kind that will make your boss call you to congratulate you and talk about your next raise—are not usually the kind realized through increasing bandwidth on the backbone. Those types of performance increases generally come from adding bandwidth within a local segment from the workstation to the local server.

Selecting a High-Speed Backbone Protocol

If you have conducted the necessary tests and have determined that you need to implement a high-speed protocol on your backbone, it's time to establish the selection criteria for this protocol. Overall, the most important features for a backbone protocol are

- Manageability
- Fault tolerance
- Scalability
- Packet size
- Packet overhead
- Maximum network span

Because manageability and fault tolerance are so important on the backbone, these two qualities must be paramount when you are selecting a high-speed protocol for this implementation. A protocol that currently supports only limited management systems is clearly a bad choice, as is a protocol that can't support a backup ring, spanning tree, or other disaster recovery system.

Easy and broad scalability is also another necessary feature of a backbone protocol because the protocol will need to be able to ensure low response times, even as you are adding servers. Important things to remember are the number of stations the protocol can support on a single LAN, as well as the packet size. Internetwork and server-to-server packets tend to be larger than local segment packets. Therefore, a protocol that can support large packet sizes tends to be more efficient on a backbone. As well, the amount of overhead (addressing and management information) per packet should be low to eliminate unnecessary traffic on the backbone.

Furthermore, consider maximum network extent. Backbones tend to be spread out over buildings or campuses, so be sure that the protocol you select can span your network without a lot of expensive repeating devices.

Finally, the backbone is not the place to pinch pennies. Losing a backbone link could cost you your job, so don't select backbone equipment on the basis of cost alone. Remember, the protocol that you select for your backbone doesn't have to be the same protocol you use throughout your network. Therefore, implementing a more expensive protocol on the backbone doesn't condemn you to overrunning your cabling budget on every segment.

TIP: *Later chapters in this book discuss each protocol in detail, and make recommendations on where they would be best implemented. However, we recommend that you take a look at Fiber Distributed Data Interface (FDDI) first. This protocol is fault tolerant deluxe. FDDI supports dual-homed, dual-attached backbones, which means that each server on the ring can be connected to as many as two hubs on the same ring, so there is always an alternate path. It also supports counterrotating rings which provide great fault isolation. Finally, FDDI has a built-in network monitoring and management protocol called Station Management (SMT) designed as an integral part of it.*

CHAPTER 3

Down on the
Farm

The second most likely place to have a bandwidth crunch (after the backbone) is in a *server farm*. If you have one of these, you're probably not experiencing the network throughput your users need. However, because the term is used so loosely, you're probably not even sure whether you have one, much less how to improve its performance. So, in this chapter we'll begin by defining the structure of the server farm, illustrated in Figure 3-1, and then discuss the specific requirements it demands of its transport protocol. Next we'll discuss the indications of insufficient bandwidth in a server farm environment and how to alleviate it.

Do Servers Grow on Farms?

Many manufacturers of high-speed networking devices recommend their products for use in server farms. However, rarely do these same manufacturers define what they mean by "server farm." Often, they mean anything from a backbone to a UNIX workgroup. For the purposes of this book, however, let's define a server farm as a group of servers that share processing responsibility for a common information system. This type of environment is often called a *distributed computing system*, or more recently, a distributed information access architecture. Before you can design a network to support a distributed computing system, you first need to understand the function of this architecture and the tools used to implement it.

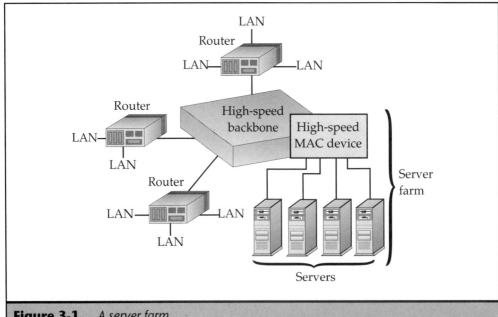

Figure 3-1.   *A server farm*

A distributed computing environment, such as the one shown in Figure 3-2, generally has two goals:

- Allow enterprise-wide access to information
- Distribute processing load across specialized platforms

Enterprise-Wide Access to Information

Enabling all users throughout the enterprise to access corporate information is truly the most important goal of a distributed computing environment. It is the driving force behind developing a distributed computing environment, and so we will address this goal first.

How It All Began

For decades now, companies have developed and maintained databases—at times huge and very expensive—containing vital corporate information of all kinds. These

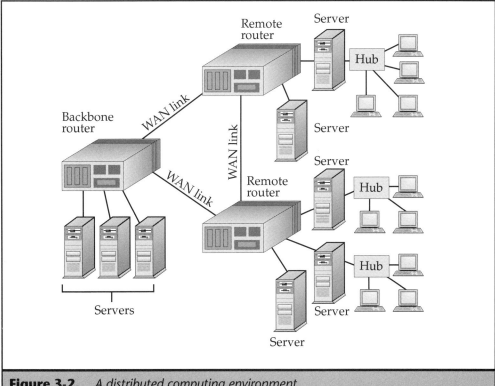

Figure 3-2. *A distributed computing environment*

databases were developed independently on a variety of computing platforms using many different development tools and programming languages. All of these databases fulfilled their intended functions (some better than others), but they existed for the most part as islands of information. The users who needed access to the information had to have specialized software loaded on their specialized workstations, which were in turn connected by specialized cables to the specialized host computing platform that held the database.

During the past decade or so of mergers, takeovers, consolidations, and downsizing, however, maintaining these large, expensive, and disparate databases has become both unwieldy and uneconomical. Executive managers wanted fast, seamless, integrated access to *all* corporate information. MIS managers wanted to be able to access all databases from one desktop platform rather than having to support a terminal, a UNIX workstation, and a PC for each user so that he or she could access all the various corporate databases. Users didn't want to have to learn how to work on three different workstations and six different host platforms to pull their daily reports, then have to spend hours manually consolidating them. Furthermore, as companies discovered that many of their databases could be moved from expensive mainframe platforms to more economical local area and wide area networks, they began pressuring their data processing departments to port applications and databases to these less expensive platforms.

The result of these different forces—corporate mergers, downsizing, the emergence of local area networks, and plain old economic pressures—is the emergence of distributed computing systems. A distributed computing system is a logical evolutionary step from centralized computer systems and even client-server computer systems, as shown in Figure 3-3.

Issues and Concerns About Distributed Computing Systems

A distributed computing system is really client-server computing on a grander scale. While in a client-server system, data is located on one server; in a distributed computing system, the data is located on many servers. Furthermore, these servers can be located anywhere: in the next room or in the next state.

Obviously, a distributed computing system has a lot of advantages over the old centralized computing systems, including fault tolerance. Because data is replicated on several servers, users are protected from loss or downed systems. A distributed computing system also makes more computing power available as it is needed. However, there are some problems associated with implementing a distributed computing system. Among these are

■ *Management* Because distributed computing systems by definition include multiple platforms, the time required to manage them increases exponentially over that required for a centralized system. Also, distributed computing systems are often the result of merging existing systems, which involves finding and resolving integration problems.

- *Data synchronization*   Keeping all data updated and consistent across all computing platforms is a major management challenge.

- *Time synchronization*   The system must have some means of resolving updates when more than one user creates a transaction to change the same field in the same record at the same time.

- *Security and control*   Multiple platforms means multiple points of access, and general concerns about data location, content, control, and management.

Distribute Processing Load Across Specialized Platforms

A distributed computing system is very similar to a client-server environment except that rather than a single server with many clients, there are many servers **and** many clients who can—and do—access any one of those servers at any time. This opens up many possibilities for efficient use of computing hardware, but also presents challenges as to how to make the best use of each platform.

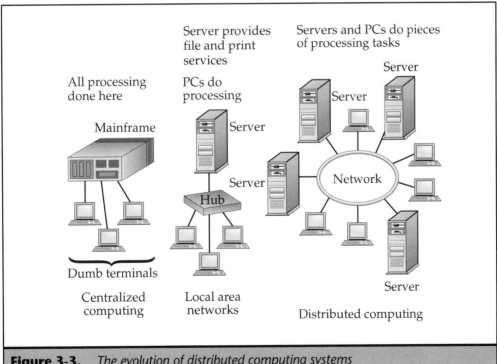

Figure 3-3.   *The evolution of distributed computing systems*

In some ways, distributed computing is similar to multiprocessing. A multiprocessing computer system divides processing functions into multiple discrete tasks, then assigns these tasks to each of its multiple processors. The multiprocessing computer balances the load so that no one processor becomes overwhelmed. Distributed application processing does the same thing, except that it balances processing across *computers* rather than just across processors in the same computer platform. Furthermore, there are, theoretically at least, more kinds of computing resources available in the distributed computing system, such as random access memory and disk storage space. For example, in many offices around the world, thousands of megabytes of memory lie idle every evening as workers turn off their desktop systems and leave for the day. It is possible, however, for a distributed application to use this idle memory.

Distributed systems have some clear advantages. First, in a client-server environment, inexpensive personal computers can relieve the server of many tasks. Likewise, relatively inexpensive local area network servers can handle some of the processing that once required CPU cycles from a mainframe. Furthermore, using multiple server platforms allows network managers a flexibility in hardware upgrades, moves, and changes that simply wasn't possible in centralized mainframe systems.

However, as we mentioned, distributed computing systems present their share of challenges, mostly in the area of network design. For example, distributed computing systems theoretically allow a client system to locate other computer systems on the network to process all or part of a task. The criteria for delegating processing tasks might include load balancing or processing power. Developing applications that can seek out appropriate computer platforms and take advantage of them is a challenge in and of itself. However, these distributed applications must be supported by a network that is fast enough, manageable enough, and fault-tolerant enough to make such distributed processing possible. For example, the only way to make our scenario of using workstation memory during idle periods possible is by using extremely high speed links to make memory of one platform available for use by another.

Implementations of Distributed Computing Systems

In the move to consolidate corporate data and port it to the most efficient and economic platforms available, certain types of distributed computing systems have become standard for commercial environments. These different types of systems determine the design of the networks that support them, so we'll take some time to describe these tools and their requirements.

Distributed Application Processing

As we mentioned earlier, distributed computing environments can employ *distributed applications*. A distributed application is one that can take advantage of multiple computing platforms by running different processes on different computers attached to the same network. Groupware applications, for example, are distributed applications because they let users work with the same data at the same time or take advantage of the network to share information easily. Document processing, scheduling, electronic mail, and workflow software are examples of groupware. Some applications automatically integrate data from systems attached to the network. For example, object linking and embedding (OLE) in Windows for Workgroups and Windows NT lets users take information stored in other places on the network and "paste" it in their own documents. The original source of the information can still be updated by other users. When the original data is changed, the copies of that data that are pasted in other users' documents are automatically changed as well.

Distributed Databases

By definition, a distributed computing system has data located at multiple sites. Users everywhere should be able to access all data no matter where it is located. Users should therefore only have to concern themselves with the data, not with the design of the network.

These *distributed databases* generally reside in server-based database management systems (DBMS) and mainframe-based information systems. In the centralized computing model, users accessed only their local database server. In the new distributed computing model, however, users can—and do—access any server in the enterprise. The network challenge here is providing transparent access from any user on the network to any database. Furthermore, distributed databases may also require some level of local control so that managers at the local site can secure the data.

Data Warehousing

While data warehousing is not itself a distributed computing system—and is actually the antithesis of distributed computing—it is a practice that often enables distributed computing systems to exist. Data warehousing is the practice of extracting working copies of databases and storing these copies on a database warehouse server or servers— usually large multiprocessor computers. The data is extracted from various distributed databases, cleansed, and transformed in the information warehouse, making distributed access quicker and easier (as well as often providing more accurate results). This practice allows users to access actual, current corporate data, running involved and processors-intensive queries, without affecting the production systems. This not only protects the integrity of vital data and production systems, it also is often the most efficient way of allowing access to multiple databases of differing designs. It is also one of the more practical ways of storing and managing historical information, accounting detail, and other data that may be too unwieldy to manage on local systems.

Many companies have used data warehousing successfully to preserve their distributed computing systems while simultaneously allowing users "one stop shopping" for all the data contained in the various distributed databases. As a result, data warehouses are becoming increasingly popular.

To keep the data in the warehouse sufficiently current to meet the needs of its users, data may have to be transferred from the production databases to the warehouse (after cleansing and normalization) many times a day. This frequent transfer of data places special demands on the network, because the data will need to be transferred quickly enough to keep the warehouse up to date (if you need to update the warehouse every six hours, but a data transfer takes eight hours, you've a real problem on your hands) while not bringing the network traffic for the production databases to a standstill.

One thing to keep in mind when you are designing a network to support a data warehouse is that usually the primary reason for implementing data warehousing is cost. Therefore, any additional cost incurred to develop a network for a data warehouse system will likely be closely scrutinized by corporate management. As a result, a lower cost, high-speed networking alternative is probably the best choice for this environment.

Building Blocks of Distributed Computing Systems

So far we have discussed the goals of distributed computing systems as well as some of the ways these systems are implemented. All of these systems are designed and built using a common set of database tools and techniques. Understanding these basic "building blocks" of distributed computing systems will help you better understand their networking requirements, so we'll describe them in some detail.

Relational Databases

The relational database has become the data structure of choice for most corporate distributed computing systems. One reason is that its structure is, by definition, transparent to its users. Here's how it's designed: All relational databases consist of only two-dimensional tables with rows. The rows are not in any particular order. Rows *are*, however, supposed to have a unique primary key that defines a sort order or other criteria. A single column is common to every row in the table, as shown in Figure 3-4.

The model doesn't specify exactly how tables are represented physically, so they could take pretty much any form—indexed files, for example. However, all the users see is a table with rows and columns.

Structured Query Language

Almost every relational database product available supports a Structured Query Language (SQL) interface. SQL, invented by IBM and now standardized by the American National Standards Institute (ANSI), started life as a database query language for the VM/370 and MVS/370 operating systems. Today, SQL is used to access data on all different types of database systems, including mainframes, midrange systems, UNIX systems, and network servers.

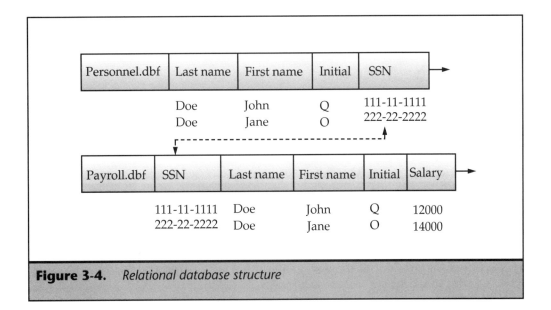

Figure 3-4.   *Relational database structure*

SQL is both a data definition language and a data manipulation tool that can be used to develop complex queries. SQL takes advantage of the inherent strengths of relational databases: efficient optimizers that make all the decisions about data access at the time the database is compiled or at execution. Therefore, SQL specifies the targeted values of the queries or updates, but specifies nothing about how the data is to be accessed. For example, in SQL you can't save a pointer or select indices.

SQL plays a key role in a client-server environment. It provides a standard interface between the user's front-end application and the DBMS engine. This interface can be implemented through application programming interfaces embedded in the programming language (embedded application program interfaces—APIs) or called externally (call-level APIs). In either case, SQL effects the communication between the front-end application—which usually resides on the user's desktop computer—and the back-end database—which usually runs on a server located elsewhere on the network.

Middleware

Middleware is software that lets users access data on a server using a wide variety of front-end applications. Using middleware is the latest trend in client-server networks, because it lets users select any front-end application they want to access any "back-end" server on the network, hiding the underlying network from applications. This allows users and programmers to use and develop applications without having to know anything about the networks on which they will run or the communication protocols that will be used on those networks. This lets the programmers concentrate on the applications and the users concentrate on doing their work. It also provides a mechanism for integrating legacy database applications with new ones. Clearly, middleware is especially helpful for programmers developing applications that will run on networks that use different network communication protocols.

Caught in the Middle

Like its name suggests, middleware acts as an intermediary between front-end applications and back-end engines, as shown in Figure 3-5.

Its role is something like that of a diplomat mediating an agreement among countries that don't share common cultures or languages. The diplomat provides language translation services as well as a standard etiquette by which all parties agree to conduct themselves. Therefore, citizens of Country A may know nothing about the culture of Country W, but they know if they conduct themselves by the standard etiquette, or *protocol*, they will be able to carry on trade with them successfully. Likewise, middleware translates between the APIs of front-end and back-end applications and provides a standard interface to which developers of both types of applications can write for successful interaction.

Middleware is crucial to client-server computing for a couple of reasons. First, it hides the differences among various vendors' SQL. Although SQL is supposed to provide a standard interface between front-end applications and back-end data, each vendor has slight differences in how they have implemented SQL. Thus, middleware plays an important role in making back-end data available to all vendors' SQL.

Second, it keeps application development generic. For example, without middleware, a programmer developing an application for a multiprotocol environment would have to develop a variation of the application to work with each of the protocols present in the network. Middleware, however, was developed to negotiate the multiprotocol environment, so all the programmer has to do is write the application to the middleware interface and middleware takes care of the rest.

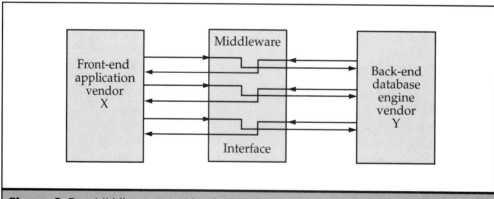

Figure 3-5. *Middleware provides the interface between front-end applications and back-end database engines*

Types of Middleware

Middleware comes in three flavors. Each has a different impact on network traffic, so we'll briefly discuss each of them. The three types of middleware are

- Conversations
- Messaging systems
- Remote procedure calls

CONVERSATIONS   A *conversation* is a continuous stream of requests and replies between two or more systems. Because of its continuous nature and many-to-many orientation, conversations are generally used in situations where full synchronization of databases is critical.

MESSAGING SYSTEMS   *Messaging systems* are store-and-forward systems that can be likened to a voice mail system. They allow applications to leave messages—in the form of commands and data—for other applications to pick up and process at a later time.

Because messaging systems aren't real-time and require no synchronization among systems, messaging systems are connectionless. Because messaging systems don't operate in real-time, they are generally deployed in widely dispersed networks and/or networks with low transfer rates. Obviously, therefore, middleware based on messaging systems is not crying out for a high-speed network to support it.

REMOTE PROCEDURES CALLS   *Remote procedure calls* (RPCs) are requests from one machine to another over a network, as shown in Figure 3-6. In an RPC, the requester waits for a response before issuing the next request. Consequently, RPCs are usually real-time calls that take place over connection-oriented interfaces. The Open Software Foundation has written specifications for an environment called the Distributed Computing Environment (DCE) that includes a set of middleware RPCs that can break processing tasks down into smaller routines, any of which can then be run on any server on a network.

Developing Standards in Middleware

As middleware becomes more prevalent and more crucial in the development of distributed computing environments, different organizations and companies are attempting to develop standards that will allow interoperability among all front-end and back-end systems. Currently, the major standards seem to be Microsoft's Open Database Connectivity (ODBC) standard and the Independent Database Application Program Interface (IDAPI) which was jointly developed by IBM, Novell, and Borland. At the time of this writing, Microsoft's ODBC appears predominant.

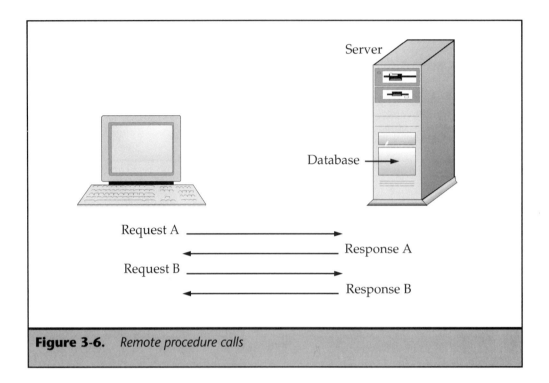

Figure 3-6.   *Remote procedure calls*

Data Propagation

Data propagation is really just copying data in whole or in part. As well as copying, data propagation may also involve some level of data processing, such as summarizing or aggregating. The concept of data propagation plays a key role in designing a distributed computing system because it is the means by which the data is distributed to various platforms around the network.

A carefully planned system of data propagation, such as the one shown in Figure 3-7, allows database administrators to divide processing tasks among the server platforms that are best able to perform them. It lets administrators break large processing tasks into several smaller tasks and distribute them throughout the network. It also allows them to maintain security by providing users with only those parts of the data absolutely necessary to perform their jobs. This explains why it is so popular for financial analysis and decision support systems.

Data propagation has many costs associated with it. As a result, you must carefully plan your data propagation strategy. Data propagation obviously increases network traffic, data storage requirements, data communications facilities, and management time. Management is especially crucial, because maintaining the consistency of the directories, synchronizing data, and providing adequate storage on the various server platforms require careful planning and frequent review. As well, the security of data

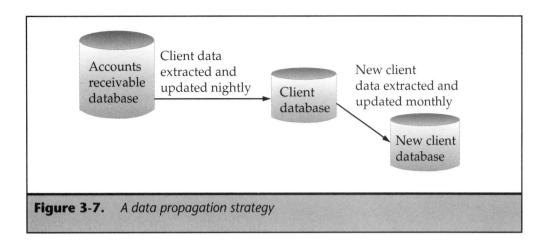

Figure 3-7.   *A data propagation strategy*

both over the wire as it is being propagated and on the hard drives of the server platform may be critical.

Network Requirements of a Server Farm

Now that we've had a fairly thorough discussion of the what, why, and how of a server farm, it's time to translate that into network needs. From the preceding discussion, we can see that a network that connects a distributed computing environment like the one illustrated in Figure 3-8 must support

- A wide variety of communications protocols
- Real-time connection-oriented requests to servers
- Quick updates to a directory naming service
- High-speed replication of data to various servers
- High-speed transfers of extracted data to data warehouse computers
- Database connectivity
- Security
- Rapid synchronization of data
- Transparency to users
- Quick response to users, even during extract transfer replications and backups
- Fault tolerance
- Easy installation and configuration, because you will probably be moving it around frequently to balance the load on servers

- Driver support for many different server platforms
- Support for fiber-optic cabling and other high-speed, high-security media

TIP: Security may be far more important on a server farm than on other portions of the network. This is because distributed computing systems are most frequently used to handle accounting systems and decision support systems that include sensitive financial data.

Indications of Bandwidth Drought on the Farm

The empirical evidence that your server farm is suffering from insufficient bandwidth is

- Delayed replication of databases
- Corrupted databases caused by poor synchronization
- Slow response time to users during data extract transfers
- Slow updates to directory naming service

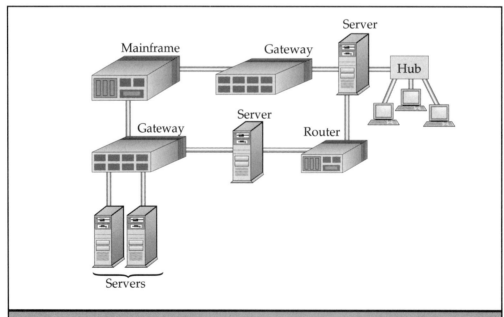

Figure 3-8. *A distributed computing system*

Other Causes and Cures for Slow Performance on the Server Farm

Even if the network supporting your server farm is suffering from one or more of the problems listed above, it is still premature to conclude that implementing a high-speed network is the solution. There are other situations that can cause slow performance on a server farm. And there certainly may be other—often less expensive—solutions.

Location of Data and Applications

Before you conclude that you need more bandwidth on the server farm, however, ask yourself whether it's possible to balance the load more equitably among the servers. If you can move databases and/or applications from busier servers to more idle servers, you may notice performance problems alleviating or disappearing altogether. Also, whenever possible, be sure all users are as close as possible—both physically and logically—to the databases they use most frequently. Although the point of a distributed computing system is that users anywhere can effectively access data anywhere, you can sometimes spot trends in data usage and keep users as close to their data as possible. This helps keep network traffic to a minimum.

TIP: *Balancing server load and keeping users close to their data is much more efficient—and much less expensive—than implementing a high-speed protocol on your server farm.*

Inadequate Hardware

You should also check your workstation hardware configuration. Client-server application front-ends tend to demand a lot of processing power from workstations, so be sure that they are up to the task. Ensure that your workstations have sufficient memory and processing power for the job.

Also, check servers to make sure that they are not the bottleneck. Database engines can put a strain on disk input/output. If your servers are waiting on disk input/output, that's probably the cause of the network slowdown, and it can be alleviated by installing a faster disk subsystem. Likewise, insufficient memory (often indicated by memory swapping to disk), low throughput to and from the network adapter (resulting in dropped packets and retransmissions), and inadequate processors can all slow your servers and cause them to be a bottleneck on your server farm.

Buying the Farm

Of course, the true and indisputable determination of where your server farm's bottleneck lies comes from in-depth analysis of your network traffic with a protocol analyzer (see Chapter 1). A protocol analyzer will help you determine whether packets are being dropped, resulting in retransmissions, and pinpoint where those packets are being dropped. It will also help you confirm whether your network has heavy internetwork traffic (data packets addressed to a node not on the same segment it originated). You can also use the protocol analyzer to determine *bandwidth utilization*, or the average percentage of bandwidth being used, on your server farm's network. If you are experiencing slow network performance and dropped packets, and if your network's bandwidth utilization over the server farm's segment(s) consistently averages over 50 percent, it's fairly safe to say that the problem is too much network traffic, and your server farm's network is a good candidate for implementing high-speed networking protocols.

CHAPTER 4

Closer to Home

When Is a Workgroup Powerful?

Servers aren't the only causes of network traffic jams. In this era of collaborative computing and client-server architectures, workstations often generate more traffic than their network protocols can handle efficiently. This heavy traffic is usually generated by *power workgroups*—users who collaborate via their computers, sending massive amounts of electronic mail to one another, constantly surfing the Internet, and often employing bandwidth-gobbling applications such as multimedia, client-server databases, groupware, and workflow software.

To understand if and when these applications might dictate a high-speed protocol for your network, we'll first take a look at each of them and how they affect network performance. Then we'll discuss the symptoms of excessive bandwidth in the workgroup, and the special requirements a workgroup has for a high-speed protocol.

Electronic Mail and Messaging

Electronic mail is everywhere. Nearly everyone who has turned on a computer has used electronic mail. They are undoubtedly one of the most widely used network applications in existence. More important to your network traffic, however, is *electronic messaging* (on which electronic mail systems are based), which is a system for exchanging data commands among applications. An electronic message may carry an electronic mail, or it may contain a request for service from a user to a remote database, which in turn replies with a message back to the user.

Despite all the benefits of electronic mail—instant communication, elimination of telephone tag, and others—it can pose a traffic problem. Often, careful management can alleviate mail-induced bandwidth problems, or even avoid them altogether. However, sometimes the only answer is more bandwidth. To understand how to manage electronic mail and messaging, let's first take a look at how it works.

An Electronic Mail System

The basic components of an electronic mail system are a mail-enabled user application, a back-end mail application, and a mail directory. The user application would reside on the user's workstation and allow the user to create, address, and send electronic mail. The back-end mail application resides on a server and would handle the delivery of the messages, including any document conversion and gateway operations required among different types of electronic mail systems. The electronic mail directory is a database of electronic mail addresses that would also reside on a server or servers. A typical electronic mail system would look something like the one in Figure 4-1.

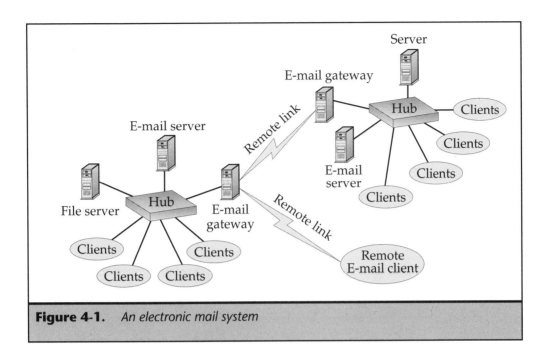

Figure 4-1. *An electronic mail system*

Electronic Messaging Systems

An electronic messaging system is something like an electronic mail system for applications rather than people. As we mentioned earlier, an application may send an electronic message containing a request to another application. The receiving application can then send its reply in an electronic message to the application making the request. Electronic messaging is a store-and-forward operation. That means the exchange of electronic messages doesn't take place in real-time—the requesting application does not wait for a reply before continuing with its other processing. While this wouldn't be acceptable in many systems, it's perfect for collaborative workgroups. That's because it allows members of workgroups to exchange information and work together *without having to establish and maintain real-time sessions with one another*. They can send information and messages that other users can read and act upon later, enabling widely dispersed users to function as a workgroup. Furthermore, you can attach text and graphics files to messages, making it easy to exchange documents, photos, and other types of images with other users.

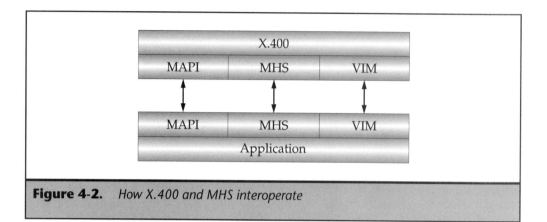

Figure 4-2. *How X.400 and MHS interoperate*

Electronic Messaging Systems, Standards, and Tools

As you can imagine, as the number of widespread workgroups increases, the amount of electronic mail and messaging increases even faster. This has the potential for causing performance problems, depending upon the traffic characteristics of the electronic messaging being used. This in turn depends upon which electronic messaging standard the messaging-enabled applications use. Some are more efficient than others, so we'll discuss the most popular ones here.

Mail Systems and Standards

A number of e-mail standards have been proposed to span all computing environments, including mainframes and local area networks. Probably the two most widely used are the CCITT's X.400 standard, and Novell's Message Handling Service (MHS). The two function at different layers in the application interface, as illustrated in Figure 4-2, and unfortunately are not always compatible.

X.400 The Consultative Committee for International Telegraph and Telephone (CCITT) has defined the X.400 store-and-forward message exchange system. The goal of X.400 is to provide message exchange interoperability among a wide variety of platforms. The basic components of X.400 are

- **User agent (UA),** which resides on the client computer as part of the front-end mail application.

- **Message transfer agent (MTA),** which accepts messages from the UA and routes them to other MTAs. The MTA may perform data conversion and translation if required.

■ **The message store (MS)**, which is a storage directory for messages that are currently undeliverable. For example, if the addressee isn't logged into the network when the MTA first tries to deliver a message, the message will be stored in the message store, where the addressee can collect it later.

■ **Access unit (AU)**, which is an interface to the mail system for dissimilar systems, such as fax machines.

■ **Directory system**, which is a database of names and electronic mail addresses.

NOTE: In X.400, the directory system is called X.500 and includes a special format for electronic mail names and addresses.

NOVELL MESSAGE HANDLING SERVICE (MHS)   Novell developed NetWare MHS to provide messaging for both LANs and wide area networks (WANs). MHS is designed to function as the messaging engine for both electronic mail systems and application message systems. Therefore, developers can use MHS to create applications that talk to other applications and exchange information. For example, queries can be made to databases on other systems using MHS as long as both client front-end and server back-end applications support the MHS interface.

Figure 4-3 shows an MHS installation. MHS is built on the client-server model, so in an MHS environment host systems provide messaging services for a group of clients. MHS hubs route messages and establish connections. Because MHS was developed to support both local and wide area networks, it supports remote connections.

Mail-Enabled Applications

As we mentioned earlier, many client-server applications use store-and-forward messaging systems to communicate with each other. *Mail-enabled applications* are

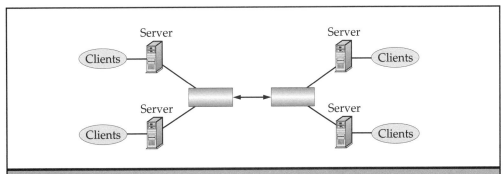

Figure 4-3.   *An MHS system built on the client-server model*

applications that use messaging systems to let the application users communicate with each other. Electronic mail is an organic, integrated function of a mail-enabled application, allowing users to create, address, and mail data and documents from within the application. Vendors are now shipping mail-enabled word processors, databases, and applications. Figure 4-4 shows how these standards interoperate.

Electronic Mail Application Programming Interfaces (APIs)

So, how do programmers design support for messaging systems into their applications? By using application program interfaces (APIs) developed to provide application support for these systems. These APIs define such things as address formats and file attachment services. Several standard APIs have emerged to provide interoperability among applications and various mail systems. Some of these standard APIs are described below.

VENDOR-INDEPENDENT MESSAGING (VIM)   Vendor-Independent Messaging (VIM), developed by Lotus Development Corporation, is an API that allows developers to create mail-enabled applications that work on many different platforms.

MESSAGING APPLICATION PROGRAMMING INTERFACE (MAPI)   Developed by Microsoft to enhance Windows interoperability, MAPI provides a way for Windows applications to access messaging systems like Microsoft Mail and Novell's MHS.

STANDARD MESSAGE FORMAT (SMF)   This is the messaging API provided by Novell for MHS.

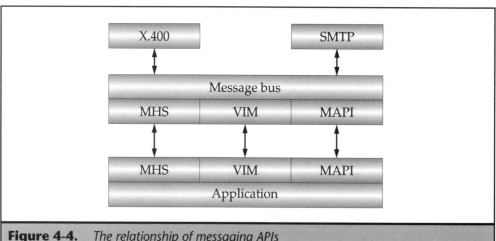

Figure 4-4.   *The relationship of messaging APIs*

The Internet

It's now a cliché to say that the Internet has revolutionized how people locate information and each other. Nearly everyone has turned to the Internet for research and communication, both for business and personal use. While this has made information in heretofore unheard of variety and quantity available to record numbers of people, the Internet is something of a curse to network designers. That's because "surfing the 'Net" involves downloading huge, graphics-laden files as well as sending and receiving electronic mail in astonishing amounts. Workgroups that use the Internet frequently are among the first to experience slow network performance.

Electronic Mail and Messaging on the Internet

Electronic messaging on the Internet employs systems and standards that are different from, but interoperate with, that of local and wide area private networks. Refer again to Figure 4-2. For example, the messaging standard for electronic mail on the Internet is *simple mail transfer protocol* (SMTP), which can support any user interface as a front end. Therefore, users can exchange SMTP-based electronic mail with anyone on the Internet without going through a gateway. Furthermore, using *multipurpose Internet mail extension* (MIME), a standard built on SMTP constructs, users can exchange multimedia e-mail messages that include both text and multimedia components.

Client-Server Applications

For the past several years, one of the most popular phrases in the computing industry has been *client-server computing*. However, it has become obvious that the concept of what constitutes client-server computing varies dramatically from vendor to vendor. For the purposes of this book, client-server computing is a distributed computing model in which users work at intelligent computers running *front-end applications* that share processing functions with *back-end applications* that run on network servers. The servers running the back-end applications provide far more than storage, file, and print services. Taking advantage of the server's often far superior processing power, the back-end applications perform applications processing tasks such as complex calculations and queries. Most commonly, client-server systems are composed of a *database management system* (DBMS) in which clients query back-end servers using *structured query language* (SQL), which we discussed in some detail in Chapter 3.

Client-Server Architecture

The client-server architecture defines a relationship between the client and the server. The client can't be a dumb terminal. It must have its own processing ability, but it doesn't have to bear all the burden of processing as it generally does in the file server model. There are several possible client-server configurations. One of the most common is shown in Figure 4-5, in which clients access a distributed database located on several servers.

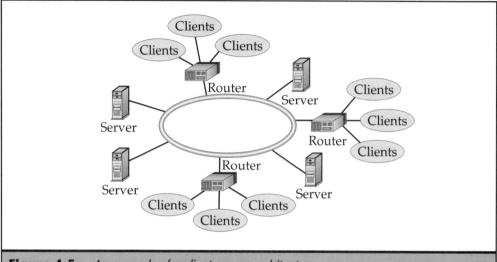

Figure 4-5.   *An example of a client-server architecture*

How to Build a Client-Server Application to Minimize Traffic

Currently there are no strict standards on how to build client-server architectures or applications. There are, however, four broad models for client-server systems, each with its own strengths and weaknesses. Therefore, you can base your client-server system on the model that suits your network's particular needs, whether those be minimal server load, minimal client load, or minimal network traffic.

Standard Model

The client portion in this model does little more than transmit requests to the back-end server portion. The server then responds to the requests. This model probably puts the greatest traffic burden on the network, especially if the server responses involve large amounts of data.

Stored Procedures

Think of stored procedures as macros stored on the server. The client sends a request to the server and receives a response, just like in the standard model. However, in this model the client doesn't send quite as many requests to the server because stored on the server are these macros, or procedures, triggered by requests from the clients, which automatically perform a complete task. This model moves closer to the object-oriented model in which procedures are stored with data.

Object-Oriented Model

In this model, data and procedures are encapsulated in objects. In the object-oriented model, procedures and data are stored together as a single object, minimizing network traffic. Objects communicate with one another using message-passing procedures, managed by a mechanism called an *object request broker* (ORB). The ORB receives a request from a client, then locates the most appropriate service on the network to respond to a request. By combining procedures and data into objects, and giving the system the intelligence to find the best network resources to process the object, this model generally results in optimum performance with minimum traffic generation.

Data Warehouse

In this model, data is stored in a back-end server "warehouse" that is not usually directly accessed by the users. Instead, a system sitting between the user and the warehouse extracts the appropriate data from the warehouse and prepares it for delivery to the user. Furthermore, this system may already have the requested information, so it may be able to reply to client requests without accessing the warehouse server. This system minimizes the processing burden on the warehouse server, but can result in more network traffic in those instances when the secondary or intermediate server is unable to reply to a client request.

Effects of Client-Server Computing on Network Traffic

In some instances, client-server computing reduces the amount of traffic on the network. The reason is that in the file server model, when a user wants to work on a particular file, he or she requests it from the server. The server then sends a copy of the entire file as well as the program the user will use to work on it across the network to the workstation, which does all the processing. When the user finishes working on the file, he or she sends the entire copy of the completed data across the network to the server. You can see how network traffic increases at the beginning and end of working on a file.

However, the file server model was made for a "feast or famine" model of network traffic. When users began working on files, the network traffic was heavy as entire copies of the data (executable) and overlay files were transmitted to the workstation. When they completed work, network traffic was heavy as an entire copy of the data was transmitted back to the server. However, in between these operations there was almost no traffic between workstation and server.

The client-server model has pretty much eliminated the flood of traffic at the beginning and end of tasks. Network traffic is reduced because the server only gives the client the information requested, not large blocks of information that the workstation must process. However, it has made for a consistently higher level of traffic at any given time.

Multimedia

Multimedia is the bane of any network traffic management scheme. Multimedia involves sending not only text, but also voice, video, and graphics files across the network, often in real-time. Multimedia files are huge, requiring not only large amounts of disk space for storage, but (more critically for us) massive bandwidth for transmission. More and more applications, especially groupware applications, are including multimedia support. Therefore, we can only warn you that it is probably a matter of when, not if, multimedia support becomes an issue on **your** network.

Some multimedia applications are less bandwidth-greedy than others. Image and graphics files, while large and complex, generally don't require synchronized delivery of multiple frames like video and sound files usually do. By the same token, store-and-forward messages that don't require immediate delivery don't demand the high-bandwidth transmission rates necessary for real-time video, which must have dedicated bandwidth during the transmission and a fast transmission rate.

NOTE: *Flicker-free full-motion video requires a delivery speed of 30 frames per second (fps). Viewers find the quality of video with a delivery speed below 10 frames per second to be unacceptably "jumpy."*

Workflow Software

Workflow software combines electronic messaging with document management and imaging. The concept is to move a document through various stages of processing by sending it to people within a group who have the equipment and skills to manipulate the document or the authority to sign and validate it.

Typical environments where workflow software is beneficial would be a tax preparation firm. A document containing an income tax return would travel through the firm as shown in Figure 4-6. Raw data for the tax return would be entered by a typist working from original client documents. Once the data entry is completed, the tax return document would go into a queue for review by a first-level accountant, who would actually perform the necessary calculations and apply the necessary tax regulations to complete the return. When the first-level accountant's work is completed, the tax return document would then go into a queue for review by a senior accountant, who would check the return for accuracy and completeness. Once the review is finished, the tax return document would be printed and presented to the taxpayer for signature and approval. At that point, the tax return would go into a queue awaiting electronic filing. When the return was filed and confirmation received, the document would then be archived.

NOTE: *In this example, as in many workflow environments, software must provide a high level of security, perhaps through some implementation of passwords and login authentication.*

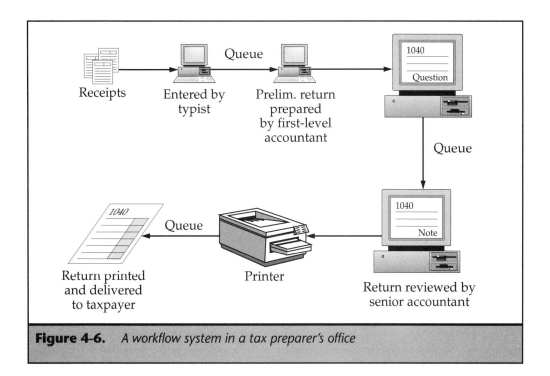

Figure 4-6. *A workflow system in a tax preparer's office*

What distinguishes a workflow system from other document processing systems is that in a workflow system, documents:

- Contain routing information
- Allow simultaneous access
- Have a filing system, queue, and workflow manager
- Allow "user sign off" at various stages
- Lock all or part of approved documents to prevent further modification

Groupware

Groupware is exactly what its name implies: software used by a group of people to enable them to work together more efficiently and effectively. It lets users conduct discussions and debates, schedule meetings, and work collaboratively. By definition, it should allow several people to:

- Access the files and documents simultaneously
- Make and track modifications to files and documents
- Monitor projects

Groupware in Action

An example of groupware is Windows for Workgroups' object linking and embedding (OLE) features. It lets users collaborate on one document simultaneously, letting them create and modify text, graphics, and spreadsheet information. The resulting document, called a *compound document* and illustrated in Figure 4-7, actually contains links to a file on the workstation of the person who created a given element. If that file is changed, the element linked to it in the compound document also changes. Therefore, the next time any user anywhere opens the compound document, the document is automatically updated.

There are lots of companies offering groupware now. Among them are the following:

■ Microsoft Windows for Workgroups is a workgroup-based network operating system and a suite of applications and interfaces that aid in collaborative computing.

■ Novell's Groupwise is a workgroup suite that provides e-mail, project management, workflow, and calendaring and scheduling applications.

■ Lotus Development's Notes is a groupware environment for developing and using document processing, messaging, and database applications.

■ Intelligent Messaging Service (IM) from Banyan Systems is a product that includes both e-mail and workflow software. IM also provides a messaging system that supports other collaborative applications such as NetScape's Collabrashare.

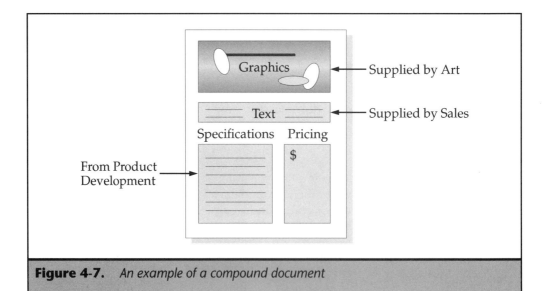

Figure 4-7. *An example of a compound document*

Groupware Tools

With so many vendors offering so many different types of groupware, all of which offer similar, overlapping functionality, you may be wondering whether each of these implementations is proprietary and thus restrictive. The answer is both yes and no. Yes, each company's implementation of groupware is proprietary, but fortunately each employs—to varying degrees—standard interfaces that enable the collaborative environment. Among these technologies are the following.

Standard Generalized Markup Language (SGML)

Like the American Standard Code for Information Interchange (ASCII), *Standard Generalized Markup Language* (SGML) is a standard means of storing data in documents. However, unlike ASCII, SGML defines procedures for sharing within the same document data that was created in other environments. SGML files can have attributes that define each element of a document (such as page style, footers, and paragraphs) that can be transferred to any other application that supports SGML.

Windows Open System Architecture (WOSA)

Windows Open System Architecture (WOSA) is a Microsoft API that allows developers to build messaging functionality into their Windows applications that allows users to access information across multiple platforms within a single enterprise.

Group Therapy

Now that you know how much bandwidth a workgroup can consume, how can you determine whether your network traffic problems are being caused by the workgroup or by something else? Luckily, there are a few signs of an overactive workgroup. First, if you have workgroups using multimedia applications, especially full-motion video systems like the one shown in Figure 4-8, they should be prime suspects when the network starts to slow. Furthermore, if slow performance is limited to just one segment on your network (not a backbone or server farm), chances are the problem lies in the activities of the workgroup or workgroups on that segment rather than with the server. As well, if network timeouts, packet collisions, and packet retransmissions seem to occur only in one segment, and all the network adapters, hubs, and cables test out fine, it's fairly safe to say that the workgroup on that segment is the culprit.

Location of Applications

Before you conclude that more bandwidth in the workgroup is what you need, however, ask yourself whether it's possible to move all the applications the workgroup needs onto the same segment as the user without slowing down performance for users on other segments. Be sure all users are as close as possible—both physically and logically—to the network resources they use most frequently. This at least eliminates unnecessary internetwork traffic.

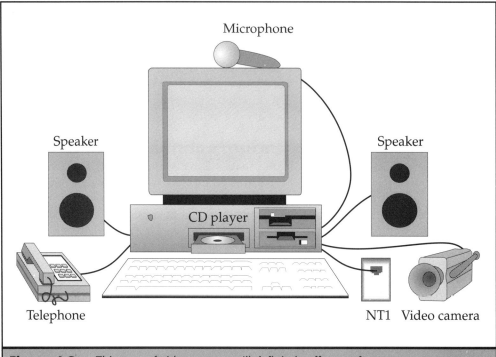

Figure 4-8.   *This type of video system will definitely affect performance*

Inadequate Hardware

Next, check your workstations and servers. Ensure that they have sufficient memory and processing power for the job. Also, check servers to make sure that they are not the bottleneck. If your servers are waiting on disk input/output, that's probably the cause of the network slowdown and it can be alleviated by installing a faster disk subsystem. Likewise, insufficient memory (often indicated by memory swapping to disk), low throughput to and from the network adapter (resulting in dropped packets and retransmissions), and inadequate processors can all slow your servers and cause them to be bottlenecks on your power workgroup segment.

"Chatty" Communication Protocols

Just as with backbones, another cause of congested workgroup segments is the *communication protocol* used by your network operating system. Among the functions of the communication protocol are creating service connections, getting network station addresses, and other tasks associated with transferring data from a station on one network to a station on another network. The communication protocol operates at the network layer as described on the International Standards Organization's Open Systems Interconnection model (see Appendix A). Communication protocols include Internet protocol (IP) and NetWare's Internetwork Packet Exchange protocol (IPX).

Some communication protocols generate a lot of traffic because for every request for service they send, they require a response from the station that is granting the services. Because of this constant "conversation" between the requester and grantor of services, these protocols are called "chatty" protocols. IPX, for example, is the classic example of a "chatty" protocol—request then response, request then response. Often these requests and responses are larger than one packet. Therefore, a chatty protocol significantly increases the number of packets being transmitted. Consequently, chatty protocols are not a good choice for deployment in power workgroups.

Transmission control protocol/Internet protocol (TCP/IP), on the other hand, is not a chatty protocol. Rather than sending a request for service, waiting for a reply, then sending the next request for service, TCP/IP sends all requests for service in a single burst, sometimes called a "packet burst." It then receives multiple responses from the grantor of those services. This makes it a better choice for a power workgroup protocol than IPX.

To ease the congestion that IPX can cause, Novell has introduced PBURST NLM, a NetWare Loadable Module that enables the server and workstations to function in packet burst mode, sending all service requests in a single burst. However, PBURST is not turned on by default. You will have to load PBURST manually or add the LOAD PBURST command to your STARTUP.NCF file.

Small Packet Size

Also, bigger is better when it comes to packet size in segments that are using multimedia applications. That's because multimedia applications involve large files with rapid delivery rates, and one large packet obviously represents less traffic than a lot of little ones. This has a couple of indications. First, you should select a protocol with the largest packet size available. Second, if you're running NetWare, you may have to make some adjustments.

Your NetWare servers could be needlessly creating more traffic because they are limiting packet size to a 512KB maximum. By default, NetWare servers route a default packet size of 512KB. This is because 512KB used to be the largest packet that all routers could route. However, most routers these days will route at the maximum packet size for each protocol. Therefore, if you have a NetWare network, check to make sure your routers can handle a larger packet size. If they can, contact Novell for the workaround that will enable the server to default to a larger packet size.

Finally, look at the history of the workgroup. If you've had to make smaller and smaller segments to isolate high-bandwidth users from the rest of the network, any recurring or persistent performance problems are probably workgroup-related.

Group Encounters

Of course, the true and indisputable determination of where your workgroup's bottleneck lies comes from in-depth analysis of your network traffic with a protocol analyzer (see Chapter 1). A protocol analyzer will help you determine whether packets are being dropped, resulting in retransmissions, and pinpoint where those packets are being dropped. It will also help you confirm whether your network has heavy internetwork traffic (data packets addressed to a node not on the same segment it originated). You can also use the protocol analyzer to determine *bandwidth utilization*, or the average percentage of bandwidth being used, on your workgroup's segment. If you are experiencing slow network performance and dropped packets, and if your network's bandwidth utilization over the server farm's segment(s) consistently averages over 50 percent, it's fairly safe to say that the problem is too much network traffic, and your workgroup's segment is a good candidate for implementing high-speed networking protocols.

Group Things

When selecting a high-speed networking protocol for the workgroup, there are a few issues unique to this environment that you should consider:

- **Applications transparency** Applications transparency means existing applications can run over the new network protocol. As we will see in Chapter 16, this is especially important when considering asynchronous transfer mode.

- **Computer compatibility** When converting to a new network protocol, each computer in the workgroup must be equipped with a new network interface card. The NIC must be compatible with the bus type, operating system, and model of the connected workstation. It is important that the NIC card has been tested with the specific product you are using. Also, choose a vendor that has experience with NICs across a variety of platforms.

- **Physical network compatibility** Ideally, the new network protocol should support the type of cable that is already installed in the workgroup. Another consideration is the wiring hub location. Be sure you have enough space, power, and air conditioning to meet the requirements of any new equipment.

- **Special multimedia considerations** To maintain deterministic frame delivery, video traffic should not be directed through routers. Therefore, you'll need to keep video users within the same area or network segment. Furthermore, prioritization of real-time video traffic can ensure that it has enough bandwidth in the available signal to ensure quality delivery. Switched micro-segmented Ethernet, asynchronous transfer mode (ATM), and new 100Mbps Fast Ethernet technologies can provide the bandwidth.

CHAPTER 5

The Wide Area

Why Are We Talking About Wide Area Protocols in This Book?

In many organizations, there is a distinct division of responsibilities between "network management" and "telecommunications management." Network managers handle all aspects of the local area network up to the building walls or the campus gate. All data communications outside the local area network are administered by the telecommunication managers. Whether or not this is the case in your organization, you probably still need to read this chapter, as well as the other wide area networking chapters in this book.

If you are a network manager, you probably already know that most wide area equipment vendors assume you know enough about data communications over the wide area to select and manage their wares. If you're a telecommunications manager, you know that the fastest growing part of your job is wide area data communications, and that requires an understanding of local area networking. In either case, you'll need an understanding of wide area networking and how it interoperates with local area networking.

The most compelling reason to read the wide area networking chapters in this book, however, is that *your users don't know the difference between local and wide area data communications—and they don't want to.* Network operating systems and networked applications are becoming very "wide area aware," and are so good at hiding the location of data and programs that users mistake wide area performance problems for local performance problems. For example, I know of a situation in which a user complained about how doggedly slow the network was because it had taken her almost a minute to retrieve a document. Upon investigation, I discovered that the document was on a server in another city, and she was accessing it over a 19.2Kbps dial-up line. The network operating system and the document management application she was using had done a great job of making the location and retrieval transparent to the user. It was so transparent, in fact, that I had a hard time explaining to the user that the problem wasn't an underpowered server or workstation, or a slow LAN, but rather a wide area link that was many times slower than the local links—and couldn't be cost-justifiably upgraded.

This brings up another reason for studying the wide area. Whether you are in telecommunications or network management, because of the previously mentioned wide area transparency of applications and NOSes, you will have to troubleshoot wide area problems, as well as recommend and justify the cost of wide area solutions. So read on!

The Wide Area Defined

A wide area network (WAN) uses *dedicated* or *switched* connections to link computers in geographically remote locations that are too widely dispersed to be directly linked to the local area network media. These wide area connections can be made either through the *public network* or through a *private network* built by the organization it serves.

A typical WAN and the equipment required for WAN connections is shown in Figure 5-1. A *router* sends traffic addressed to a remote location from the local network over the wide area connection to the remote destination. The router is connected either to an *analog line* or a *digital line*. Routers are connected to analog lines via *modems* or to digital lines via *channel service unit/data service units* (CSU/DSUs). The type of *carrier service* determines the exact type of equipment the wide area will need to function.

Dedicated versus Switched Lines

Wide area networks can include either *dedicated* or *switched* lines. A dedicated line is a permanent connection between two points that is usually leased on a monthly basis, as shown in Figure 5-2.

A switched line service doesn't require permanent connections between two fixed points. Instead, it lets users establish temporary connections among multiple points that last only for the duration of the data transmission, as shown in Figure 5-3.

There are two types of switched services available, *circuit-switching services* that are similar to the services used to make garden variety voice telephone calls, and *packet-switching services*, which are better suited to data transmission, as explained next.

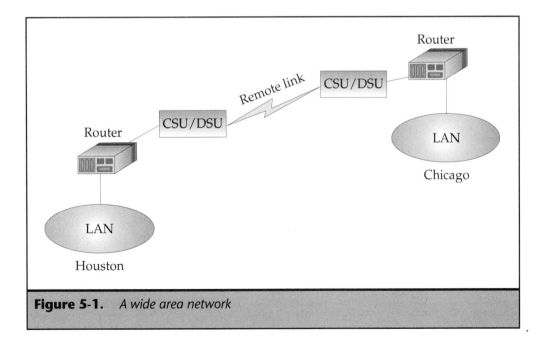

Figure 5-1. *A wide area network*

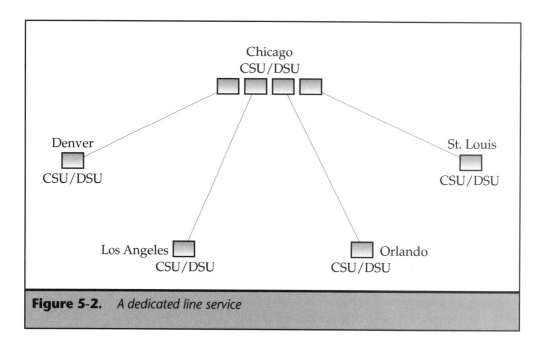

Figure 5-2. *A dedicated line service*

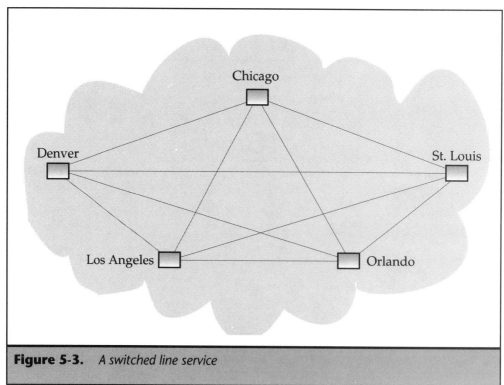

Figure 5-3. *A switched line service*

Circuit-Switching Services

In a circuit-switched connection, a dedicated channel, called a *circuit*, is set up between two points for the duration of the call. It provides a fixed amount of bandwidth during the call, and users pay for only that amount of bandwidth for amount of time on the call. Occasionally there is a delay at the beginning of these calls while the connection is being made, although new switching techniques and equipment have made this connection delay negligible in most cases.

Circuit-switching connections have a couple of serious drawbacks. First, because the bandwidth is fixed in these connections, they don't handle bursts of traffic well, requiring frequent retransmissions. Given that WAN connections are relatively slow anyway, retransmissions can make the performance crawl. The second drawback is that these virtual circuits have only one route, with no alternate paths determined. Therefore, when a line goes down, either the transmission stops or one of the users intervenes manually to reroute the traffic. Figure 5-4 illustrates a circuit-switched network.

Packet-Switching Services

Packet-switching services do away with the concept of the fixed virtual circuit. Data is transmitted one packet at a time through a network mesh or *cloud*, with each packet having the ability to take a different route through the network cloud. This is illustrated in Figure 5-5. Because there is no predefined virtual circuit, packet switching can increase or decrease bandwidth as required, and therefore handles bursts in packets elegantly. Taking advantage of the multiple paths of the network cloud, packet-switching services can route packets around failed or congested lines.

Which Switch?

Whether to choose circuit-switching or packet-switching services depends upon two things:

- The type of traffic your network generates
- Your budget

If the traffic generated on your network is delay sensitive, such as that generated by video applications, you'll need the fixed, guaranteed bandwidth of a circuit-switched service. Unfortunately, these services are very expensive. On the other hand, if your traffic can stand delays, especially if it is "bursty" in nature, packet-switching services are reliable and also more economical than circuit-switched services.

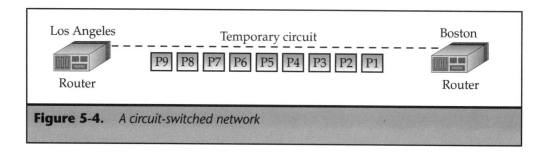

Figure 5-4. *A circuit-switched network*

Public Networks

Public networks are the wide area telecommunications facilities owned by common carriers and resold to users by subscription. These common carriers include

- Local exchange carriers
- Interexchange carriers
- Value added carriers

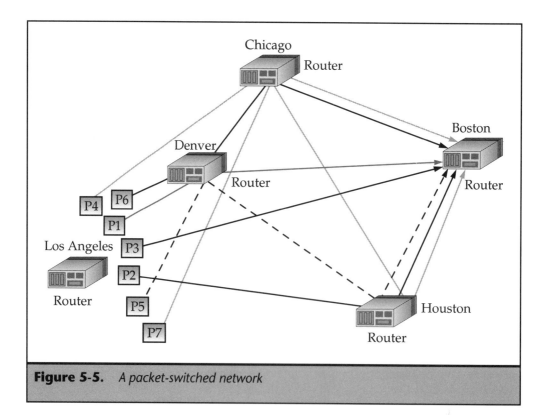

Figure 5-5. *A packet-switched network*

Each type of common carrier may offer wide area data services, and they often compete against one another in this market. Therefore, it's a good idea to check service availability and pricing with all of them.

Local Exchange Carriers (LECs)

Local exchange carriers are companies such as the Regional Bell Operating Companies (RBOCs), GTE, and other companies that handle local telephone and telecommunications connections. Until recently, these companies were restricted by federal law to handling local communications, providing *point of presence* (POP) facilities for long-distance carriers, and offering wide area communications services only within their local service areas, known as *local access and transport areas* (LATAs). However, recent legislation has permitted them to compete with long-distance carriers and eventually to discontinue providing POP facilities to their competitors in the long-distance markets.

Interexchange Carriers (IXCs)

An interexchange carrier (IXC) is a long-distance telecommunications carrier, such as AT&T, MCI, and US Sprint. Customers can choose the IXC of their choice. While many IXCs use the local point-of-presence facilities that local exchange carriers were required to provide, some IXCs built their own POPs, allowing customers to bypass the LEC and connect directly into the IXCs' long-distance services.

Just as the Telecommunications Act of 1996 has allowed LECs to go into the long-distance business, it has also allowed IXCs to compete in the local exchange carrier service market. Therefore, look for the lines between the LECs and the IXCs to disappear in the near future.

Value Added Carriers (VACs)

VACs, such as CompuServe Information Services and GE Information Services, often provide WAN services as a sideline to their core business. Typically, a VAC has a national *private data network* (PDN) it established for its own use, and resells the excess capacity of that PDN to its customers. Using a PDN saves you the trouble of acquiring the various carrier services and setting up your own switching equipment, because the switching is done in the carrier's network. The VAC also handles the management and maintenance of the WAN services, and may even be able to do some protocol conversion for you.

Private Networks

A private network is just that: a private communications network built, maintained, and controlled by the organization it serves. At a minimum, a private network requires its own switching and communications equipment. It may also use its own carrier services, or it may lease them from public networks or other private networks that have built their own communication lines.

A private network is extremely expensive. The organization that builds one must be prepared to maintain and manage its own switching and communications equipment, as well as either build its own microwave or other long-haul carrier service or negotiate to lease such service at a reasonable price. However, in companies where tight security and control over data traffic are paramount, private lines are the only guarantee of a high level of service. Furthermore, in situations where data traffic between two remote points exceeds six hours a day, employing a private network may actually be more cost effective than using the public network.

Figure 5-6 shows a private network connecting two separate sites.

A Word About Routers and Routing

Routers play a crucial part in determining the efficiency of a WAN connection. Routers connect the LAN to the WAN, learning the destination of devices on the internetwork and determining the best path for data traffic to take to reach its destination. For users of delay-sensitive applications, the router can either make the wide area connection completely transparent or a frustrating swamp. For switched-services customers, who pay only for the bandwidth they use, an efficient router can save huge amounts of money in carrier service fees.

When selecting a router for your WAN, be sure to test how efficiently it uses the carrier service. Does it terminate the connection when no traffic is being transmitted? Does it allow you to select the criteria for route determination—cost, shortest route, etc.? Does it correctly select the transmission route based on this criteria?

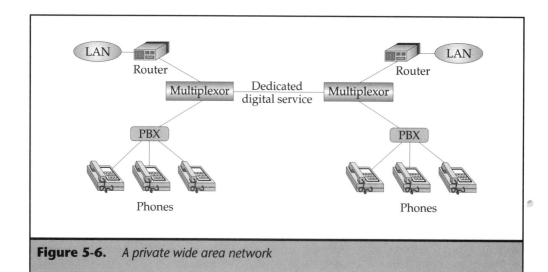

Figure 5-6.   *A private wide area network*

TIP: When purchasing wide area routers, try to get a substantial trial period or return period. This will enable you to test the router thoroughly before making a final commitment.

Analog Lines

Analog lines are garden variety voice lines that were originally developed to carry voice traffic. Analog lines are a part of plain old telephone service (POTS), and as such they are everywhere. Although digital data traffic isn't compatible with analog carrier signals, you can transmit digital traffic on analog lines by using a modem, which modulates digital signals onto analog carrier services. The maximum achievable transmission rate of digital traffic over analog lines is about 43,000 bits per second, although the international standard for this rate of transmission hasn't been completed. Currently the fastest modems available transmit about 32,600bps, which is the transmission rate of the CCITT ITU V.34bis standard. Even when modems are available that transmit at the higher rate, it will still be significantly slower than the transmission rates achievable with digital lines.

Digital Lines

Digital lines are designed to carry data traffic, which is digital in nature. Therefore, your computer equipment won't need a modem to load data onto the digital carrier signal. Instead, it will use a channel service unit/digital service unit (CSU/DSU), which simply provides an interface to the digital line. Digital lines can transmit data traffic at speeds up to 45Mbps and are available as either dedicated or switched services.

Carrier Services

Different networks require different transmission rates, data prioritization, and levels of service. They also have different budgets available for wide area connections. Luckily, there are a variety of wide area carrier services available. We'll briefly describe the most popular.

Switched Analog Lines

As we mentioned earlier, traditional analog voice lines are made up of the POTS we all know. They are widely available and inexpensive, and can theoretically support a data bandwidth of up to about 43,000 bits per second, although the current practical limit as established in the V.34bis standard is 32,600bps with compression. Analog lines come in two basic flavors:

- Dial-up lines
- Dedicated lines

DIAL-UP LINES   In dial-up access, a connection is made only when there is data to transmit. It is especially good for traffic that is not delay sensitive, such as file transfers and electronic mail.

DEDICATED LINES   These analog lines provide the same data rates as dial-up lines, except that customers have a contract with the carrier that stipulates, in return for a flat fee, that the lines will always be available for the customer's immediate use.

Circuit-Switched Services

Circuit-switched services are switched carrier services that establish a virtual connection before transmitting data. Two of the most commonly used are switched 56 service and integrated service digital network (ISDN).

SWITCHED 56 SERVICE   This is a digital data service that transmits at 56Kbps. Because it is digital, it doesn't require a modem. Instead, it uses a CSU/DSU to provide an interface between the router and the carrier service. Switched 56 is most often used as a backup to higher speed data services as well as for fax transmissions and file transfers.

INTEGRATED SERVICE DIGITAL NETWORK (ISDN)   ISDN is the first all-digital dial-up service. It will be discussed in detail in Chapter 13, so for now it is enough to note that it is a high-speed digital circuit-switching service that provides integrated voice and data services on which many other high-speed offerings are based, including switched T1 services.

The basic ISDN service unit, called the basic rate interface (BRI), has three channels (although some carriers don't offer all three in their packaging of the BRI): two provide 64Kbps data channels (called the "bearer channels" or "B channels") and the other is a 16Kbps signaling channel (called the "D channel"). The ISDN primary rate interface (PRI) provides 23 B channels and one D channel. In either interface, the D channel provides call setup and monitoring, keeping the B channels free to transmit data.

Packet-Switching Services

Packet-switching services, described in greater detail earlier in this chapter, do not function on the model of the virtual circuit. Connections don't need to be established before data transmission begins. Instead, each packet is transmitted separately, and each may take a separate path through the mesh of network paths that make up the packet-switching network. Although it is not as well suited for delay-sensitive traffic as circuit-switching services, packet-switching services do handle bursty traffic better. The most popular packet-switching services are X.25 and frame relay.

X.25   X.25 networks have been around since 1976, when it was mostly used to provide remote terminal connections to mainframes. They perform extensive error checking that ensures reliable delivery. However, X.25 networks are not suitable for most LAN-to-LAN traffic because of the time and bandwidth consumed by this extensive error checking. Still, X.25 operates at speeds up to 2Mbps, which is much higher than the previously described carrier services.

FRAME RELAY   Frame relay, which began life as a service of ISDN, provides services similar to X.25, but is faster and more efficient. Frame relay doesn't employ the extensive error checking of X.25. We will discuss frame relay in greater detail in Chapter 13.

Cell-Switched Services

In cell-switched services, the smallest unit of data switched is a fixed-size "cell" rather than a variable-size packet. This cell-based technology allows switching to be accomplished in hardware without complex and time-consuming frame-by-frame route calculation. This makes switching both faster and less expensive.

ASYNCHRONOUS TRANSFER MODE (ATM)   ATM, which will be discussed in detail in Chapter 16, can currently transfer data at rates of 25Mbps to 622Mbps and has the potential to transfer data at rates measured in gigabits per second. Many carriers already offer ATM services, with many more scheduled to do so in the near future.

SWITCHED MULTIMEGABIT DATA SERVICE (SMDS)   Like ATM, switched multimegabit data service is another cell-based service provided by the regional Bell operating companies (RBOCs) in selected areas. SMDS uses cell switching and provides services such as usage-based billing and network management.

Digital Services

Digital services are often used to carry voice, video, and data. Digital circuits can transmit data at speeds up to 45Mbps. Usually, digital lines are made possible by "conditioning" analog lines to handle higher data rates. The lines are usually leased from a local exchange carrier and installed between two points (point-to-point) to provide dedicated, service.

T1   The standard—and most widely used—digital line service is the T1 channel. A T1 channel provides transmission rates of 1.544Mbps and can carry both voice and data. The 1.544Mbps bandwidth of a T1 is usually divided into twenty-four 64Kbps channels. This is because a digitized conversation requires 64Kbps of bandwidth, so when T1s are divided into 64Kbps channels, voice and data can be carried over the same T1 service.

FRACTIONAL T1   Fractional T1 is for those who need 64Kbps wide-area channels but don't need a full T1. A customer can start with a number of fractional T1 lines and grow into a full T1 line when and as necessary. When a customer orders fractional T1 service, the carrier sets up a full T1 interface, but only makes the contracted bandwidth available until more is needed. The lines are fractional, meaning that they can be divided into channels for voice or data.

T3   A T3 line is equivalent to 45Mbps, or 28 T1 lines, or 672 64Kbps channels.

Symptoms of a Bandwidth Shortage Over the Wide Area

As we mentioned earlier, right now the wide area will always seem slower than the rest of your network. That's because currently most wide area carrier services simply aren't designed to carry the megabits per second bandwidths that local area protocols can sustain. This will change as ATM becomes available over the wide area. However, until then, users who access programs and data over wide area connections will not receive anything near the performance they are accustomed to receiving over the local area.

If users complain of slow performance when accessing remote data and applications, you can almost be certain the problem is a slow remote link. However, to be thorough, check the following to make sure that the problem can't be solved locally.

- ■ Hardware (may be inadequate)
- ■ Location of applications and data
- ■ Traffic patterns
- ■ Packet size
- ■ Communications protocols

Inadequate Hardware

As always, check your workstations and servers. Ensure that they have sufficient memory and processing power for the job. Also, check servers to make sure that they are not the bottleneck. If your servers are waiting on disk input/output, that's probably the cause of the network slowdown, and it can be alleviated by installing a faster disk subsystem. Likewise, insufficient memory (often indicated by memory swapping to disk), low throughput to and from the network adapter (resulting in dropped packets and retransmissions), and inadequate processors can all slow your servers and cause them to be a bottleneck.

Location of Applications

Before you conclude that more bandwidth in the workgroup is what you need, however, ask yourself whether it's possible to move all the data and applications, or at least the applications, onto the local area network. This goes back to ensuring that all users are as close as possible—both physically and logically—to the network resources they use most frequently. This at least eliminates unnecessary internetwork traffic, which is especially important when the internetwork link is over a wide area connection (with its generally much slower transmission speeds).

Traffic Patterns

Try to limit the data that travels over wide area connections to that which *absolutely has to*. That means making sure that, whenever possible, database and application maintenance, server backups, and software upgrades are done locally rather than over the wide area link.

Packet Size

Your NetWare servers could be needlessly creating more wide area traffic because they are limiting packet size to a 512KB maximum. By default, NetWare servers route a default packet size of 512KB. This is because 512KB used to be the largest packet that all routers could route. However, most routers these days will route at the maximum packet size for each protocol. Therefore, if you have a NetWare network, check to make sure your routers can handle a larger packet size. If they can, you may want to implement the *Large Internet Packet* parameter on your NetWare Server.

"Chatty" Communication Protocols

Just as with backbones, another cause of congested workgroup segments is the *communication protocol* used by your network operating system. Among the functions of the communication protocol are creating service connections, getting network station addresses, and other tasks associated with transferring data from a station on one network to a station on another network. The communication protocol operates at the network layer as described on the International Standards Organization's Open Systems Interconnection model (see Appendix A). Communication protocols include Internet protocol (IP) and NetWare's Internetwork Packet Exchange protocol (IPX).

Some communication protocols generate a lot of traffic because for every request for service they send, they require a response from the station that is granting the services. Because of this constant "conversation" between the requester and grantor of services, these protocols are called "chatty" protocols. IPX, for example, is the classic example of a "chatty" protocol—request then response, request then response. Often these requests and responses are larger than one packet. Therefore, a chatty protocol significantly increases the number of packets being transmitted. Furthermore, if a route fails, the delay required to rebuild routing tables using this chatty protocol can delay the establishment of a new route. Consequently, chatty protocols can slow a wide area link tremendously.

Novell has solved many of these problems by replacing IPX with a new routing protocol, called NetWare Link Services Protocol (NLSP). NLSP doesn't use the request-reply routines that IPX does. Instead, it uses a link-state routing based on the open shortest path first and intermediate system-to-intermediate system routing algorithms. This makes routes easier to manage and faster to recalculate should a path fail. It also lets network managers program a preferred route selection based on cost, traffic congestion or priority, line speed, or other criteria.

Transmission control protocol/Internet protocol (TCP/IP), on the other hand, is not a chatty protocol. Rather than sending a request for service, waiting for a reply, then sending the next request for service, TCP/IP sends all requests for service in a single burst, sometimes called a "packet burst." It then receives multiple responses from the grantor of those services. This makes it a better choice for a wide area link than IPX.

To ease the congestion that IPX/SPX can cause, Novell has introduced PBURST.NLM, a NetWare Loadable Module that enables the server and workstations to function in packet burst mode, sending all service requests in a single burst. However, PBURST is not turned on by default. You will have to load PBURST manually or add the LOAD PBURST command to your STARTUP.NCF file.

Tests to Confirm Insufficient WAN Bandwidth

Just as with the local area, the true and indisputable determination of where your wide area bottleneck lies comes from in-depth analysis of your network traffic. This analysis will reveal whether lack of bandwidth is the culprit, or whether there is some other problem on your wide area link that is causing the poor performance.

However, unlike on the local area, for the wide area connection analysis you will have to rely on your carrier service provider to conduct these tests and report the results. From my experience, relying on these test results requires a leap of faith—don't be surprised if the report comes back with "nothing wrong." Even when you receive such a report, wait a couple of days to see if network performance improves anyway. On many occasions I've had a wide area link magically improve after I notified the carrier service we were having problems, even when the carrier service's investigation turned up "No Trouble Found."

 TIP: *When you first report a performance problem to your wide area carrier, just ask for a traffic analysis. Don't tell them you're considering upgrading to a faster wide area protocol.*

Requirements for Wide Area Protocols

If you have conducted the necessary tests and have determined that you need to implement a high-speed protocol on your wide area connections, it's time to set the selection criteria for this protocol. Overall, the most important features for a wide area protocol are almost the same as for the backbone protocol:

- Performance
- Manageability

- Fault tolerance
- Packet size and overhead
- Cost

Performance

Performance is paramount in a wide area connection because, with the exception of ATM, wide area protocols are much slower than local area network protocols. Therefore, to limit performance degradation as much as possible, select the fastest protocol you can manage.

Manageability

Manageability and fault tolerance are critical on the wide area, and yet they are largely out of your hands unless you have a private network. The majority of network and data communications managers will have to work with the public network providers to manage, troubleshoot, and repair their wide area links. Therefore, it's essential that you select both a protocol *and a vendor you feel is capable of supporting that protocol*.

Packet Size and Overhead

Packet size and overhead are more critical on wide area connections than on any other segments. This is because

- Wide area network protocols are often slow anyway, and unnecessary overhead and error checking, as well as smaller, less efficient packets, will simply slow them even more, and
- Many carrier services charge their customers only for the bandwidth they use, so larger, more efficient data packets will save bandwidth and money.

Internetwork and server-to-server packets tend to be larger than local segment packets. Therefore, a protocol that can support large packets sizes tends to be more efficient on a backbone. As well, the amount of overhead (addressing and management information) per packet should be low to eliminate unnecessary—and potentially expensive—traffic over the wide area link.

Cost

Finally, the wide area is not the place to pinch pennies, and yet wide area protocols, with their frequent dependence on outside carrier services, can be wildly expensive to implement. The wide area is one place where it's very important to make sure that you have all the features your network requires, but no "extras" that you can live without.

TIP: *Later chapters in this book discuss each protocol in detail, and make recommendations of where they would be best implemented.*

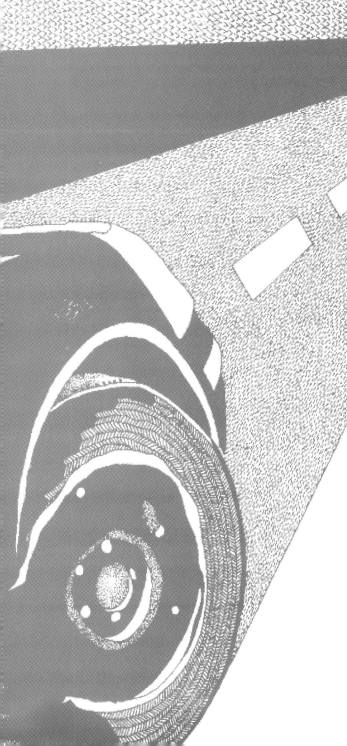

CHAPTER 6

The Cost of Converting to High Speed

Now that you know where to expect slowdowns, and why they occur, it's nearly time to start talking about how to speed things up. However, before we do that, we need to prepare you for sticker shock. High-speed networking is not cheap, it's not easy, and therefore it's not always worth it. Therefore, before you launch into an implementation project, I recommend that you:

- Determine exactly which segments will benefit from a high-speed protocol, as detailed in the first four chapters of this book

- Carefully estimate the costs of converting to a high-speed protocol

To help you "put a pencil" to these potential expenses, I have prepared worksheets that outline the major cost components of a high-speed network and describe how to calculate the cash outlays associated with each. These worksheets appear at the end of the chapter. The actual prices for each of the specific protocols are discussed in the chapters covering those protocols.

To Speed or Not to Speed

Before you can estimate costs, you'll need to determine which segments of your network you want to upgrade. This can be your most difficult planning task, because you'll want to implement high-speed networking widely enough to provide you with adequate bandwidth for the foreseeable future, but not implement any more than you'll really need during that time because of the high costs associated with it. Here are a few guidelines to help you develop a good scope for your network conversion project:

- **Upgrade your network to see you through the next 18–24 months.** Upgrades intended to last less than that amount of time will be outdated nearly before they are complete. The future beyond 24 months is too unpredictable. Under *no* circumstances should you claim that no further upgrades will be required for more than two years—the networking industry is changing too fast to make such dangerous assertions!

- **Whenever possible, upgrade your cable plant universally.** For example, if you're going to have to upgrade high-speed segments from Category 3 to Category 5 cable, go ahead and upgrade your whole network to Category 5. The incremental cost of upgrading cable is fairly low, and having a versatile cable plant will save you time and money in the future.

- **Upgrade the busiest 20 percent of your network.** The 80–20 rule usually applies in networking as well, so upgrading the top 20 percent of bandwidth-starved segments should cover most of your problem areas.

NOTE: *A little speed and a lot of management go a long way. As we will discuss in later chapters, there are many things you can do to prevent a bandwidth crunch on the segments that you **don't** upgrade to a high-speed protocol. Among these bandwidth management tools are virtual networking, microsegmentation, and full-duplex protocols.*

Hardware Worksheet

The cost of equipment is probably the first and most obvious expense related to installing a high-speed network. What may not be so obvious, however, are the many costs directly and indirectly related to installing new hardware. The Hardware worksheet outlines the equipment and related costs you will have to consider, along with the quantity and the cost of each.

Servers

When upgrading servers, be sure to contact your NOS vendor to find out exactly which network adapters and drivers are fully certified for the version of the NOS you now have. Remember, high-speed networking is relatively new, so the version of the network operating system you currently have installed may not support high-speed protocols. If it doesn't, a NOS upgrade—with all the attendant heartache—will be in order. Furthermore, a new version of the operating system—or even a high-speed NIC driver—may require other hardware upgrades, such as increased memory or disk space. Be sure to ask your vendors about system hardware requirements, and figure any upgrades into your cost estimate.

Hubs

The number of hubs you require depends on two things:

- How many ports you will be converting to a high-speed protocol
- The port density of the hubs you want to purchase

If you are purchasing stackable hubs, the smallest unit you can buy is a hub. Note that some stackable hubs require separate terminators, so be sure to include the cost of these terminators in your estimate.

If you have purchased or are planning to purchase a chassis-based unit, the smallest unit will be a chassis module. In either case, be sure to include the cost of special cables and connectors required to attach the high-speed ports to your existing network.

Finally, remember to include the cost of any changes that you'll need to make in your wiring closet to accommodate the new hubs, such as additional racks and patch panels.

Routers

Your routers may require new physical interfaces, either internal or external, as well as software and firmware upgrades to work with a high-speed protocol. They may even have to be replaced altogether. In either case, some manual configuration will be necessary, so be sure to include all the associated costs.

Switches

You may need to purchase or upgrade existing switches. Upgrading your switches may involve high-speed interfaces or firmware upgrades. Be sure to quiz your vendor to make sure you know everything involved in preparing your switches for high-speed networking.

Workstations

Implementing high-speed networking at the workstation involves many of the same considerations as upgrading servers. Contact your workstation vendor to make sure the network adapters you have chosen are compatible. Select network adapters with PCI or EISA buses if at all possible. Also, make sure the workstations are running a version of the operating system that supports the network adapter driver, and that they have sufficient memory and hard disk storage to accommodate the operating system and drivers. And remember, to get the desired performance, you may need to replace the workstation altogether.

And a Smooth Road

Don't forget that you may need to upgrade your cable plant. The Hardware worksheet will make sure you consider what kind of work will have to be done and the number of cable drops that will need this kind of work. Also, remember that new media will require new patch cables—which may seem insignificant at first, but add up to no small expense in most shops!

Service Cost Worksheet

You may need help with all of this. Use the Service Cost worksheet when considering the cost of any outside service providers you may retain to help you with your high-speed networking implementation. This will include contract programmers to help you enhance applications, network integrators to help you upgrade your servers and network operating system, as well as your switches and routers. Don't forget PC maintenance companies that can help you upgrade your desktop workstations. Finally, you may need to hire cabling contractors to help upgrade racks, risers, and patch panels in your wiring closets.

Staffing and Staff Development Worksheet

Hiring and/or training a staff to install and maintain a high-speed network is a significant expense. Because, as we have mentioned earlier, high-speed networking technologies are relatively new, chances are your current staff hasn't been adequately trained in them. Therefore, before you dive into a high-speed network implementation, you'll need to make sure that your staff has acquired the necessary skills both in troubleshooting and management. This means they need to learn not only how to physically connect devices to the high-speed network, but also to optimize drivers and operate management applications for the protocol.

Preparing your staff to handle these responsibilities includes sending them to courses and seminars, purchasing books and other reference materials, and possibly hiring temporary staff to keep your network running while your regular staff acquires expertise in high-speed networking.

Sometimes developing existing staff isn't enough. You may even have to hire additional staff that are already experienced in high-speed networking. If that's the case, be sure to include recruiting and hiring costs into your implementation budget. The Staffing and Staff Development worksheet can help you estimate your budget.

Time Estimate Worksheet

One of the hardest figures to estimate is that of time. Using the Time Estimate worksheet, come up with an estimated time to upgrade each server, hub, router, workstation, and switch; then, multiply that by the number of units of each piece of equipment you will convert.

Don't forget, the cost isn't limited to just time spent on the actual installation and configuration of your high-speed network. A major expense of converting your network protocol will be the costs of downtime, reduced productivity of everyone in your organization while systems are being optimized and the inevitable conversion problems are being solved, and reduced productivity of your staff while they become comfortable with the new equipment, software, and systems. Also, don't forget the opportunity cost associated with a network conversion: what won't get done well, or get done at all, while your staff is concentrating on implementing the high-speed protocol?

Applications Worksheet

In some instances, you will need to upgrade applications as well as hardware. For example, you may need new network management applications to monitor and manage the new protocol. In the case of asynchronous transfer mode (which we will discuss in detail in Chapter 16), applications on both the clients and the servers may need to be upgraded to support the transport protocol. As well, if you will be upgrading the network and/or desktop operating systems, application upgrades may be necessary or desirable to get the required performance and support of the operating system.

Live Fast, Die Young

Another issue to consider before undertaking a conversion to high-speed networking is the emotional cost. Whether and when it is worthwhile to install a high-speed network depends a lot on the condition of your company and your department. As you will learn in excruciating detail in later chapters, implementing a high-speed network is an expensive, laborious, time-consuming, and nerve-wracking project. Therefore, if your company is in the midst of, say, a reorganization, a financial crisis, or an SEC audit, the stress of such a conversion will more than likely far outweigh its benefits. The same is true of your department. If you're having morale problems *before* you begin a high-speed networking conversion, you may not even have a department left when it's complete.

If You Still Find It's Worth It

Okay, you've figured in the cost of equipment, staff, applications, services, and morale, and it still seems cost-effective to implement a high-speed networking protocol. Now it's time to select the specific protocol or protocols that will best meet the needs of your network. In the next section, we will discuss in detail the high-speed networking protocols that are currently available for both the local and wide area.

Hardware Worksheet

Servers:

Equipment	No. of Units	Cost per Unit	Total
Network adapters			
NOS upgrades			
Memory upgrades			
Disk upgrades			
Driver upgrades			
Other hardware upgrades			

Total

Hubs—Number of ports to upgrade:

Equipment	No. of Units	Cost per Unit	Total
New hubs			
Modules			
Chasses			

Total

Routers:

Equipment	No. of Units	Cost per Unit	Total
New routers			
Router interfaces			
Firmware upgrades			
Software upgrades			

Total

Hardware Worksheet (*continued*)
Switches—Number of switched ports needed:

Equipment	No. of Units	Cost per Unit	Total
New switches			
Switch upgrade modules			
Firmware upgrades			
Total			

Workstations:

Equipment	No. of Units	Cost per Unit	Total
New			
Operating system upgrades			
Network adapters			
Memory			
Disk space			
Total			

Cable, Media, and Wiring closet:

Equipment	No. of Units	Cost per Unit	Total
New drops			
Upgraded drops			
Additional pair terminate			
Patch cables			
Connectors			
Terminators			
Racks			
Patch panels			
Total			

Service Cost Worksheet

Service	No. of Hours	Cost per Hour	Total
Contract programmers			
Client applications			
Server applications			
Management applications			
Network integrators			
Server upgrades			
Network operating system upgrades			
Cabling contractors			
Wiring closet upgrades			
Rack installation			
Riser wiring/ installation			
Patch panel installation			
Total		X	

Staff Development Worksheet

Staff Development Costs:

Seminars	No. of Enrollees	Cost per Enrollee	Total
Management systems			
Cabling			
Switches			
Routers			
Hubs			
General protocol			
Total			

Courses	No. of Enrollees	Cost per Enrollee	Total
Management systems			
Cabling			
Switches			
Routers			
Hubs			
General protocol			
Total			

Books and Reference Materials	No. of Units	Cost per Unit	Total
Management systems			
Cabling			
Switches			
Routers			
Hubs			
General protocol			
Total			

Staffing Worksheet

Temporary Staff Costs	No. of Hours	Cost per Hour	Total
Network management			
Programming/analyst			
Hardware maintenance			
Network administration			
Total			

New Staff Recruiting Costs	No. of Positions	Cost per Position	Total
Advertisements			
Search firm fees			
Orientation costs			
Total			

Time Estimate Worksheet

Installation Time	No. of Hours	Cost per Hour	Total
Servers			
Hubs			
Routers			
Switches			
Workstations			

Upgrades and Optimization	No. of Hours	Cost per Hour	Total
Servers			
Hubs			
Routers			
Switches			
Workstations			

Application Upgrades	No. of Hours	Cost per Hour	Total
Workstations			
Servers			
Network management			

Total

Time Estimate Worksheet (*continued*)

Segment	No. of People on Segment	Average Cost per Hour for Person on Segment	Estimated Downtime in Hours	Total Cost of Segment Downtime

What Won't
Get Done

Total
Downtime
Lost

Application Worksheet

Client Applications	No. of Licenses	Cost per License	Total
Upgrade			
New			

Server Applications	No. of Licenses	Cost per License	Total
Upgrade			
New			

Management Applications	No. of Licenses	Cost per License	Total
Upgrade			
New			

Total

WAN Services Worksheet

	Quantity	Cost per Unit	Total Cost
Wide Area Service Links			
Customer Premises Equipment			
Local Access Links			

PART TWO

How to Speed Up: Local Area Solutions

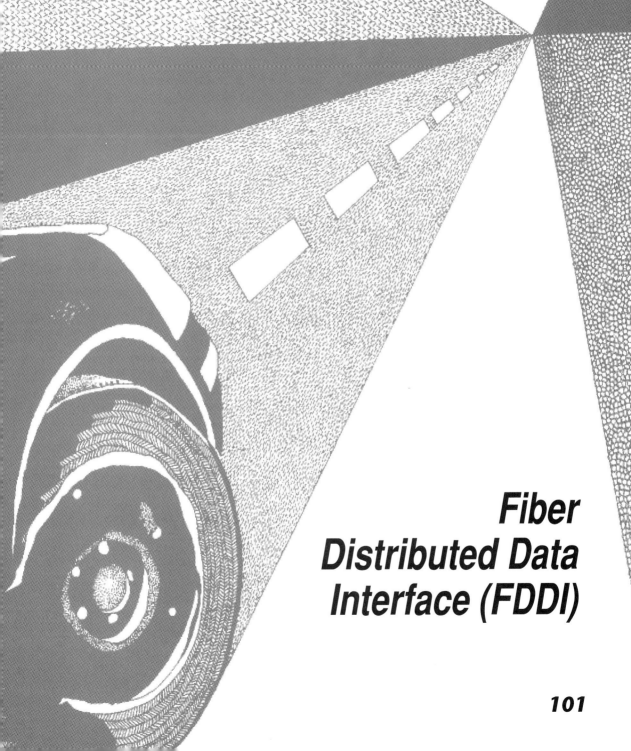

CHAPTER 7

Fiber Distributed Data Interface (FDDI)

Solution for:

Network Architecture
- ○ Workgroups
- ☑ Power Workgroups
- ☑ Server Farms
- ☑ Backbones
- ○ Wide Area

Network Application
- ○ Database Applications
- ○ Workgroup Applications
- ☑ Multimedia
- ☑ Image Processing
- ○ Wide Area

Fiber Distributed Data Interface, or FDDI, was perhaps the first 100Mbps transport protocol available for local area networks. When it first appeared in the late 1980s, FDDI was expensive both to install and to manage. This was largely because the protocol ran only on fiber-optic cabling, which was scarce and difficult to install. Therefore, it was reserved almost exclusively for backbone use. Although most FDDI nodes are still mostly found on backbone segments, with the introduction of the protocol's copper wire implementation—twisted-pair-physical media dependent (TP-PMD)—along with a drop in the cost of installing optical fiber, this protocol is finding its way to the desktops more often than ever before. Although, with the recent advent of other high-speed transport protocols that require less investment of time and money to implement, FDDI may have missed its chance for widespread deployment, it still may be the right choice for your network's backbone or power workgroup.

What Makes It the Same—and What Makes It Different

While there is nothing magic about FDDI as opposed to the other local area network transport protocols discussed in this book, FDDI **is** a significant departure from protocols we find defined in the IEEE 802 committee specifications. FDDI is a standard developed by the X3T9 committee of the American National Standards Institute (ANSI), and was originally conceived to transport data over fiber-optic cabling at 100Mbps. Since then, a copper cable implementation called TP-PMD has emerged, but has never enjoyed widespread popularity. Therefore, we will focus on the fiber-optic cabling implementation.

In its most basic form, an FDDI network is a group of computers, each with an FDDI network adapter installed, passing data packets around a ring. When operating in default mode, a computer receives a data packet from its neighbor on one side, then retransmits the packet to its neighbor on the other side.

In this scenario, each computer in the network is acting as a repeater, regenerating the data packet when it retransmits it. However, most FDDI adapters have a *bypass mode*, in which the device lets data packets pass by without retransmitting them. Bypass mode is used to keep the FDDI ring intact even when a computer is inactive. However, because a computer operating in bypass mode is not acting as a repeater (regenerating the data packets it receives), if too many computers placed next to each other in the ring are operating in bypass mode, the data signal may become very weak and limit the span of the network.

While a computer retransmits every data packet it receives, it sends a data packet of its own origination only when it receives the *token*. A token is a special data packet that serves the sole purpose of letting computers know that it has permission to originate a data packet on the ring. When a computer receives a data packet that it originated—after that packet has completely traversed the ring—the computer doesn't retransmit the packet again. If it did, packets would continue circling the ring ad infinitum, eventually overwhelming the network with unnecessary traffic. Instead, when the originating computer receives its data packet, it removes the data packet from the ring.

The network just described is a very basic FDDI ring. As we will see, the functions of an FDDI network quickly become more complex.

Framing the Data

FDDI uses a frame type different from that described in either the IEEE 802.3 (Ethernet) or IEEE 802.5 (Token Ring) standards. Although a comprehensive discussion of the types and contents of FDDI frames is beyond the scope of this book, it is important to understand that FDDI has its own frame structure. Figure 7-1 illustrates the composition of a frame.

FDDI carries much the same information in its header field as do other protocols. The header contains information on originating station, frame classification, and unique frame identification.

The Class field identifies the frame as belonging to one of the eight (soon to be twelve) frame classes now defined in the FDDI protocol. Currently these are

- Neighbor information frames (NIF)
- Extended service frames (ESF)
- Parameter management frames (PMF)
- Status report frames (SRF)

- Status information frames (SIF)
- Echo frames (ECF)
- Resource allocation frames (RAF)
- Request denied frames (RDF)

The Type field identifies to which of the six frame types the frame belongs: token, void, media access control (MAC), station management (SMT), implementor, and logical link control (LLC). The Ver ID field shows the version of SMT protocol. The Transaction ID field is a unique identifier for each frame. The Station ID field gives the FDDI (not the MAC) address of the originating station. This is because some FDDI stations have multiple MAC addresses, and therefore need identifiers for the protocol. This Station ID field also comes in handy if you are using hot-swappable FDDI devices, because it will maintain a constant ID for the station even when the MAC addresses change.

Determining the Path

As mentioned earlier, FDDI is a protocol that employs a token-passing scheme to determine station access. Stations send and receive data packets when they receive the token—data transmission is not managed by a central controlling station as it is with 100VG-AnyLAN. This token-passing scheme guarantees each station on the network a certain amount of bandwidth. If you take the number of nodes on the network and multiply it by the amount of time it takes each node to transmit a data packet, then you have the maximum amount of time it can take for any station to receive the token. This is what makes FDDI a deterministic network: each node will receive a minimum throughput that you can calculate.

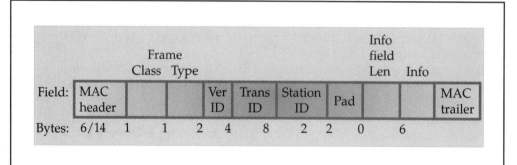

Figure 7-1. *Structure of a Fiber Distributed Data Interface frame*

While throughput on an FDDI network is fixed at any given time, it varies according to the number of nodes transmitting on the ring. Therefore, to join an FDDI segment, a station must follow a fairly strict set of procedures, which are part of FDDI's integrated management capabilities called *station management protocols,* or SMT (these are discussed later in the "Manageability" section of this chapter). These ring initiation protocols first initialize and test the link from the new station to the ring. Next, the station initiates its connection to the ring using a distributed algorithm called *claim token.* The claim token process determines whether a token already exists, and if so, reconfigures the token's path to include the new station. However, if no token is detected, the claim token protocol requires that all stations attempting to join the FDDI segment transmit special packets, called *claim frames.* The stations use the claim frames to determine both

- An exact value for token rotation time
- Which station will initiate the new token

Once the token has been created and transmitted, it is used to arbitrate shared access for the stations using a timed token protocol. The first station to join the ring establishes and tests its link with the ring, then generates a token that is passed from station to station. When a station receives the token, it can then transmit a fixed amount of frames. To transmit information onto the ring, a station claims the token that is otherwise circling the ring.

FDDI has prioritization mechanisms implemented via bandwidth allocation. The first mechanism, called synchronous bandwidth allocation (SBA), enables managers to assign a fixed amount of bandwidth to a certain station or stations, thus giving them greater access to the token. In SBA, bandwidth is allocated to stations as a percentage of *target token rotation time* (TTRT), which is the preset time it takes the token to make one rotation of the ring. Obviously, the total bandwidth allocated via SBA should not exceed 100 percent of the available bandwidth. See Figure 7-2.

The second mechanism, referred to as the asynchronous class of service, takes the bandwidth that is not allocated via SBA and divides it equally among the stations on the ring. The asynchronous service works like this: each station keeps a *token rotation timer* that tells the station when next to expect the token. When the token next appears, the station compares the *target rotation time* (TRT), or expected time of arrival, to the TTRT, which is the preset time for the token to make one rotation. The TTRT is usually set at 8 milliseconds. If the TRT is less than the TTRT, the station can grab the token and send asynchronous data frames. If the TRT is greater than the TTRT, the token is late, so stations that have only asynchronous class of service must defer to stations with Synchronous Bandwidth Allocation.

During times of heavy traffic, the TRT can get so long that stations sending data packets with low priorities can be completely restricted from access to the ring for a time. Eventually, however, all the stations with high-priority packets will send their data, lowering the TRT and thereby letting stations with low-priority transmissions have a chance to claim the token.

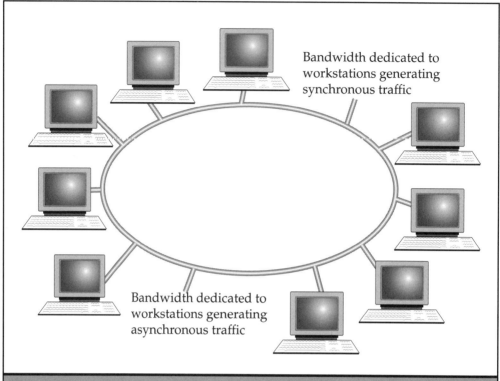

Figure 7-2. *Synchronous bandwidth allocation ensures that bandwidth is available to the stations that need it most*

Cabling Considerations

FDDI networks are composed of a set of counterrotating dual rings and attached devices and segments. The set of counterrotating dual rings is called the *trunk* ring. While devices can be directly attached to the trunk ring, as described in our initial description of a basic FDDI network, they can also be attached to the trunk ring via *concentrators*. Concentrators are devices similar to multistation access units (MAUs) in the Token Ring world that provide trunk connections to multiple stations. Devices that are directly attached to the trunk must be *dual-attachment stations* (DAS); in other words, devices that are attached to both of the counterrotating rings. Devices that are attached to the trunk ring via a concentrator are *single-attachment stations* (SAS)— stations that attach to one ring only.

Making the Connection

In FDDI, network connections are made through a series of strictly defined protocols that require that all FDDI ports have one of four identities: A, B, S, and M. Table 7-1 defines the various port types.

Port Type	Function	Location
A	Exit point from station to secondary (backup) ring	All dual-attachment stations
B	Exit point from station to primary ring	All dual-attachment stations
S	Connects stations to one ring only	All single-attachment stations
M	Distribution ports that extend both primary and secondary rings	Concentrators

Table 7-1.   *The Four Types of Network Connections Supported by FDDI*

All stations on an FDDI network must have both an A and a B port. A *tree* connection occurs when an A, B, or S port connects to an M port. In this configuration the node isn't attached directly to the trunk ring, but rather to a port on a concentrator attached to the trunk ring. See Figure 7-3.

Supported Media

FDDI can run on both multimode fiber (PMD) and single-mode fiber (SMF-PMD), as well as Category 5 unshielded twisted-pair cable and 150-ohm shielded twisted-pair cable (TP-PMD).

The Topology

The general topology used in FDDI networks is a dual ring with trees (see Figure 7-4), but there are variations:

- Dual rings without trees. This just means that all the stations are directly connected to the dual ring via DAS connections. See Figure 7-5.

- Wrapped ring with or without trees. A *wrapped ring* is really a dual ring in which a cable fault or break has occurred. When the protocol senses a cable fault, it reroutes traffic from its direct path to the destination station to the roundabout secondary data path, essentially "wrapping" the data back around the ring until it reaches its destination. See Figure 7-6 for an example of a wrapped ring without trees. This type of topology is obviously inefficient, and should be used only as a disaster recovery measure in the event of a cable fault. Wrapped-ring configurations should be rectified as quickly as possible.

- Single tree. This is simply an FDDI network consisting of one tree. See Figure 7-7.

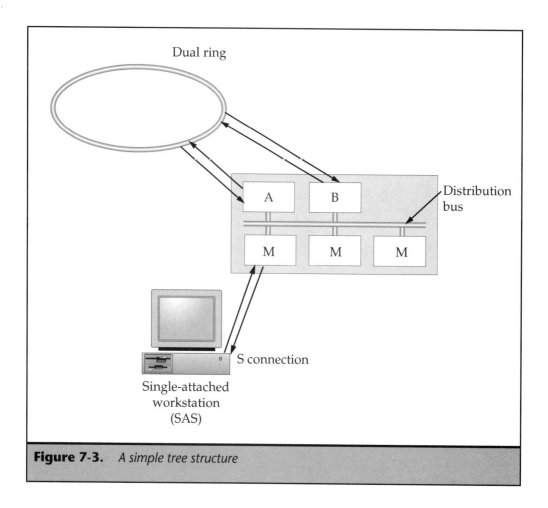

Figure 7-3. *A simple tree structure*

Whichever of these topologies you use, the cardinal rule remains the same: *FDDI supports a maximum of two data paths:* a primary data path and a secondary data path.

Cost of Ownership

FDDI is an expensive protocol to implement. Hubs cost an average of about $1,500 per port, and network adapters for the desktop average a little over $1,000 each. What's more, if you use fiber-optic cable, you're going to encounter a major expense in training your staff to install and/or work with this medium. And then you're going to have to spend money to keep them, because there is a fairly strong demand for employees who are familiar with fiber-optic technology. Still, fiber-optic cabling has the capacity to support protocols that far exceed FDDI's current bandwidth, so depending upon your network strategy, it could be a good investment.

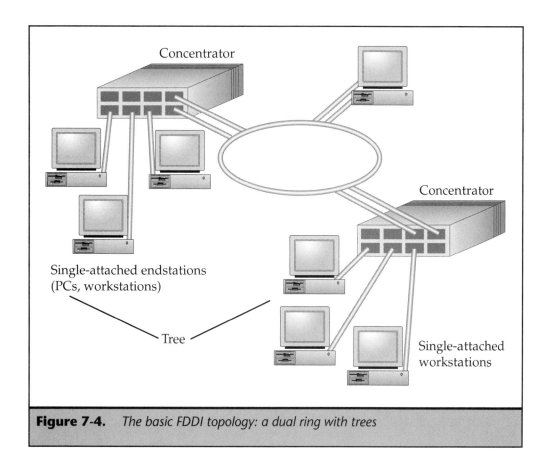

Figure 7-4.   *The basic FDDI topology: a dual ring with trees*

As we mentioned earlier, FDDI runs on either optical fiber or Category 5 UTP. However, the pinout for FDDI is different than that for Ethernet, so you'll need FDDI patch cables (it's a good a idea to color code these patch cables). Therefore, be prepared for some trouble calls resulting from Ethernet patch cables inadvertently being plugged into TP-PMD ports.

Scalability

FDDI is probably the most scalable of all the high-speed local area network protocols, with the exception of ATM. Its deterministic protocol, along with its synchronous and asynchronous bandwidth allocation mechanisms, make it easy to add stations while ensuring that response times meet the needs of the applications. What's more, FDDI supports up to 500 stations on a single LAN, and its maximum network extent is 200 kilometers when running over fiber-optic cabling.

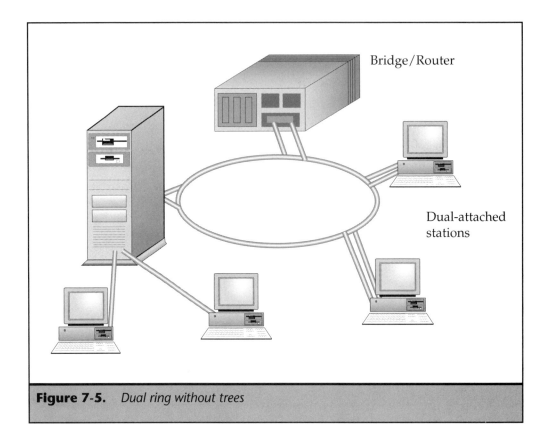

Figure 7-5. *Dual ring without trees*

FDDI's large packet size makes it a very efficient transport protocol for large packet sizes. However, for the current average packet size of between 256 bytes to 512 bytes, FDDI has extremely high overhead per packet.

If you are integrating FDDI into an existing 10Base-T network, there are many hubs available that support switching between the two protocols. Also, several vendors have recently announced the development of FDDI switches, which may enhance the performance of FDDI networks as they grow.

Setup and Configuration

As we mentioned earlier, installing FDDI is relatively difficult. However, because FDDI has been around for several years now, it should be fairly easy to find technical assistance. The initialization scheme required for stations wanting to enter the ring may cause some headaches during the initial configuration. However, once the FDDI network is up and running, it proves to be a solid and stable machine that needs very little maintenance.

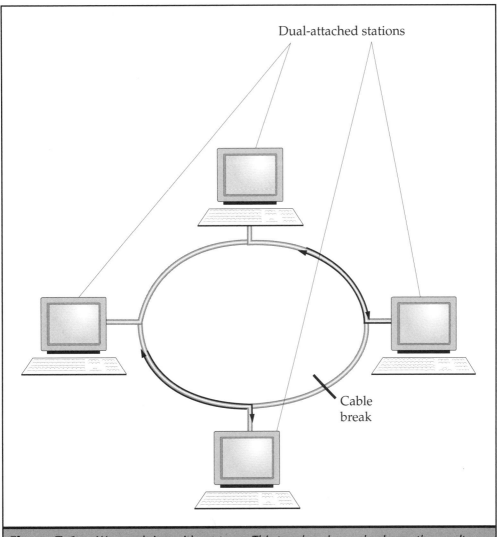

Figure 7-6. *Wrapped ring without trees. This topology is nearly always the result of a cable break*

Manageability

FDDI is both extremely fault tolerant and manageable. Because FDDI supports dual-homed, dual-attached backbones, each server on the ring can be connected to as many as two hubs on the same ring, so there is always an alternate path. Also, its support for counterrotating rings provides great fault isolation while simultaneously keeping the network running.

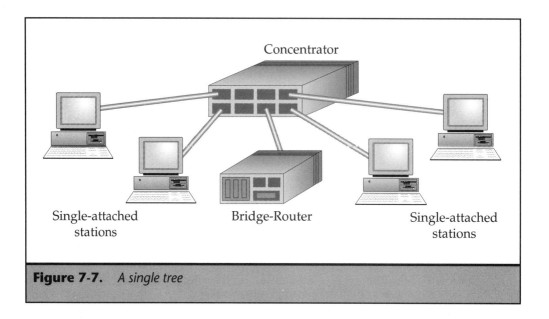

Figure 7-7. *A single tree*

Unlike Ethernet, FDDI has a built-in network monitoring and management protocol called *station management* (SMT). Unlike the rest of the protocols in this comparison book, FDDI was designed with SMT as an integral part of it. SMT includes both network monitoring facilities at the link, node, and network levels, as well as remote network management capability via management information bases (MIBs). It provides capabilities for fault isolation and recovery, statistics gathering, data error monitoring, and noise monitoring. In addition, it provides connection and configuration management. Even the previously-described ring initiation procedures are a part of the station management protocol. However, providing these management and monitoring facilities also adds to the overhead of the protocol, and therefore can limit the efficiency and cost effectiveness of the protocol, especially in desktop implementations.

Performance

FDDI has been a proven performer for some time. The elegance of the bandwidth allocation mechanisms really shows up in multimedia and video applications. As you run video applications, for example, you can add workstations to the FDDI ring without experiencing the slightest stall or shudder.

Furthermore, FDDI has a maximum data packet size of 4,500 bytes, which makes more efficient use of available bandwidth than 100Base-T with its 1,500-byte maximum. This larger packet size is especially helpful in applications with a large average packet size. In short, FDDI's performance gets very high marks.

Evolving to Survive

A related standard, FDDI-II, has emerged to transport data that cannot sustain delays. An example of this would be real-time, full-motion video. To accomplish the "zero-delay" standard, FDDI-II borrows from the circuit-switching technology of long-distance telephone carriers. FDDI-II multiplexes bandwidth into dedicated circuits that ensure packet delivery. These circuits can then provide isochronous, or *circuit-based*, services that offer a regular, fixed-length transmission slot that essentially provides a dedicated channel between stations. FDDI-II can support as many as 16 such circuits. Bandwidth on these circuits is allocated to stations on the basis of need, so maximum bandwidth varies from 6.144Mbps to 99.072Mbps. In turn, each of these channels may be subdivided into 64Kbps circuits. FDDI-II supports a maximum of 96 64Kbps channels.

FDDI-II has some drawbacks, however. First, all nodes on the network must be FDDI-II. If all nodes aren't, then the FDDI-II devices begin operating as FDDI devices. This lack of compatibility is not only inconvenient, it's extremely expensive because you will have the cost of replacing FDDI devices with FDDI-II devices as well as the cost of redesigning your network to make sure that all FDDI devices are on their own ring.

Summary

While FDDI has proven itself as a solid, fault-tolerant, high-performance vehicle for backbone deployment, there are several obstacles to implementing it at the desktop. Its high price, high overhead, and complete departure from the familiar 10Base-T cabling rules may prevent its widespread use at the desktop. You will probably have to spend a significant amount of time and money in finding, training, and then retaining expertise in fiber-optic cabling. Also, due to differences in pinout between Ethernet and FDDI, if you have both protocols at your site, there may be some confusion—and resulting troubleshooting—resulting from misplaced patch cables.

Recommended for:

- Multimedia and video because synchronous bandwidth allocation mechanism can ensure adequate bandwidth
- Server farms and backbones because of manageability and fault tolerance
- Backbone segments

Not Recommended for:

- Standard desktop deployment because of relatively high cost and high overhead associated with SMT

Strengths:

■ Extensive management support built into the protocol

■ Largest network diameter of all 100Mbps network options

■ Established protocol with fairly broad vendor support

Weaknesses:

■ Relatively expensive

■ Relatively difficult to install

■ High overhead associated with SMT

CHAPTER 8

100VG-AnyLAN

Solution for:

Network Architecture	Network Application
☑ Workgroups	☑ Database Applications
☑ Power Workgroups	☑ Workgroup Applications
○ Server Farms	☑ Multimedia
○ Backbones	☑ Image Processing
○ Wide Area	○ Wide Area

In June 1995, the IEEE certified the 100VG-AnyLAN specification for the 802.12 standard. Long before that date, however, its proponents—led by Hewlett Packard Company, Inc.—heralded it as the ultimate trade-in opportunity for 10Base-T networks. Ethernet users have been told that the conversion from 10Base-T to 100VG-AnyLAN is so inexpensive and easy that there is no reason *not* to go with 100VG-AnyLAN. However, while 100VG-AnyLAN is a logical and cost-effective migration path for some applications, *caveat emptor* is the rule for the cautious network manager.

So Close, But So Far from 10Base-T

Although 100VG-AnyLAN has many similarities to the familiar 802.3 protocol, it employs data access and signaling methods that differ drastically from both Ethernet and Fast Ethernet. Rather than the familiar collision-based CSMA/CD protocol that the 802.3 and 802.3u standards use, the 802.12 data access method is known as *Demand Priority Access* (DPA), in which the workstation initiates data transfers and the hub acknowledges data and directs the transfer. This differs from CSMA/CD in two critical ways:

- Data transfer is controlled by the hub rather than the network adapter.
- Collisions are eliminated because each node is guaranteed a turn at sending data.

Theoretically, this deterministic protocol increases available bandwidth by eliminating collisions and retransmissions. However, being a complete departure from

802.3, it therefore will likely require some rethinking on the part of your technical staff and some redesign for your network.

Getting Framed

Although 100VG supports the frame formats of the existing 802.3 and 802.5 protocols (but not both simultaneously), the 802.12 transport protocol is nothing like either. The emerging IEEE 802.12 standard for transmitting 100Mbps over voice-grade unshielded twisted-pair wire represents a significant departure from the existing Ethernet standard in the area of data access.

Setting Priorities

One of the key differences between the 802.3 and 802.12 standards is also one of the prime advantages of the latter protocol: its ability to recognize two levels of priority in transmission requests. The 802.12 100VG-AnyLAN protocol recognizes normal-priority and high-priority transmission requests, with high-priority requests taking precedence. The priority level can be set either by the workstation or by the application, although as of this writing there were no generally-available applications that took advantage of this ability to set priority. If a normal-priority request remains pending for more than 300ms, it is moved to the high-priority service queue.

DPA does more than simply allow you to set transmission priority. It also improves performance by removing the network overhead associated with the CSMA/CD access method. In CSMA/CD, all workstations contend for access to the channel. Collisions, which are fairly frequent, require detection and retransmission of the packet. Furthermore, the DPA scheme has a performance edge on CSMA/CD. This is because as collisions become more frequent as traffic increases on CSMA/CD networks, the resulting packet retransmissions slow performance. The DPA network, which has no contention for transmission and hence no packet collisions, is able to handle more traffic.

100VG-AnyLAN has something of a security advantage over the 802.3 standard as well. The 100VG-AnyLAN hub transmits packets only across ports attached to the destination address of the packet. This reduces the opportunity for unauthorized monitoring of transmissions.

The Architecture

The 100VG-AnyLAN topology must be in a physical star, with no loops or branches. The centerpiece of this topology, as specified by the DPA scheme, is a central hub, called the root hub, that controls the traffic. Each lower level hub maintains its own per port address table that contains the addresses of the stations connected to each of its ports. If this sounds like the familiar polling architecture of yore—that's because that's exactly what it is.

How the Demand Priority Access Scheme Works

When a station sends a transmission request, the request is first received by the hub to which the station is directly attached. If the directly connected hub is the only hub in the network, it is the root hub and thus the central controller for network transmission. It will therefore service the transmission request in the station's turn in the polling and priority sequence. However, if the directly connected hub is not the root hub, it will send the station's transmission request on to the next higher level hub, which in turn will transfer the request on if it is not the root hub. Eventually, the transmission request reaches the root hub, which will then allow the local hub to service the transmission request in its turn. See Figure 8-1 for a bird's-eye view of the progress of a data packet across this topology.

Here We Go Round the Network

A 100VG-AnyLAN network functions something like a "round-robin," because each hub is polled in sequence, and each hub in turn polls each of its ports in sequence. Here's the process: Between packet transmissions, stations and hubs send a signal to each other indicating that the channel is available to make a transmission request. This signal is called an *idle signal*. When a station has a packet to transmit, it sends a *transmission request signal* to the hub. The transmission request signal includes the priority of the transmission request. The transmitting station then waits for a response, originating from the root hub, which grants it permission to transmit one packet onto the network.

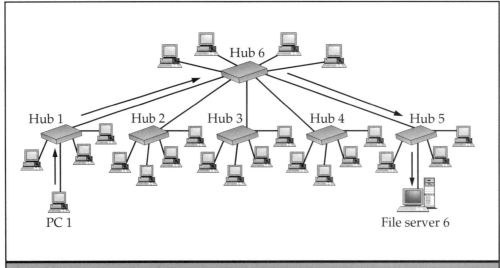

Figure 8-1.   *The path of a packet across a 100VG-AnyLAN network*

In 100VG-AnyLAN, the root hub controls all the data transmission. If the hub that receives the transmission request is the only hub in the network, it is the root hub, so it waits for any transmission in progress to complete, then services the port that is next in the polling sequence, giving that port permission to transmit one packet. However, if the hub is connected to a hub higher in the network, it waits for any network transmission in progress to complete, then signals a transmission request to the higher level hub. In the same manner, the higher level hub will pass the transmission request to the next higher level of hub—if any— until the transmission request eventually reaches the root hub.

The root hub determines which lower level hub can then begin servicing transmission requests. When the right to service network requests passes to a hub, it services requests in port order (i.e., port 1, then 2, up to port N), and then passes control back to the higher level hub. If a high-priority request is made anywhere on the network, however, the control passes immediately to the hub that has that request, and returns to the original hub after all high-priority requests have been serviced throughout the network. High-priority transmission requests occurring anywhere on the network always take precedence, and the root hub always allows the local hub that received the request to service the request, then return control to the hub whose turn it is. See Figure 8-2.

Joining the Club

Because of the deterministic nature of 100VG-AnyLAN, a station can't simply join the network and start transmitting. It must register itself with the root hub, which will assign the new station a place in the polling sequence. It works like this: when a station or hub wishes to join the network, it transmits and receives frames to and from the attached port. This is called a *training sequence* of frames. The training sequence helps the hub determine whether the new device is a station or another hub, which frame type it is using (either 802.3 or 802.5 frames), and whether the port will be allowed to operate as a promiscuous listener. If the connecting device is a station, the training sequence also determines the MAC address of the connecting station. While training is occurring, the network suspends its polling operations; fortunately, completing the training sequence takes about 5 microseconds. Based on the results of the training sequence, the hub either allows the new device to join the network or denies it access and transmits the reason why it will not be admitted.

Cable Design Considerations

The cabling rules for 100VG-AnyLAN are very similar to 10Base-T. In fact, of all the high-speed transport protocols, 100VG-AnyLAN has cabling rules closest to that for 10Base-T. However, there are some important differences.

Wiring Issues

In the 802.3 standard, one pair of wires is dedicated to transmitting data and another to receiving. Currently, in the 802.12 100VG-AnyLAN standard, all four pairs of wires

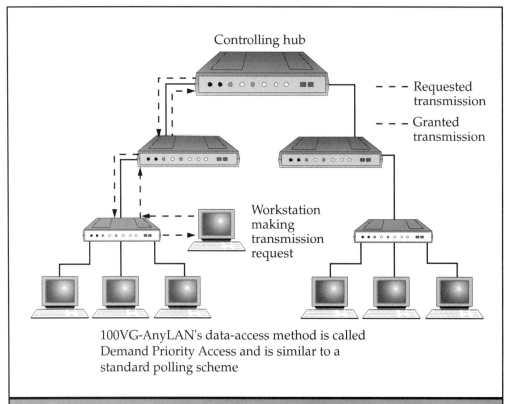

Figure 8-2.   *How Demand Priority Access handles transmission requests*

both transmit or receive data (a two-pair implementation is planned), enabling each pair to operate at a signal rate of 25MHz. Because the deterministic protocol eliminates collisions, data throughput is theoretically at 100 percent, resulting in a 100Mbps network operating rate.

By sending out 25MHz signals, the protocol keeps radio frequencies within required standards. It also allows the use of voice-grade cable (Category 3). Using 4-pair wiring, the 25MHz signal enables 100VG-AnyLAN to send and receive data simultaneously. 100VG-AnyLAN supports Categories 3, 4, or 5 UTP cable, Type-1 STP cable, and fiber-optic cable. Depending on the cable type, network span varies from 100 meters to 2,000 meters. See Figure 8-3.

Because 100VG-AnyLAN supports such a wide variety of cable types, you may be able to preserve your investment in your current network cable infrastructure. However, keep in mind that because 100VG-AnyLAN currently requires all four pairs of Category 3 UTP, you must be sure that all four pairs are terminated—and that may cost you some extra bucks.

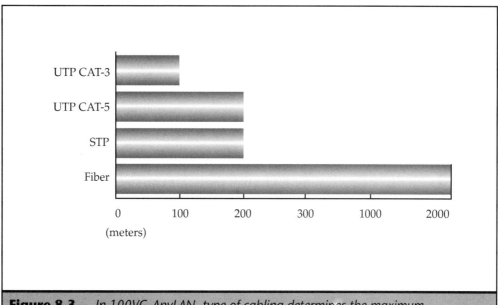

Figure 8-3. *In 100VG-AnyLAN, type of cabling determines the maximum network span*

TIP: *Be sure that your twisted-pair cabling has twists all the way up to the pins of the cross-connect blocks. A section of untwisted pairs can cause crosstalk.*

NOTE: *100VG-AnyLAN doesn't support flat cable in a twisted pair topology.*

Hub Issues

The maximum number of hub levels in a 100VG-AnyLAN network is five. However, your network will perform best if you keep it to three levels of hub cascading. Because three is the maximum number of hub levels allowed by 802.3, your network is probably already designed this way. However, each level of hubs shortens the maximum distance allowed between a root hub and an end node by 1km. Table 8-1 will help you determine the maximum distance between the root hub and an end node.

As a final cabling plant note, keep in mind that you shouldn't have more than seven bridges or switches between any two nodes in a network. This is a result of the IEEE 802.1d spanning tree protocol, not a limitation of 100VG-AnyLAN.

Type of Media	Number of Hubs Between Root Hub and End Node	Number of Levels in Network	Recommended Maximum Distances Between Root Hub and End Node
Category 3	1	2	100m
Category 3	2	3	75m
Category 3	3	4	50m
Category 3	4	5	25m
Category 5	1	2	200m
Category 5	2	3	150m
Category 5	3	4	100m
Category 5	4	5	50m
Fiber optic	1	2	4km
Fiber optic	2	3	3km
Fiber optic	3	4	2km

Table 8-1. *The Maximum Distances Allowed Between End Node and Root Hub*

Preparing for 100VG-AnyLAN

One of the most unsettling things about plunging into 100VG-AnyLAN is its current limited vendor support. Lack of competition in this market not only potentially limits the technical expertise available, but also may keep prices higher than for other better established protocols. So, let the buyer beware.

You should scrutinize your cable plant before implementing 100VG-AnyLAN, carefully removing any 25-pair cables connected to devices operating in promiscuous mode (in which the device monitors all frames it receives), including:

- A cascaded (hub-to-hub) link, because the default configuration of an uplink port is promiscuous. The entire cable path from hub to device must be unbundled cable. Otherwise, the result will likely be severe crosstalk, retransmissions, and unreliable performance.

- Links between routers and hubs.

■ Links between bridges and hubs.

■ Links between a network analyzer and a hub. Network analyzers have to be configured as promiscuous so they can capture all network data.

You'll also have to check to make sure the distance between hubs does not exceed the specifications for 100VG-AnyLAN. Refer again to Table 8-1 for more information.

TIP: *Spend a significant amount of time reviewing your cable plant to comply with 100VG-AnyLAN media and distance requirements. Also, if you are internetworking 100VG-AnyLAN with a 10Base-T network, be prepared to resegment your network to accommodate 100VG-AnyLAN bridging limitations.*

Scalability

While the deterministic Demand Priority Access scheme makes 100VG-AnyLAN easily scalable with little drop in performance, growing a 100VG-AnyLAN network has its obstacles. Most of the scalability problems we noted are ones that you are most likely to encounter when migrating in phases from 10Base-T to 100VG-AnyLAN. For example, like all high-speed protocols, 100VG-AnyLAN requires a translational bridge between itself and 10Base-T. Furthermore, while there are no limitations on the number of nodes on a single shared 100VG-AnyLAN, it's a good idea to limit the number of nodes to 250 to maintain performance.

The rules governing network span in a 100VG-AnyLAN network depend not only on the type of cable used (see Figure 8-3), but also on the number of hub levels employed. Maximum network span for 100VG-AnyLAN networks varies from 100m to 2,000m, depending upon the media used. The maximum network length with Category 5 cabling is around 200m. Refer again to Figure 8-3 for information on maximum network span. Also, you can cascade up to five hubs (it supports four repeater hops per network segment, just like Ethernet). However, we recommend that you review your network design carefully and compare it to the 100VG-AnyLAN cable rules so you can be alerted to any potential problems. That's because each level of hubs shortens the maximum distance allowed between a root hub and an end node. For example, when using fiber-optic cabling, each level of hubs shortens the maximum distance from root hub to end node by 1km. Table 8-1 will help you determine the maximum distance between the root hub and an end node for fiber-optic cabling. Figure 8-4 illustrates the maximum distance between a root hub and an end node. In this example of a 3-hub cascade using fiber-optic cabling, the maximum distance allowed is 3km.

TIP: *Minimize the levels of cascading. Every level of cascading adds to arbitration overhead, which slows performance.*

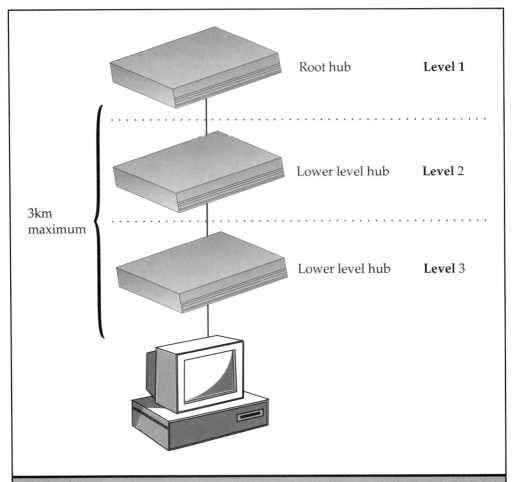

Root hub — **Level 1**

Lower level hub — **Level** 2

3km maximum

Lower level hub — **Level** 3

Figure 8-4. *The distance allowed between a root hub and an end node varies depending upon the number of cascaded hubs in between and type of media*

At this writing, there were no switching devices available or announced for the 100VG-AnyLAN protocol, although we understand that at least one company has plans to implement it later this year. High speed notwithstanding, the ability to add switching—along with management tools suitable to monitor simultaneous parallel paths—to a 100VG-AnyLAN network would enhance its scalability and make us feel more comfortable about its ability to support growth.

Manageability

Because 100VG-AnyLAN supports standard Ethernet packet types, interoperability problems are nonexistent. However, the protocol currently has no management tools that support bandwidth allocation and management.

Right now, the only security offered is the private-mode operation described earlier, which, when enabled, allows ports to receive only those packets addressed to the device attached to it. All ports not associated with the destination address receive an idle signal while the packet addressed to that destination is being transmitted. Although this level of security is sufficient for most installations, it may not be sufficient for extremely high security sites.

Performance

Performance is the strong suit of 100VG-AnyLAN. Because 100VG-AnyLAN can handle packet sizes of either 4,500 bytes or 1,500 bytes, it can support the current smaller average packet sizes and still maintain fast and efficient performance.

The real strength of 100VG-AnyLAN is highlighted when running multimedia applications. Even full-motion video runs under heavy network load with nary a flicker, thanks to the DPA scheme that assigned high priority to all the video frames. Furthermore, Hewlett Packard has stated that they have plans to add full-duplex capability 100VG-AnyLAN (which can be implemented only in two-pair environments such as two-pair shielded twisted-pair or two-pair fiber, support for which is currently unavailable), which will increase performance even more. All in all, however, the performance is extremely impressive right now.

Continuous Improvement

100VG-AnyLAN has improved since its introduction in 1994. When it was originally introduced, it didn't support redundant paths or the spanning tree protocol. Now, however, it supports redundant paths between any two hubs made via the spanning tree protocol, provided only one such path is active at any one time.

Summary

The Demand Priority Access scheme makes 100VG-AnyLAN a robust protocol that's especially well-suited for multimedia and video applications. However, the protocol's lack of fault tolerance and dearth of management facilities make it less than ideal for backbone deployment. Finally, because it almost but not quite complies with 10Base-T cabling rules, network managers should approach a broad-scale implementation with caution.

Recommended for:

- Multimedia and video applications because of its capability to prioritize and ensure packet delivery
- Installed base that doesn't include 25-pair cable, because 100VG-AnyLAN doesn't operate over 25-pair cable connected to devices running in promiscuous mode
- Power workgroups, because its deterministic data access scheme will ensure consistent performance under high traffic

Not Recommended for:

- Backbones, because the centralized polling design can potentially cause a single point of slowdown or even failure
- Installed bases that have network spans that don't comply with 100VG-AnyLAN specifications

Strengths:

- Low price of components
- Can prioritize packets

Weaknesses:

- Limited security
- Limited—but growing—vendor support
- Considerable preparation required before implementing into a legacy 10Base-T network

CHAPTER 9

100Base-T

Solution for:

Network Architecture	Network Application
☑ Workgroups	☑ Database Applications
☑ Power Workgroups	☑ Workgroup Applications
○ Server Farms	○ Multimedia
○ Backbones	○ Image Processing
○ Wide Area	○ Wide Area

From the beginning, the Fast Ethernet Alliance has heralded 100Base-T as the true and rightful heir of 10Base-T. With the IEEE's adoption of 100Base-T as the 802.3u standard in June 1995, the coronation is now complete. On its face, the succession seems logical, because in many ways 100Base-T appears to be just supercharged 10Base-T. For example, 100Base-T has retained the CSMA/CD media access method and most of the traditional cabling rules of 10Base-T.

Some argue, however, that 100Base-T is faster than most desktops require, yet slower than backbones demand. Moreover, the similarity but not strict conformity to 10Base-T cabling rules can cause confusion. This debate notwithstanding, it's probably the easiest high-speed protocol to merge into your existing 10Base-T environment—if you carefully choose the 100Base-T specification that's right for your network, familiarize yourself with and plan for the differences between 10Base-T and 100Base-T, and implement the protocol accordingly.

A Smorgasbord of Specs

The 802.3u specification adopted by the IEEE is defined in two parts. The first part defines the data link layer, which is the layer in the OSI reference model that describes how the protocol handles sending and receiving data between nodes that are connected directly to one another. The second part of the IEEE 802.3u specification, and the part that is most significant to the network manager, is the physical layer specification. This is the part of the specification that defines the type of media over which you can run the 100Base-T protocol. The 100Base-T physical specification comes in four different flavors. Each is designed to accommodate 100Base-T on a different type of physical cable plant and is exacting in its requirements. Therefore, be sure to select the physical layer specification that suits your existing cable plant or be prepared to upgrade your cabling to meet the standard required by the specification.

■ **Media-independent interface (MII)** is the specification that provides MAC-layer connectivity to 100Base-T. This is similar to that of the attachment unit interface (AUI) connection in 10Base-T. The MII interface defines the way the 100Base-T protocol accesses the physical transmission media. In other words, the MII describes a generic 100Base-T interface that can connect to a transceiver that will connect in turn to 100Base-TX, 100Base-T4, or 100Base-FX. See Figure 9-1.

NOTE: The MII specifications allow only a 1-meter distance between the network adapter and the transceiver.

■ **100Base-TX** is the specification for running 100Mbps Ethernet over 2-pair unshielded twisted-pair (UTP) cable and 2-pair Type-1 shielded twisted-pair (STP) cable. This is probably the most familiar of the 100Base-T specifications. It provides for 125MHz signaling over each pair of cables, which can supply only 80 percent throughput due to its encoding scheme (called 4B5B). The 100Base-TX specification is described for both RJ-45 and DB-9 connectors. As you can see in the diagram in Figure 9-2, pinout for the 100Base-TX RJ-45

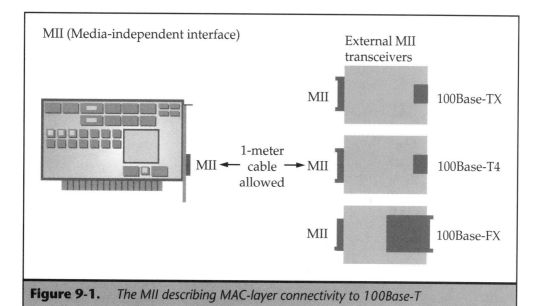

Figure 9-1. *The MII describing MAC-layer connectivity to 100Base-T*

cabling is identical to that for 10Base-T, transmitting over wires 1 and 2 and receiving over wires 3 and 6.

CAUTION: Although you may be able to run 100Base-TX over Category 3 STP for short distances, don't try it. The errors caused by this implementation will outweigh the benefits of the increased bandwidth.

■ **100Base-T4** is the specification for running 100Mbps Ethernet over 4-pair Category 3, 4, or 5 UTP cabling. Until September 1995, there were no commercially available devices that supported this standard, but at the time of this writing there is increasing interest in and industry support for this specification. 100Base-T4 provides for 25MHz signaling over 3-pair, with 133 percent throughput as a result of its encoding scheme (called 8B6T). The 100Base-T4 specification allows only RJ-45 connectors. As you can see in Figure 9-3, the RJ-45 cabling is similar to 10Base-T, adding two bidirectional pairs that 10Base-T does not have. Choosing the 100Base-T4 specification may be an expensive proposition, however. Although the majority of network sites run either Category 3 or Category 5 UTP, most are running on 2-cable pairs. What's more, the additional 2-cable pairs required to meet the 100Base-T4 specification

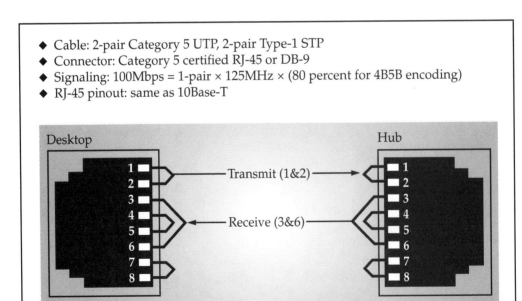

- ◆ Cable: 2-pair Category 5 UTP, 2-pair Type-1 STP
- ◆ Connector: Category 5 certified RJ-45 or DB-9
- ◆ Signaling: 100Mbps = 1-pair × 125MHz × (80 percent for 4B5B encoding)
- ◆ RJ-45 pinout: same as 10Base-T

Figure 9-2. *100Base-TX is 100Mbps 802.3u running on 2-pair twisted-pair cable*

are often unavailable, having been appropriated for telephones, printers, or other uses.

■ **100Base-FX** is the 100Mbps Ethernet physical layer specification for 2-strand 62.5/125 micron fiber-optic cabling. It supports standard MIC, ST, or SC connectors. Signaling for 100Base-FX uses the 4B5B encoding scheme, which provides 80 percent of total output. Therefore, signaling is at 125MHz over a single strand. Currently, there isn't a great deal of interest in the industry or the network management community in running 100Base-T over fiber-optic cabling. This is probably because sites that currently have fiber-optic cabling are already running at 100Mbps using the FDDI protocol. Sites that don't currently have fiber can very likely implement 100Base-T more cost effectively using copper.

It's important to pick the 100Base-T specification that is designed for the physical cable plant you have or are planning to build. That's because the various Fast Ethernet specifications are not interchangeable, and also because crafting the appropriate cable plant represents a significant portion of the cost of implementing 100Base-T. The decision table in Table 9-1 can help you select the appropriate physical layer interface for your 100Base-T network.

◆ Cable: 4-pair Category 3, 4, or 5 UTP
◆ Connector: Standard RJ-45
◆ Signaling: 100Mbps = 3-pair × 25MHz × (133 percent for 8B6T encoding)
◆ RJ-45 pinout: 10Base-T + 2 bidirectional pairs

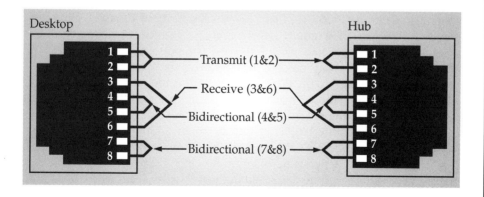

Figure 9-3. *100Base-T4 is 100Mbps 802.3u over 4-pair twisted-pair cable*

If You Have	And You Are Using	Choose This Specification
Type-1 or Category 5 STP	2-cable pairs	100Base-TX
Category 5	2-cable pairs	100Base-TX
Category 5	4-cable pairs	100Base-T4
Category 4	2-cable pairs	You must upgrade your cabling
Category 4	4-cable pairs	100Base-T4
Category 3	2-cable pairs	You must upgrade your cabling
Category 3	4-cable pairs	100Base-T4
Fiber-optic cabling		100Base-FX

Table 9-1. *How to Choose the Correct 802.3u Specification for Your Cable Plant*

Understanding the Differences Between 100Base-T and 10Base-T

As we mentioned earlier, 100Base-T bears a lot of similarity to 10Base-T. Obviously, implementing 100Base-T will require that you replace your network adapters and hubs. Fortunately, the actual cost of the 100Base-T components is very low. Strong industry support indicates that competition may drive these costs even lower, currently ranging from $600 to $1,000 per managed port including network adapter. At the time of this writing, these prices were still dropping rapidly. However, there's much more to implementing the protocol than simply replacing equipment. Although it's also fairly easy to integrate 100Base-T into an existing 10Base-T network, there are some very important differences between how the two protocols work. The success of your high-speed network depends upon your knowing and preparing for these differences. These differences are discussed in the following sections.

Interoperability and Obstacles

To plan a successful implementation, you should be aware of certain technical characteristics of the 100Base-T protocol. Knowing these will help you determine whether 100Base-T is the appropriate protocol for the segment you have in mind, as well as alert you to any potential difficulties you may experience after implementing 100Base-T.

Narrowing the Window of Opportunity

One of the biggest obstacles in implementing a 100Mbps CSMA/CD protocol is the extremely short slot time available. *Slot time* is the window of time required for a network station to detect a collision. Figure 9-4 illustrates the effect of slot time on packet transmission. In 10Base-T, the slot time is 512 bits. A transmitting station "listens" to the network, waiting for an opening in the traffic so that it can send a packet. When an opening occurs, the station must transmit its packet before another packet comes hurtling down the network. This period of time that it has to transmit the packet and listen for a collision before another one comes is called the slot time. In 802.3, slot time is set at 5.12 microseconds (the time it takes to transmit 512 bits traveling at 10Mbps). This is the amount of time the station has to transmit a packet successfully, or "claim the channel" as it is called in 802.3 jargon. In fact, 5.12μs is all the time the transmitting station has to transmit the packet *and receive a collision signal if the transmitted packet collides with another packet.* That's because if the transmitted packet collides with another packet, the transmitting station must receive notification of the collision before the end of the slot time so that it can retransmit before another packet takes over the channel.

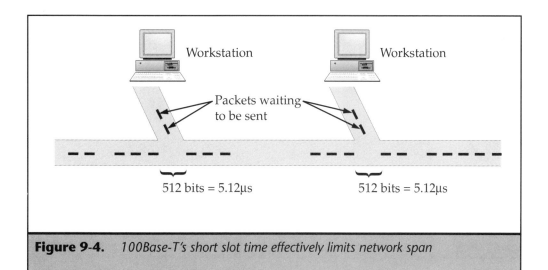

Figure 9-4. *100Base-T's short slot time effectively limits network span*

With the advent of 100Base-T, data throughput has been increased tenfold over 10Base-T, but the slot time of 512 bits has not been increased. A similar situation would be if you ordinarily merged onto a highway traveling 30 miles per hour in your car. As long as all the rest of the traffic on the highway is traveling at 30mph, you need only wait for a gap of about three car lengths to safely merge into the traffic. Imagine then, if your car and all the rest of the traffic began traveling at 300mph, but you still attempted to merge onto the highway when there was only a three-car-length space available. Collisions would seem inevitable, wouldn't they? And so they are with 100Base-T. Therefore, to ensure that collision notifications are received by the transmitting station before the end of the slot time, the network span must be shrunk proportionately. For 100Base-T, this limits the maximum network span to approximately 210m.

Changes in Latitude

The 100Base-T standard doesn't allow the latitude in configuring segments that 10Base-T does. It allows only two repeater hops per segment, unlike 10Base-T's three hops per segment. To observe the 210m maximum span, these repeater hops can be a maximum of only 10m apart. Obviously, this will affect how you design your cable plant. See Figure 9-5.

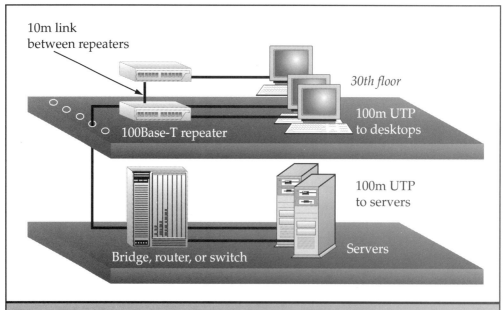

Figure 9-5. *The entire span of a 100Base-T network cannot exceed 210m*

Scalability Considerations

Before you select 100Base-T, it's important to understand the limitations of the protocol. Most of the drawbacks of 100Base-T are due to its limited scalability. Because of its close kinship to 10Base-T, it suffers from some of the same problems (such as increased collisions and resulting slow performance) when subjected to heavy traffic. However, full-duplex Ethernet is a technology that has been implemented in 100Base-T protocols to help ease the same problem.

Full-Duplex Fast Ethernet: Why and How

The CSMA/CD access protocol itself may inhibit scalability. As you add more users and more bandwidth-intensive applications, the increased collisions may well prevent acceptable performance. However, 100Base-T switches, especially those that offer full duplex, may mitigate the collision problems of the CSMA/CD protocol. To explain how full duplex increases bandwidth, let's begin with an explanation of 100Base-T signaling.

There are two pairs of wires in star-wired 10Base-T and 100Base-T environments—one for transmitting and one for receiving. However, transmission and receipt cannot take place at the same time. Full-duplex Ethernet, on the other hand, allows transmission over one pair of wires and receipt over the other pair simultaneously, providing nearly full utilization of both pairs and thus sustainable high data rates. By installing MAC devices that support full-duplex Ethernet, you can double the effective bandwidth. Full-duplex Ethernet can coexist with normal half-duplex Ethernet and make use of the existing 10Base-T wiring.

LIMITATIONS OF FULL-DUPLEX FAST ETHERNET   As attractive as it sounds, full-duplex Ethernet has a couple of serious drawbacks. The first is that it requires an investment in NICs, hubs, switches, firmware, and driver upgrades that support full-duplex operation. For example, Grand Junction offers its implementation of full-duplex Fast Ethernet, called CollisionFree, at an upgrade price of $400 per switch. The second drawback is that it makes sense only in a few situations. Specifically, this protocol is effective only in point-to-point connections, and then only when there is traffic available to flow in both directions at the same time. Still, in backbone implementations where there is a great deal of traffic among servers, full-duplex Ethernet is a technology that may be worth considering to make maximum use of the bandwidth available.

The Good News About Scalability

The good news about 100Base-T scalability, as we mentioned earlier, is that it is fairly easy to integrate with existing 10Base-T networks. Despite the fact that it supports fewer hops than 10Base-T and thus may require some recabling, the 100Base-T protocol has a relatively small packet size for high-speed networks, and it handles smaller packet sizes well. Given the current 512-byte average packet size on networks, this gives 100Base-T an edge as a "transition-to-high-speed" protocol. Furthermore, many vendors offer hubs, switches, and network adapter cards that function both at 10Mbps and 100Mbps. These devices automatically sense whether they are attached to a 10Base-T or 100Base-T network and adjust their speed accordingly. This makes it relatively easy and cost-effective to convert from 10Base-T to 100Base-T in phases.

Manageability Issues

Because 100Base-T is so similar to 10Base-T, many of the familiar 10Base-T management tools are available for use with 100Base-T networks, such as protocol analyzers and hub management systems. This means that 100Base-T is not only very manageable, but very manageable at a reasonable price since very little new development effort was required. Nonetheless, at this writing, the industry has still not provided the wide selection of management tools for 100Base-T that it has for 10Base-T. We expect this situation to change quickly as 100Base-T deployment becomes more widespread.

Setup and Configuration Considerations

Because of its many similarities to familiar 10Base-T, installation and configuration of 100Base-T devices is extremely easy. Because there is no initialization routine required of stations wanting to enter the ring, it's very easy to add new stations. To make things even easier, it even uses the same pinouts as 10Base-T, as mentioned earlier.

Cabling Considerations

Probably the biggest consideration in implementing 100Base-T is the cable plant. Differences in cabling rules between 100Base-T and 10Base-T are few but critical. For example, the maximum network span of 100Base-T is 210m. Therefore, you may have to recable portions of your network if you have made use of 10Base-T's 2,500m span. What's more, 100Base-T supports only two network hops, rather than three as with 10Base-T, and therefore you may have to reconfigure the segments that you are converting to 100Base-T to conform with this requirement.

 CAUTION: 100Base-T doesn't adhere fully with 802.3 cabling specifications! A careful pre-implementation review of your existing cable plant is critical.

Special Concerns for 100Base-T4

There are also some issues unique to those who select 100Base-T4. Because 100Base-T4 requires four cable pairs to operate over Category 3 cable, if all four pairs aren't terminated at your site, you'll have to upgrade the cable plant. If yours is a legacy cable plant, be sure to review it very carefully to be certain all four pairs are terminated. If not, you'll have to correct this situation before you can proceed with your 100Base-T4 implementation. This can be both costly and tedious, so factor that into your decision to use 100Base-T4.

Summary

100Base-T is probably best described as a high-performance economy model. It is probably the easiest of the high-speed network desktop protocols to implement. At $600 to $1,000 per managed port and falling, it nearly competes with 10Base-T in cost. It also saves you money as well as time by building on proven technology and expertise. It's easy to integrate into an existing 10Base-T network. However, because it is modeled so closely after 10Base-T, it has some of the slower protocol's inherent obstacles limiting its scalability.

Recommended for:

■ Applications that require intermittent communication between client and server, such as database applications, because the CSMA/CD protocol offers its best performance under traffic that is intermittent as opposed to continuous.

■ Word processing and other standard desktop applications. As a general high-speed replacement, 100Base-T is hard to beat for its ease of implementation and leverage of existing expertise.

■ Geographically centralized power workgroups, because of short span (210m) and a limit of two repeater hops.

■ Certain very specific backbone implementations only if the full-duplex feature is enabled. 100Base-T will certainly provide better performance than 10Base-T, but because the CSMA/CD architecture slows under heavy traffic, it may not offer as much improvement as one of the deterministic high-speed protocols.

Not Recommended for:

■ Applications that require constant, precisely timed communication between client and server, such as multimedia and video applications. This is because the CSMA/CD architecture can't deliver packets predictably.

■ Backbones, because the CSMA/CD architecture tends to slow significantly under heavy traffic.

Strengths:

■ Inexpensive

■ Easy to integrate into existing 10Base-T installations

■ Uses the same pinouts as 10Base-T

■ Uses much the same cabling rules as 10Base-T

Weaknesses:

■ Limited scalablity because:

  ■ Allows only two repeater hops per segment

  ■ Maximum network span is only 210m

  ■ CSMA/CD access method may impede response time as more users and bandwidth-intensive applications are added

 TIP: As much as 100Base-T looks and acts like 10Base-T, it's not. The cabling rules are just different enough to cause you trouble, so be prepared to spend time locating and reconfiguring those portions of your cable plant that don't comply with 100Base-T specifications. However, more than any of the other protocols compared here, 100Base-T lets you lever your investment in staff training and expertise.

CHAPTER 10

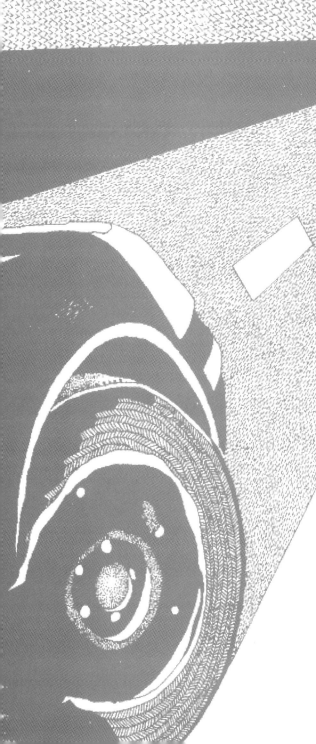

Thomas-Conrad Networking System (TCNS)

Solution for:

Network Architecture
- ☑ Workgroups
- ○ Power Workgroups
- ○ Server Farms
- ○ Backbones
- ○ Wide Area

Network Application
- ☑ Database Applications
- ☑ Workgroup Applications
- ○ Multimedia
- ○ Image Processing
- ○ Wide Area

The Thomas-Conrad Networking System, now owned by Compaq Computer Corporation and commonly known by its acronym, TCNS, is the high-speed descendant of ARCNET. TCNS began shipping in 1990, making it the second oldest 100Mbps local area network protocol (FDDI is the oldest). TCNS currently has about 60,000 nodes installed. Despite its maturity and established base, however, TCNS is really a solution only for very specific circumstances. Those circumstances include ARCNET upgrades, server mirroring, and sites that already have a legacy cable plant of RG62A/U cable.

The Successor of ARCNET

TCNS has been called Fast ARCNET, and it shares a lot with its predecessor. For example, when TCNS first appeared in 1990, it ran only on RG62A/U cable, just like ARCNET. Also like its forerunner, TCNS networks are either simple point-to-point networks or the familiar ARCNET "string of stars"—a distributed-star topology. See Figure 10-1.

TCNS employs active hubs (hubs that require power) that form the actual physical ring. Thomas-Conrad calls these hubs SmartHubs because in addition to providing basic connectivity, they also perform a variety of basic management functions such as conditioning, relaying, amplifying network signals, and monitoring reconfigurations on each hub port. The SmartHubs also provide the intelligence for managing the token-passing scheme.

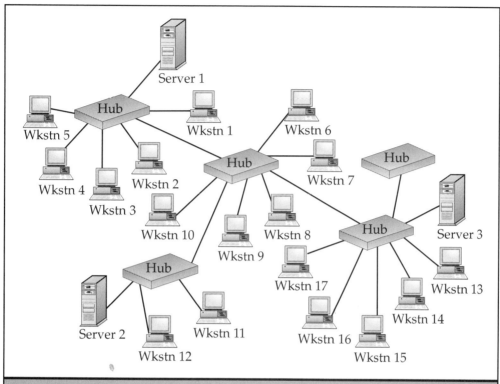

Figure 10-1. *TCNS employs the same distributed-star topology as traditional ARCNET*

The Architecture

Like ARCNET, TCNS uses a token bus data access method, which gives workstations control of the bus in the order that the workstations joined the ring. When the first workstation in the network powers on, it signals itself as station number 1 on the network, thereby having an *interface unit* of 1. This workstation will retain this same interface unit for as long as it is powered on. When the next workstation on the network powers on, it will take the interface unit of 2, and so on. Control of the bus is granted by the passing of the token from the station with the lowest interface unit to the next highest interface unit. When a workstation receives the token, it places a fixed amount of data on the network. If a station doesn't need to transmit data, the token immediately passes to the station with the next highest interface unit. When the token is passed from the workstation with the highest interface unit, it passes to the token with the lowest interface unit, and the process begins all over again.

The total amount of time it takes for the token to pass from the workstation with the lowest interface unit to the workstation with the highest interface unit is known as the *scan time*. The longer the scan time, the higher the response time and the lower the performance of the network. Because this is a deterministic protocol, the time required to pass the token from one workstation to another is fixed. Therefore, you can accurately predict how adding workstations affects scan time.

Cabling Considerations

Thomas-Conrad has expanded media support for TCNS to include not only RG62A/U, but also Type-1 shielded twisted-pair (STP), optical fiber, and even Category 5 unshielded twisted-pair (UTP). The Category 5 implementation requires all four pairs of cable (see Figure 10-2 for pinout), so you will have to be sure your cable plant meets that specification.

Distances vary with the type of cable and connectors used. Table 10-1 summarizes the maximum network span for each cable type. Of course, copper media such as coax, STP, and UTP are the best choices for small or medium-sized workgroups that span only a few hundred feet. Fiber-optic media should generally be reserved for special deployments in which long distances, electrical noise and interference, and/or security are issues. In addition, fiber-optic cable is lighter and smaller in diameter than copper media, so it can be installed in places where copper cables might be too bulky or heavy.

Cost of Ownership

TCNS devices are probably the least expensive of any high-speed local area networking equipment. However, the cost of the devices is only a small part of the price you'll pay for TCNS. For example, because of its proprietary nature, it can be difficult to integrate into other protocols, requiring the use of routers. TCNS routing can be done at the server if the servers are running the Novell NetWare network operating system. Otherwise, the routing must be done via standalone PCs on which

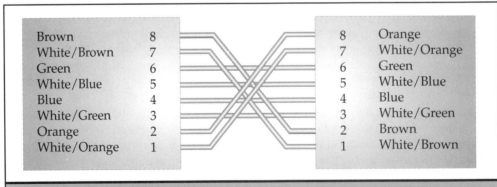

Figure 10-2.   *The cable pinout for TCNS running on Category 5 UTP cable*

Cable Type	Connector Type	Maximum Network Span
RG62A/U	BNC	100m
Shielded twisted-pair (Type-1)	DB-9	150m
Fiber-optic cable (62.5/105 micron recommended)	ST	900m
Unshielded twisted-pair (Category 5)	RJ-45	100m

Table 10-1. *Summary of the Maximum Network Span for TCNS Networks*

special TCNS routing software must be loaded. The routers are placed between the TCNS network and all other networks so that TCNS packets can be routed to nodes on the non-TCNS network and vice versa. See Figure 10-3.

There is also the question of cable support. As we mentioned earlier, TCNS requires RG62A/U coax (a legacy from ARCNET), fiber-optical, Type-1 (just like Token Ring), or Category 5 UTP. With the exception of Category 5 UTP, all of these are expensive options.

Scalability

Scalability is TCNS's forte. Like ARCNET, TCNS is limited to 250 nodes per network. Also like ARCNET, this protocol uses a token bus access method. This makes it easily scalable with little discernible drop in response time. What's more, the TCNS topology and cabling rules have no restrictions on the number of hubs between nodes. This somewhat "free-form" approach to network design is a mixed blessing: It gives you more flexibility than most of the other high-speed protocols, but also allows you to create an unsupportable mess if you don't structure and document carefully.

Setup & Configuration

Like its ARCNET ancestor, TCNS is simple and quick to install *if* it is the only protocol you will be using on the network. However, if you want to integrate TCNS into another network, you are going to have your hands full. As a proprietary protocol, TCNS wasn't really designed for interoperability. Although with technical support from Thomas-Conrad and a good measure of persistence you can usually configure TCNS to overcome its interoperability problems, all of these configuration solutions will involve PC-based routers.

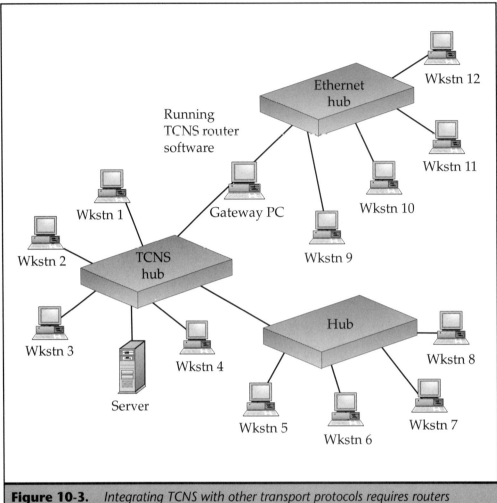

Figure 10-3. *Integrating TCNS with other transport protocols requires routers*

Because TCNS uses the ARCNET MAC-layer specification described earlier in "The Architecture" section, it is compatible with existing ARCNET drivers. Because most popular network operating systems support ARCNET drivers, you will probably find that your current network operating system will also support TCNS.

Manageability

TCNS receives its lowest marks in manageability. Although Thomas-Conrad does have a network hub management tool, called HubTalk, the protocol itself is essentially without management tools. In addition, HubTalk really only provides out-of-band management of the physical hub device, which lets you turn hub ports on and off remotely.

Furthermore, SNMP support is currently limited to a single agent (available from Thomas-Conrad) that the company admits will only help you identify attached devices, but won't collect information on them. There are also no protocol analysis tools available.

Performance

TCNS is a stable, if not stellar, performer. Throughput from the server averages 45Mbps. Client throughput runs at about 30Mbps.

This deterministic protocol shows its strength in multimedia and video applications because it guarantees each station a fixed amount of bandwidth, thus ensuring that packets are transmitted without delays. Furthermore, its low packet overhead (due largely to its lack of management features) leaves more bandwidth for payload transmission.

Special Applications of TCNS

In cooperation with Novell and IBM, Thomas-Conrad has developed special drivers for TCNS so it can function as a high-speed NetWare SFT III mirrored server link. TCNS has now been tested and approved by Novell for this use. This makes TCNS a good choice for this specialized implementation.

It's Getting Better, But...

Thomas-Conrad announced its commitment to continuing enhancements to TCNS, and the company seems to be making good on its promise. As a result of this promise, Thomas-Conrad launched SNMP support as well as expanded media support. However, although TCNS now runs on a variety of cable types (see Table 10-1), at the time of this writing SNMP support is severely limited. For example, it won't work with anything but NetWare. Furthermore, Thomas-Conrad seems to be pulling back on its support for TCNS, focusing instead on its 100VG-AnyLAN initiative.

Summary

Of all the high-speed protocols discussed in this book, TCNS is the most limited. The low price of its components and its excellent scalability just don't compensate for its lack of manageability, challenging interoperability, and proprietary design.

Strengths:

- Very inexpensive
- Low overhead

■ Very flexible cabling and topology rules

Weaknesses:

■ Essentially no management capabilities

■ Proprietary, single-vendor solution

■ Interoperability with other protocols is often very difficult

Recommended for:

■ Transaction-oriented and/or time-critical applications such as CAD/CAM

■ Distributed database management, because of its predictable performance and low overhead

■ Workgroups with existing RG62A/U and Type-1 cabling

■ Upgrading legacy 3270 and ARCNET networks, because it uses existing RG62A/U cabling and is fairly easy to install and maintain

■ Mirrored server links, because of the specially designed driver, low overhead, and cost

Not Recommended for:

■ Backbones, because of lack of management capabilities

■ New installations, because there are several other more manageable and equally inexpensive solutions

CHAPTER 11

Fibre Channel

Solution for:

Network Architecture	Network Application
○ Workgroups	○ Database Applications
☑ Power Workgroups	○ Workgroup Applications
☑ Server Farms	☑ Multimedia
○ Backbones	☑ Image Processing
○ Wide Area	○ Wide Area

Fibre Channel didn't begin life as a network transport protocol. In fact, the specification was not originally intended to work as a network protocol at all. It was first designed and developed to interconnect high-speed peripherals—for example, a cluster of high-performance computers—to a shared mass storage device. The result of this intent was a generic architecture that was a combination of both *network* and *channel* connection technology that concentrates on high-speed transmission and guaranteed delivery of data. This makes it suitable not only for connecting peripherals to hosts, but also for network connectivity over the short haul.

Going Through Channels

A *channel connection* provides either a direct or switched point-to-point connection between devices, such as a computer's processor and a peripheral device. The function of a channel isn't sophisticated in concept: it's supposed to transmit data as fast as possible from point A to point B. The destination address is not only predetermined, it is hard-wired—the data really *can't* go anywhere but its destination. Any error-correction it performs is simple and is done in hardware. Routing and address resolution aren't done because they aren't required. Therefore, there's no address and error-correction information that needs to be carried in the data packet, so the packet overhead is very low. Because of their point-to-point nature and consequently limited processing demands, channel connections are largely implemented in hardware.

Network connections, on the other hand, are multipoint connections that rely on addressing schemes to make sure that the data gets to the appropriate destination.

Each data packet traveling along a network connection must contain an address, which each device on the network reads to determine whether the packet is intended for it. Furthermore, network connections routinely have relatively sophisticated error-detection and correction capabilities. Therefore, the packet must contain the address and error-correction information in its header, resulting in higher packet overhead than in a channel connection. However, network connections can support functions, such as routing, that a channel simply isn't designed to support.

Fibre Channel has features of both a channel and a network. It is a high-speed channel that connects devices to a *network fabric*. The network fabric describes the matrix of connections, from a single cable connecting two devices to a mesh created by a switch connecting many devices. The fabric can be pretty much any combination of devices, including hubs, loops, mainframes, and switches. A fabric can be created specifically to suit the application being supported. In any event, no matter how complex the network fabric is, as far as an individual Fibre Channel port is concerned, it manages a simple point-to-point connection between the workstation and the network fabric.

Fibre Channel's greatest asset is speed. Ethernet, at 10Mbps, transmits data far slower than computers can produce it. Therefore, the primary goal of Fibre Channel is to provide computing devices with a throughput mechanism that is closer to the speed of their processors. And speed it has—it delivers bandwidth from 133Mbps to 1.062Gbps over a wide variety of cable types, including multimode fiber, coaxial cable, and shielded twisted-pair wire, and can support a network span of up to 10km. In fact, Fibre Channel is so efficient and fast that it can deliver speeds of 100MBps (notice that is mega*bytes* per second) in both directions simultaneously, which means it is effectively a 200MBps full-duplex channel.

Fibre Channel is extremely versatile because it is protocol independent. It is a *generic transport mechanism*, meaning that it can support command sets from several different other channel protocols, such as Small Computer System Interface (SCSI), Internet Protocol (IP), and High Performance Parallel Interface (HIPPI).

Its speed and guaranteed packet delivery make Fibre Channel a good protocol for connecting network devices in a relatively local environment, such as a workgroup or even a campus environment, as shown in Figure 11-1. But because of its high performance, wide network span, and support of various topologies such as point-to-point, *arbitrated loop* (which we will discuss in detail later in this chapter), and switched fabric, Fibre Channel has broader applications than as simply a networking protocol. It can connect LANs, midrange computers, mainframes, disk arrays, and server farms as part of one giant network.

The Standard and Its Supporting Groups

The American National Standards Institute (ANSI) ANSI X3T9.3 started work on the Fibre Channel standard in 1988. At that time, the main support for the protocol came from its supporting group, the Fibre Channel System Initiative (FCSI), headed by IBM,

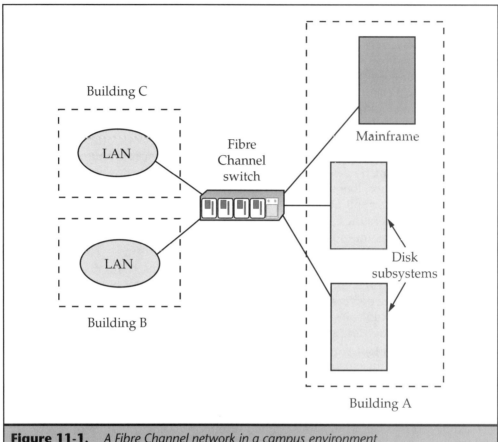

Figure 11-1.   *A Fibre Channel network in a campus environment*

HP, and Sun Microsystems. The mission of the FCSI was to develop a high-speed open connection standard for Fibre Channel workstations and peripherals. This mission was accomplished early on. During its existence, the FCSI was a major influence in the design of the protocol, developing profiles and specifications that offered interoperability between existing architectures and Fibre Channel.

Since its ratification by ANSI in the early 90s, the Fibre Channel standard has been through many enhancements. For example, in 1991 the standard was modified to include support for copper and multidrop configurations. The most changes came in 1995, when the Fibre Channel Systems Initiative and Fibre Channel Association announced that the ANSI X3T11 committee overseeing the technology had adopted 2Gbps and 4Gbps data rates, a 400 percent increase over the previous 1Gbps ceiling. Shortly thereafter, the Fibre Channel System Initiative pronounced its job complete and passed its mantel as the standard bearer for Fibre Channel to the Fibre Channel

Association (Austin, Texas), which has a little over 85 member companies. The Fibre Channel Association will pick up where FCSI left off. For information, contact the Fibre Channel Association, a 100-member consortium of Fibre Channel vendors, in Austin, Texas, at (800) 272-4618; e-mail FCA-info@amcc.com (see Appendix C).

How Do They *Do* That?

Fibre Channel transports data in much the same way a router does. It reads the destination addresses of incoming packets, encapsulates the packets, and sends them across the fabric. Underlying data formats, packet structures, or frame types are not important to Fibre Channel devices.

As mentioned, Fibre Channel establishes point-to-point connections between devices. These connections are like switched circuits, and multiple circuits can exist simultaneously. The circuits are duplex connections that can provide 100MBps of transmission speed in both directions simultaneously. When a device wishes to transmit over a switching device or network, it simply requests a connection to that device. If the network is currently busy, the port tries to make the connection later.

The current Fibre Channel standard supports four transmission speeds: 133Mbps, 266Mbps, 530Mbps, and 1.062Gbps. Fibre Channel network equipment that supports 266Mbps and 1.062Gbps are now shipping from various vendors such as Ancor Communications, Inc., of Minnetonka, MN.

The Fibre Channel frame, as shown in Figure 11-2, supports a data payload of 70 to 2,112 bytes with a 24-byte frame header (preceded by a 4-byte Start of Frame delimiter). It is this relatively large payload supported by a very low overhead that allows such high end-to-end throughputs: 25MBps for 266Mbps Fibre Channel and 100MBps for 1.062Gbps Fibre Channel—speed close to that of the backplanes of some server systems.

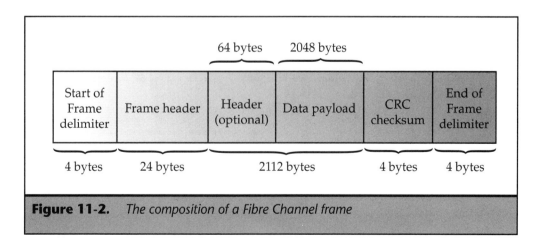

Figure 11-2. *The composition of a Fibre Channel frame*

The Fibre Channel architecture comprises five layers, designated FC-0 through FC-4, as shown in Figure 11-3.

Fibre Channel Layer 0 (FC-0): The Physical Interface

Layer FC-0 is the layer that defines the physical and media interfaces and the media. This is the layer that describes the electrical characteristics of the media, and includes the transmitters, receivers, connectors, and cables, upon which the Fibre Channel network runs.

The FC-0 layer also defines a system unique to Fibre Channel: the *open fibre control system*, which affects the Fibre Channel running over optical fiber. The open fibre control system is sort of a "back off and resend" failsafe system that is required because the power of the optical laser used in Fibre Channel exceeds ANSI safety standards for optical lasers. You see, Fibre Channel connections often break due to this excessive laser power. When that happens, the open fibre control system in the receiving device detects the open link, then sends a lower level laser pulse than that defined by the Fibre Channel standard. The lower level laser pulse continues until both ends of the

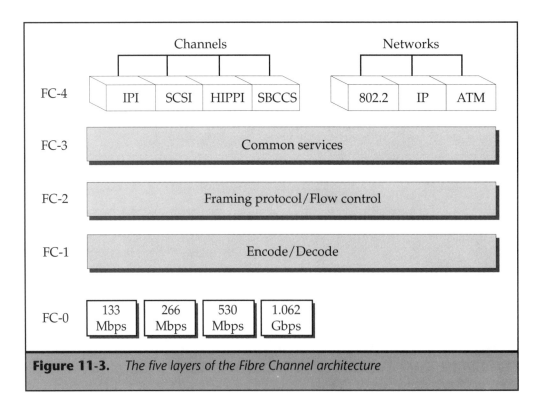

Figure 11-3. *The five layers of the Fibre Channel architecture*

connection receive it. After the physical connection has been restored, the network connection resumes a few seconds later. Figure 11-4 shows a sample FC-0 link with open fibre control.

Fibre Channel Layer 1 (FC-1): The Transmission Protocol

FC-1 describes the transmission protocol layer; that is, the layer responsible for establishing the rules for transmitting each data packet. It defines the special data encoding scheme, called 8B/10B encoding, that Fibre Channel employs for high-performance data transmission. This scheme encodes each consecutive 8 bits of data (i.e., each byte) into a 10-bit transmission character. Transmitting these uniformly sized 10-bit characters enables the protocol to synchronize data transmission, thereby providing a recovery and retransmission mechanism when errors are detected. Furthermore, Fibre Channel uses a special character, called a *comma* character, to ensure byte and word alignment. The block diagram in Figure 11-5 shows the 8B/10B encoding scheme.

Fibre Channel Layer 2 (FC-2): Signaling Protocol

FC-2 is the signaling protocol layer. It defines the method of moving data between end devices on the network, called *node ports* or *N_ports*, through the Fibre Channel switching device, called *fabric ports* or *F_ports*. The N_ports have a management system known as the Fibre Channel *Link_Control_Facility* that manages the physical and logical links between them. The FC-2 layer is concerned with defining the objects that will be managed by the Link_Control_Facility. These objects are called *ordered set,*

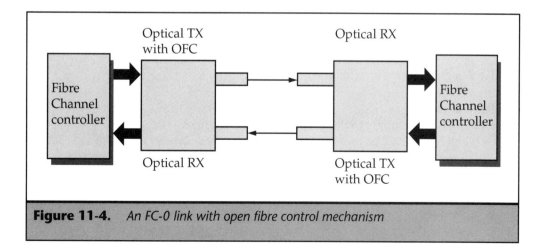

Figure 11-4. *An FC-0 link with open fibre control mechanism*

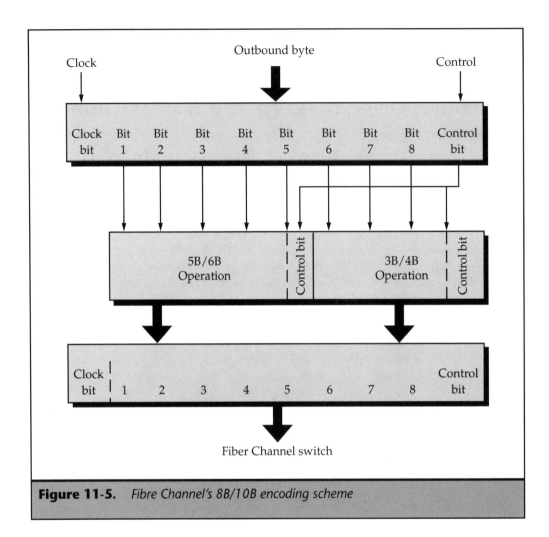

Figure 11-5. *Fibre Channel's 8B/10B encoding scheme*

frame, sequence, exchange, and *protocol.* Flow control, congestion management, and *class of service* designations are also handled at this layer.

Ordered Set

An ordered set is a delimiter or "flag" used by Fibre Channel to signal events in low-level link functions. For example, the Start of Frame delimiter is an ordered set. The structure of an ordered set is a combination of four 10-bit characters, both data and special characters. This signaling helps Fibre Channel establish a network link when devices are first powered on. It also enables a few basic recovery actions.

Frame

As we mentioned earlier, the Fibre Channel frame begins and ends with a 4-byte frame marker, followed by a 24-byte frame header containing addressing information. Next comes a large Data field that can contain up to 2,112 bytes (2,048-byte payload and an optional 64-byte header). The Data field is followed by 4 bytes for a cyclical redundancy error check and, finally, the 4-byte end of frame marker. Refer to Figure 11-2.

In classes of service that guarantee delivery, which we will define and discuss in detail shortly, each frame is acknowledged by the receiving N_port. These acknowledgments also provide notification of nondelivery of the frame to the transmitting N_port. The FC-2 layer also defines "Busy" and "Reject" signals that notify the transmitting N_port that a frame hasn't been delivered.

Sequence

A *sequence* is the unit of data transfer in the Fibre Channel. It is a frame or group of related frames describing a single operation that has been put into packets for transmission over the Fibre Channel fabric. The FC-2 layer on the transmitting end is responsible for disassembling these sequences and packaging them in the frame size that has been set up by the transmitting and receiving ports—as well as all intervening ports on the fabric. On the receiving end, the FC-2 layer assembles these frames into the operation they describe, then passes them on to the higher layers of the Fibre Channel protocol. If an error occurs during the transmission of a sequence, the entire sequence is retransmitted.

Each sequence is assigned a *Sequence Identifier*, which appears in a field in the header of each frame sent over the fabric. As well, each frame within the sequence is numbered with a *Sequence Count* identifier, which also appears in the frame header information.

This use of sequences allows Fibre Channel both to send large blocks of data without dividing it into smaller frames and to support other channel protocols, such as IP and HIPPI, transparently.

Exchange

An *exchange* is a group of sequences that make up a single operation. An operation usually involves several tasks. For example, sending a packet of data can involve connection initiation, connection acknowledgment, packet transmission, and acknowledgment of packet receipt. Each of these tasks is a separate sequence, but together make up one exchange. Only one sequence at a time can be active in an exchange, although multiple exchanges can be active simultaneously.

The relationship among ordered sets, frames, sequences, and exchanges is illustrated in Figure 11-6.

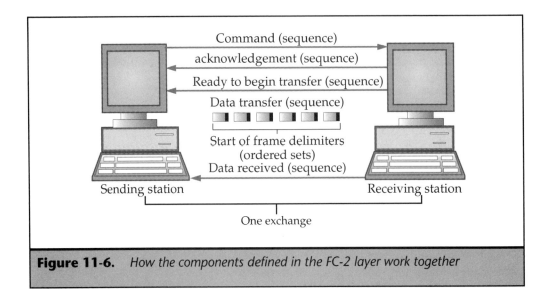

Figure 11-6. *How the components defined in the FC-2 layer work together*

Classes of Service

With Fibre Channel, flow control and delivery acknowledgment depend upon the class of service designated for the network traffic in question. Currently, three classes of service are defined within the FC-2 layer. These classes range from Class 1 service, which provides a dedicated connection with confirmed delivery of packets, to Class 3 service, which does not guarantee or confirm delivery of packets.

CLASS 1 SERVICE In Class 1, data packets are delivered in the same order in which they are transmitted, and each frame's delivery is confirmed by an acknowledgment from the receiving device. If congestion causes a frame to be dropped, a busy frame is returned to the sender, which then resends the frame. This type of service is well-suited to applications that require high-speed, guaranteed packet delivery such as full-motion video.

The Class 1 service also contains a service mode called *Intermix*. Intermix allows you to set priorities among data traffic. In Intermix, you can multiplex all classes of service over a single wire, but only Class 1 connections get guaranteed bandwidth. Frames sent within the other classes are only transmitted when bandwidth in excess of that needed for the Class 1 connection is available. This is similar to Fiber Distributed Data Interface's prioritization mechanism.

CLASS 2 SERVICE In Class 2 service, no dedicated connection is established. Instead, bandwidth is shared rather than dedicated as it is in Class 1 service. The protocol uses multiplexing to send multiple frames over the wire simultaneously. The frames aren't necessarily received in the same order they are sent, and in fact may take different paths because Class 2 service allows packets to make use of the shortest path available at the time of transmission.

However, delivery of frames **is** guaranteed in Class 2. As well, just as in Class 1 service, in Class 2 service the sending device will get a "busy frames" signal if the receiving device can't process an incoming frame, so the sender knows to retransmit the frame. Class 2 service is therefore best suited for use in networks that aren't transmitting time-sensitive data.

CLASS 3 SERVICE   Class 3 is a connectionless packet-switched service like Class 2, but it does not provide guaranteed frame delivery. Thus, devices operating in Class 3 service require buffers on both the transmitting and receiving stations to avoid lost packets. Therefore, Class 3 is best suited for data that requires high-speed, time-sensitive transmission, but in which a dropped frame is useless if not received in time. Videoconferencing and teletraining are such applications.

Fibre Channel Layer 3 (FC-3): Common Services

The next layer of the Fibre Channel architecture, FC-3, defines common services such as support for multicasts and hunt groups. These functions are

- **Multicast.** Multicast delivers a single transmission to a group address that defines multiple destination ports.

- **Hunt Groups**. This operates much like a telephone hunt group in which an incoming call can be answered by any one of a predefined group of phones. A hunt group is useful when connecting high-speed devices. It is a predefined group of ports attached to a single node, such as a set of ports belonging to a mass storage device. Frames addressed to a hunt group are delivered to any available port within the hunt group.

- **Striping.** Striping is a method of parallel transmission, similar to that of parallel printing. Fibre Channel can use multiple connections simultaneously to deliver a packet of data, *striping* the data across the connections to deliver it faster.

Fibre Channel Layer 4 (FC-4): Upper Layer Protocol Mapping

The FC-4 layer is the top layer of the Fibre Channel architecture. This layer defines the upper layer protocols (ULPs) that are interfaces to transport protocols, communications protocols, and other channel protocols. These ULPs allow Fibre Channel to support these other protocols transparently.

Cabling Considerations

Fibre Channel is in many ways a cable installer's dream, because:

- It is media independent. As we mentioned earlier, it supports single-mode fiber, multimode fiber, coaxial cable, and Type-1 shielded twisted-pair cable.

- Its huge maximum network spans on fiber media mean that it will operate on existing fiber runs.

However, the short supported distances on copper media—especially at high bandwidths—require that you review your cable plant carefully to make sure that existing cable runs don't exceed the maximum distances allowed by the Fibre Channel protocol.

Brave New Topology

Fibre Channel supports shared and switched connections just like most network protocols. However, one of the keys to Fibre Channel's versatility is its ability to support a topology that other protocols don't support well or can't support at all. That topology is a point-to-point connection with no intervening devices, which is called *Fibre Channel Arbitrated Loop* (FC-AL).

Loop the Loop

Fibre Channel Arbitrated Loop has been receiving a lot of attention lately. This topology lets you connect multiple devices in a ring without using hubs or switches. This makes it a flexible and cost-effective solution for localized high-bandwidth applications. The loop can support up to 127 ports that share bandwidth. An example of FC-AL is shown in Figure 11-7.

In FC-AL, a port is granted access to the loop based on its port address, with the lowest port address getting access first. When this port completes its transmission, the device with the next lowest port address is given access to the loop, and so on. Only one pair of ports, a sending port and a receiving port, can be active in the loop at any one time. A loop can also be attached to a Fibre Channel fabric to enable ports on the loop to communicate with ports on the fabric.

Installation and Configuration

As we mentioned earlier, because of its large network span, Fibre Channel usually requires no physical changes to an existing user's Ethernet or token-ring-based network. As a result of its use of sequences and exchanges, Fibre Channel works with common channel protocols such as IP, SCSI, and HIPPI, so your applications will probably require no modifications, either.

I'd like to point out, however, that when you are dealing with an extremely high performance protocol like Fibre Channel, the computing power of the network devices could quickly become a bottleneck. For this reason, we recommend that all devices attached to the Fibre Channel loop and/or fabric have high-performance processors and high-throughput bus architectures.

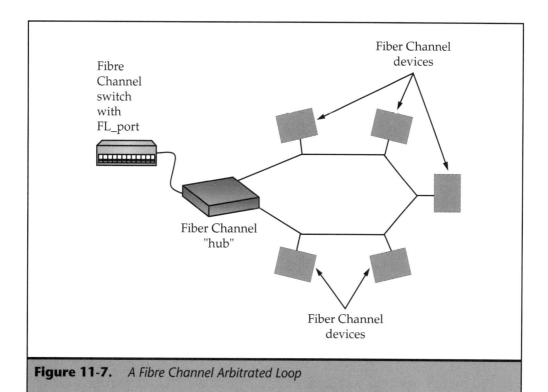

Figure 11-7. *A Fibre Channel Arbitrated Loop*

Interoperability

At first glance, Fibre Channel appears ultra-interoperable. As we mentioned, Fibre Channel can support most channel protocols such as IP and HIPPI transparently. What's more, Ethernet, FDDI, and even ATM frames or cells can be transmitted over the Fibre Channel fabric thanks to the encapsulation techniques used to create sequences and exchanges.

Furthermore, Fibre Channel is a fairly mature ANSI standard, so its specifications are well-defined and readily available. This may be one of Fibre Channel's greatest assets: it is an open, consistent interface. However, as of this writing, no vendors were shipping Fibre Channel adapters for routers. Without router support, Fibre Channel is a poor choice for backbones or other segments that have a wide variety of data paths and types of traffic.

Scalability

Fibre Channel is extremely scalable both in distance and number of networked devices. The Fibre Channel protocol supports up to 16 million nodes on a single fabric. Furthermore, because of its data prioritization and guaranteed delivery mechanisms, performance for critical applications will not drop significantly as devices are added to the network.

Also, Fibre Channel supports a network span of up to 10km. The maximum network span depends upon the type of media used and the transfer rate implemented. Table 11-1 shows the distances supported by the various media.

Taken together, this means that Fibre Channel is so scalable, aggregate data rates into the hundreds of gigabits per second or even terabits per second are feasible.

Manageability and Fault Tolerance

Fibre Channel supports a unique means of network management. Instead of having each node on the network perform its own management functions such as routing, configuration management, time synchronization, and fault management, Fibre Channel has assigned these functions to special management servers operating in the fabric. While this points to a single point of failure within the fabric, it does on the other hand free the nodes to concentrate on delivery of high-bandwidth transmission. For management reporting and monitoring, Fibre Channel supports simple network management protocol (SNMP), and most vendors implement SNMP management information base data with their network adapters and switches.

	132.8Mbps	265.6Mbps	531.25Mbps	1.062Gbps
Single-mode fiber	10km	10km	10km	10km
50-micrometer multimode fiber	n/a	2km	1km	n/a
62.5-micrometer multimode fiber	500m	1km	n/a	n/a
Coaxial cable	40m	30m	20m	10m
Shielded twisted-pair	100m	50m	n/a	n/a

Table 11-1. *The Maximum Network Span Supported by Each Type of Media Defined in the Fibre Channel Specification*

Performance

Fibre Channel is the highest performance protocol available right now in terms of raw bandwidth, throughput, and latency. As we mentioned, Fibre Channel can offer as much as 1.062Gbps bandwidth, with a real throughput (in full-duplex) of 200MBps. Furthermore, switched Fibre Channel has extremely low latency. This is because Fibre Channel dedicates separate circuits to traffic, thereby minimizing buffering and consequently latency at the switch.

Advantages: Fibre Channel vs. ATM

Fibre Channel's only real rival in the area of performance is asynchronous transfer mode (ATM), and much ink has been shed over the relative advantages of these two technologies. We will discuss ATM in detail in Chapter 16, but I would like to highlight the main points of differentiation between them:

- Ease of migration and integration. As we have discussed, Fibre Channel supports most existing applications, communications protocols, and transport protocols transparently. On the other hand, ATM requires sophisticated *LAN emulation* techniques to work with existing LANs, and these LAN emulation technologies are currently proprietary.

- Fibre Channel is fairly mature ANSI standard. All of ATM's standards have not yet been finalized.

- Voice Traffic. Fibre Channel is able to carry voice traffic easily and cost-effectively right now. ATM, as we will see, will require significant work on its ATM adaptation layer-1 protocol to accommodate voice traffic in a cost-effective way.

- Fibre Channel offers more raw throughput than ATM does.

However, before we take this comparison of the two protocols too far, I think we should consider that they are really designed to serve different segments of the high-speed networking market. Fibre Channel is really designed for a local environment comprised of high-speed devices needing access to other devices. It supports user nodes almost incidentally. ATM, as we will see, is fundamentally designed to integrate wide area and local connections seamlessly, and in many ways provides better support for user connections.

Disadvantages

Fibre Channel has two big drawbacks: it lacks good wide area integration capabilities, and there aren't a lot of people out there who know much about it. Therefore, it's best to implement Fibre Channel only for the local environment, and only if you already have or are willing to invest in the expertise to install and maintain it.

Recommended for:

■ High-bandwidth, localized applications, such as medical imaging and computer-generated animation

■ Distributed parallel processing

Not Recommended for:

■ Backbones, because of lack of integration with existing routers

■ Wide area

CHAPTER 12

IsoEthernet

Solution for:

Network Architecture
- ☑ Workgroups
- ☑ Power Workgroups
- ○ Server Farms
- ○ Backbones
- ☑ Wide Area

Network Application
- ○ Database Applications
- ☑ Workgroup Applications
- ☑ Multimedia
- ☑ Image Processing
- ☑ Wide Area

Many of you have probably not heard much about isochronous Ethernet, more widely known as isoEthernet. That's because isoEthernet has fairly limited industry support. However, because the support that it does have is from some very large and influential companies, such as National Semiconductor and IBM, isoEthernet is a contender in the high-speed networking arena. In addition, isoEthernet is viable because it can be integrated with ISDN public networks and is capable of upward migration to ATM.

The Second Coming of Ethernet

Not a high-speed networking protocol *per se*, isoEthernet is instead a technology that lets you revitalize your existing 10Base-T network by letting you take multimedia, wide area, and telephony traffic out of the LAN infrastructure and support it on a separate channel.

The IEEE 802.9a (IsoEthernet) Standard

Introduced in 1992 by National Semiconductor, isoEthernet is similar to the more familiar 10Base-T. It offers 10Mbps Ethernet support on shared, twisted-pair copper cable and it adheres to all of the cabling rules of 10Base-T. It varies from 10Base-T, however, in that it dedicates some circuits to time-sensitive traffic, such as video. The

IEEE 802.9a spec is similar to standards such as 802.3 Ethernet and 802.5 Token Ring in that it defines the media access control (MAC) and physical layers of the standard. In addition, 802.9a specifies a signaling layer based on ISDN protocols and using existing 10Base-T infrastructure. Therefore, it can be implemented in a legacy network without replacing cable or equipment.

 NOTE: *For purposes of discussing isoEthernet, I will use the terms* Ethernet *and* 10Base-T *interchangeably. Please note, however, that Ethernet and 10Base-T are not the same, and employ slightly different frame structures.*

In the Beginning, There Was Ethernet

To fully understand the difference between isoEthernet and 10Base-T, it's probably best to start with a discussion of isochronous services in general. The term "isochronous services" means that the network is capable of delivering data packets at precise time intervals. Real-time data such as voice requires isochronous connections. As a result, the public switched telephone network is a well-known example of an isochronous network. It is timed upon precise 8kHz clock signals. A digital phone line consists of a serial 64Kbps data stream with one byte every 125 microseconds. Known as bearer channels, or "B channels" for short, these 64Kbps digital phone lines are multiplexed serially with other B channels to form 128Kbps data streams that support more calls of greater bandwidth than a single B channel alone could. For example, a T1 link provides 23 B channels, which can be multiplexed to support simultaneous voice conversations and video transmissions.

Because the telephone network is circuit-switched rather than packet-switched, it provides isochronous connections between calling parties that remain dedicated for the duration of the call. Before any voice data is transmitted, a connection is established between the sending and receiving stations, and a portion of bandwidth is dedicated to this connection. Therefore, the circuit-switched telephone network supports multimedia communications well.

Local area networks using Ethernet, on the other hand, use a packet-based transmission method that doesn't require a connection to be established before the packets are transmitted. Instead, the packets are all of a uniform structure, containing origination and destination addresses in the header information that allow the network to route each packet to its destination. This means that packets from various origination addresses can travel together over the same cable. It also provides adequate LAN bandwidth to all parties. However, because the bandwidth isn't dedicated, all transactions contend with one another for bandwidth, and therefore transmission delays are unpredictable when network traffic is heavy. This makes packet-based transmission undesirable for time-sensitive traffic like voice and data.

Enter IsoEthernet

The new IEEE 802.9a isoEthernet standard was designed to overcome this basic incompatibility between packet-based LAN transmission and time-sensitive data, and to do so without interfering with existing Ethernet packet traffic or requiring expensive replacement of equipment, management systems, and cable plants. By intertwining the ISDN standard for WAN communications throughout the Ethernet LAN, the standard goes a long way toward meeting this goal.

There are three main features of isoEthernet that separate it from other desktop technologies:

- A new encoding scheme to increase bandwidth

- Time division multiplexing to separate isochronous traffic from packet-based network traffic

- The 8kHz master clock to implement timing

Two Networks in One

The isoEthernet standard really calls for two separate networks running over the same unshielded twisted-pair wiring. In addition to the 10Mbps channel allotted for 10Base-T traffic, there is also a separate 6.144Mbps channel dedicated to providing isochronous services. This channel is divided into 96 channels of 64Kbps each—in other words, 96 ISDN bearer channels ("B channels"). This makes for a total of 16Mbps of bandwidth squeezed out of the same 10Mbps 10Base-T infrastructure.

Where Do They Get the Extra Bandwidth?

To understand how IsoEthernet squeezes an extra 6Mbps out of ordinary 10Base-T, you first need to understand something about baseband signaling in Ethernet. Baseband signaling is the process of transmitting data in digital form over a baseband LAN. The job isn't a straightforward one, despite the fact that computers produce data already in digital format. This is because the encoding method used by computers is different than that used by LANs.

Computers use a digital signaling method called *unipolar nonreturn to zero* (NRZ) signaling. In NRZ, a positive voltage is used to represent a binary 1, and no voltage is used to represent a binary 0. The signaling method is called "nonreturn to zero" because the signal goes from 0 to some predefined positive voltage level and doesn't return to 0 between successive binary 1's (represented by the presence of voltage), as shown in Figure 12-1. If two successive 1 bits occur, two successive bit positions then have an identical voltage level. If two successive 0 bits occur, then they both have the same 0 voltage level. Because there is no voltage change to delineate between bits in the case of successive bits of the same value, it could be difficult to determine where—and whether—one bit ends and the next begins. Therefore, NRZ signaling depends upon precise clocking to determine the beginning and ending of each bit.

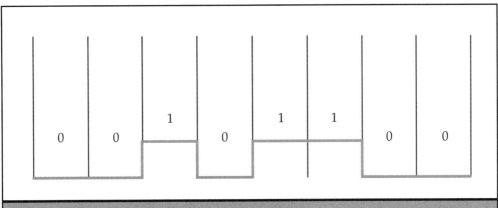

Figure 12-1. *Unipolar nonreturn to zero signaling*

To avoid expensive and high-overhead clocking in baseband LAN equipment, Ethernet and other LAN protocols have done away with unipolar NRZ signaling in favor of *Manchester encoding*. In Manchester encoding, an equal amount of positive and negative voltage represents each bit, and a timing transition always occurs in the middle of each bit. Therefore, a low to high voltage transmission represents a binary 1, and a high to low voltage represents a binary 0. This coding technique provides a good timing signal for clock recovery from received data due to its timing transitions. Figure 12-2 illustrates Manchester encoding.

As you can see from Figure 12-2, Manchester encoding is only 50 percent efficient. Therefore, the 10Mbps of Ethernet data is carried via a 20Mbps signal on the medium. While Manchester coding was chosen in 1979 for Ethernet because it was easy to

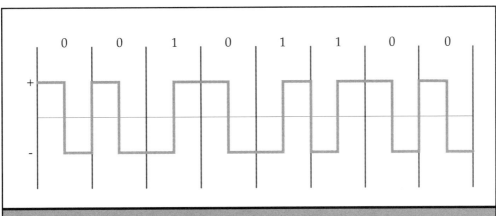

Figure 12-2. *Manchester encoding*

implement, silicon integration technology has advanced sufficiently to make it as easy to implement a more efficient line-encoding technique. As shown in Figure 12-3, isoEthernet replaces the Manchester encoding with a 4B/5B block-encoding scheme that is 80 percent efficient. Thus it provides 16Mbps in the same 20Mbps line rate used by 10Base-T. As in regular 10Base-T transmission, 10Mbps is available for Ethernet, and an additional 6Mbps becomes available for isochronous data transmission like video and voice transport.

NOTE: *Since isoEthernet provides only 6Mbps for isochronous video transmission, to provide an acceptable delivery rate, the video applications must be highly compressed.*

Two Networks, Four Channels

Contained within isoEthernet are four service channels, as illustrated in Figure 12-4. These channels are called the *circuit channel*, the *data channel*, the *maintenance channel*, and the *packet channel*.

The Circuit Channel

The circuit, or "C channel," is the switched 6.144Mbps, isochronous channel that contains 96 full-duplex, 64Kbps ISDN B channels designed to transmit digital voice and video.

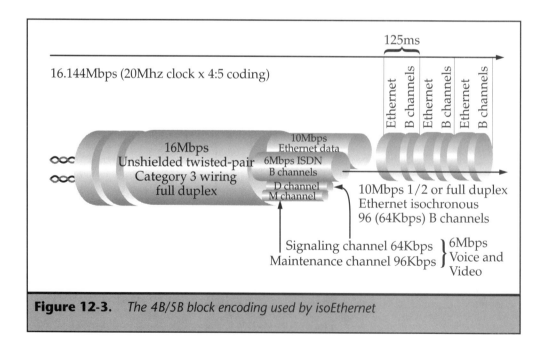

Figure 12-3. *The 4B/5B block encoding used by isoEthernet*

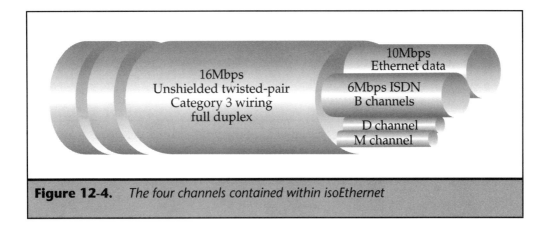

Figure 12-4. *The four channels contained within isoEthernet*

The D Channel

To ensure proper signaling and call-control services of the isochronous connections, a separate 64Kbps, full-duplex data channel, or "D channel," is in place. This channel performs the same functions as the ISDN D channel. It can also transfer such packet data as ITU-T X.25.

The M Channel

The maintenance channel, or "M channel," is a full-duplex, 96Kbps channel that provides low-level control and status information to the remote end of the link.

The P Channel

The packet channel, or "P channel," is the standard Ethernet 10Base-T line. Unlike the switched isochronous channels, the 10Mbps pipe is a shared media. A 10Mbps P channel carries normal data packet traffic unchanged from current 10Base-T Ethernet. It can be passed transparently to other 10Base-T or isoEthernet nodes sharing the same network.

Time Division Multiplexing

As illustrated in Figure 12-5, isoEthernet uses *time division multiplexing* (TDM) to isolate local multimedia applications from a company's normal LAN packet data flow, thereby maximizing the performance of both. In TDM, the transmission channel is divided into time slots, and each transmitting device is assigned one of the time slots for its transmissions. The time slots are assigned so that each transmitting device gets an equal amount of time; however, multimedia devices are usually assigned more time slots than other types of devices to make sure that they get enough bandwidth for acceptable delivery rates.

By plugging a stackable isoEthernet hub into the wiring closet, you provide a separate channel for bandwidth-gobbling voice, video, and multimedia files.

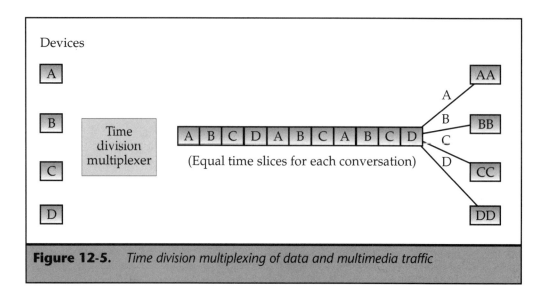

Figure 12-5. *Time division multiplexing of data and multimedia traffic*

Separating time-sensitive traffic from the packet-oriented traffic takes a tremendous amount of pressure off the standard packet oriented network and limits the contention for bandwidth inherent in 10Base-T networks. Thus, isoEthernet prevents multimedia traffic from disrupting data traffic, and eliminates the delays that make 10Base-T unsuitable for voice and video transmission.

Clockers

IsoEthernet is the only desktop protocol that implements the 8kHz clock—used by the public telephone network—at the desktop. This is a much simpler and less expensive timing mechanism than other high-speed protocols. ATM, for example, requires buffering and adaptation protocols to support synchronous traffic.

The Benefits of IsoEthernet

In applications that involve wide area support that must reach smoothly to the desktop, isoEthernet has many advantages over asynchronous high-speed protocols. Here are a few examples.

IsoEthernet and Wide Area Support

IsoEthernet makes wide area network support simple. It lets you connect the isochronous hub to a switched public service, and thereby gives you direct access to WAN services from the desktop. Therefore, a single wide area service can support many locally linked users via the 6Mbps isochronous channels. IsoEthernet provides direct desktop integration with the following services:

- T-1
- E-1
- ISDN basic rate interface
- ISDN primary rate interface
- ATM devices that support standard Q.931 signaling

IsoEthernet and Videoconferencing

Videoconferencing is one application in which isoEthernet shines. The international standard for videoconferencing is the International Telecommunications Union's H.320 standard for full-duplex audio and video compression. The compression/decompression (codec) techniques defined in this standard require an 8kHz clocking signal to maintain synchronization at both ends of the connection. WAN protocols support this clocking signal; however, most packet LANs don't. However, because isoEthernet provides the 8kHz clocking, it operates with the public switched telephone network in the WAN and delivers vidoeconferencing to the desktop without additional buffering adaptation techniques.

Manageability

IsoEthernet provides voice, video, and data over existing 10Base-T cable without requiring any changes to routers, network management systems, servers, and existing packet switches. The packet channel of isoEthernet uses the same frame type as standard 10Base-T. Therefore, all your existing 10Base-T management tools will work just fine on isoEthernet.

Scalability

The maximum network span is 100 meters. The isochronous portion allows better scalability because the bandwidth is dedicated, not shared among an increasing number of users. Furthermore, isoEthernet can also operate in "all isochronous mode," which allows end stations to achieve a maximum isochronous bandwidth of 15.872Mbps. Thus, the 15.872Mbps isochronous channel would contain 248 64Kbps ISDN B channels to service bandwidth-busting video server applications.

Cost

IsoEthernet equipment is expensive, probably because there aren't a lot of vendors producing isoEthernet devices and competing for consumers' dollars. National Semiconductor is really the only vendor supplying isoEthernet network adapters, and these are priced at about $500 each. This is a far cry from their original stated goal to provide isoEthernet NICs at only $10–$15 per unit. When you add to this the fact that you're not getting the 100Mbps bandwidth that other local area protocols provide, you quickly conclude that it's usually not cost-effective.

Security and Fault Tolerance

IsoEthernet doesn't offer any more security or fault tolerance than shared 10Base-T. Therefore, it's probably not a good choice for a backbone protocol. In fact, many supporters of isoEthernet suggest using FDDI-II or ATM as a backbone for isoEthernet.

Performance

IsoEthernet is a good performer, but not a great performer. It delivers better multimedia performance than regular shared 10Base-T, but not really any better than switched 10Base-T. It certainly doesn't outperform 100VG-AnyLAN in voice and video transmission.

However, one environment in which isoEthernet's performance excels is desktop WAN integration. Because traffic doesn't have to pass through routers and gateways—being encapsulated, translated, and bridged en route—to reach from the wide area to the desktop, isoEthernet delivers unrivaled performance. Furthermore, isoEthernet enables the transmission of PBX-quality voice over 10Base-T cabling, which packet-based protocols simply can't deliver.

Ease of Installation/Maintenance

IsoEthernet is fairly easy to install, but don't think you'll just be snapping it into your existing network. IsoEthernet runs over two-pair Category 3 UTP cabling with a distance limit of 100 meters. Therefore, currently wired corporate sites don't have to rework their cabling system. IsoEthernet can also run on Category 5 cabling. However, it will require new adapters and repeaters as well as an isochronous-capable backbone such as FDDI-II or ATM.

As with most new networking protocols, isoEthernet requires the installation of new hubs and network adapters to implement isochronous connections. However, because isoEthernet integrates Ethernet and ISDN circuits on the same adapter and across the same wire, it's easy to install in existing cable plants. Therefore, you can usually connect your current NICs, routers, and hubs into an isoEthernet card and continue working in 10Base-T as before.

In a voice system, the only new equipment necessary is hubs, software, and network-interface cards. The hubs connect to the WAN or private branch exchange (PBX) and the existing LAN on one side, and to 10Base-T or isoEthernet devices on the other, as shown in Figure 12-6. This configuration allows you to transmit voice, video, and data over Category 3 cable to the desktop.

Transmitting real-time voice and video on the isoEthernet network requires attaching an isochronous Ethernet NIC to a *compression/decompression adapter* (codec), as shown in Figure 12-7, which converts analog voice to digital signals. Unfortunately, there are no hardware codecs available that can use all of the 6.144Mbps isochronous channels. Hopefully, continued development of the market for isoEthernet will remedy this.

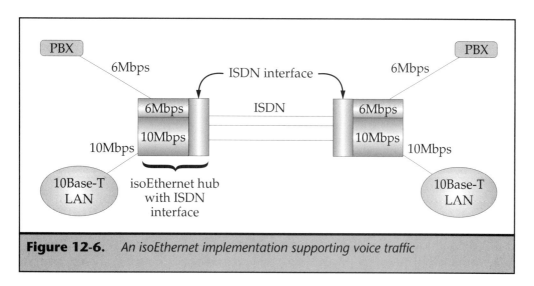

Figure 12-6.   *An isoEthernet implementation supporting voice traffic*

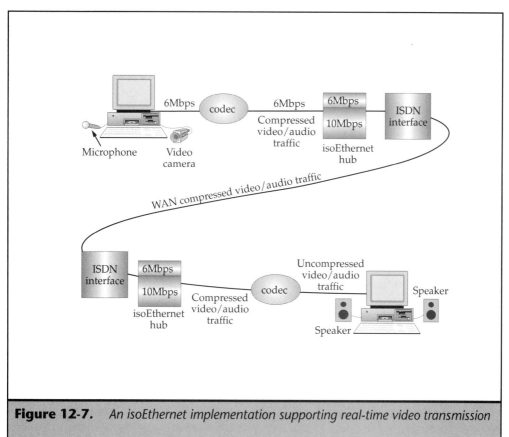

Figure 12-7.   *An isoEthernet implementation supporting real-time video transmission*

Disadvantages of IsoEthernet

Despite its benefits, isoEthernet has many serious shortcomings. One of the most critical is the lack of applications that are designed to take advantage of isochronous channels' wide area connectivity or real-time voice and video support.

Future Trends

Work is continuing on the 802.9 standard. Some new innovations we can expect to see added to the standard in the near future are

- 100Base-T (Fast Ethernet) support

- 802.9b – simplified interhub signaling

- 802.9e – integrated ATM support at 16Mbps

- Support for switched 10Base-T connections

- 802.9c – specification of the managed-objects conformance statement for compatibility testing

- 802.9d – specification of the protocol-implementation conformance statement (PICS) for compatibility testing

- 802.9f – remote line powering (a technique allowing remote powerdown of the isoEthernet network)

The Isochronous Network Communication Alliance

A group of LAN, telecommunications, and compression-product manufacturers have joined together to form the *isochronous network communication Alliance*, or *incAlliance*. As stated in the press release announcing the formation of the group, their five main purposes are

- To demonstrate high-quality, real-time, interactive multimedia- and computer-telephony integration products and services and promote them as key business tools

- To educate the industry on differences and requirements between voice, video, and data communications for LAN/WAN implementations and how these services can be integrated and synchronized

- To foster industry growth through joint applications development and interoperability testing to ensure robust, yet affordable, total system solutions

- To inform customers of the availability of new isochronous networking technologies such as isochronous Ethernet (isoEthernet) as key enablers for delivering interactive communications solutions in the networked enterprise to the desktop

■ To provide a vision and roadmap for upgrading networks without causing forklift upgrades and through adherence to and support of open LAN and WAN industry standards

The incAlliance can be contacted at 2640 Del Mar Heights Road, Suite 134, Del Mar, California 92014, telephone (619) 792-7964, fax (619) 792-7967.

Strengths:

■ Excellent wide area integration

■ Supports time-sensitive traffic over existing cabling

■ Requires little replacement of equipment

■ Easy to install

Weaknesses:

■ Lack of third-party hardware suppliers

■ Lack of application support

■ Expensive

■ Limited security and fault tolerance

Recommended for:

■ Multimedia

■ Collaborative workgroups

■ Telemedicine

■ Remote training

■ Wide area to desktop integration

■ Computer telephony integration

Not Recommended for:

■ Backbone

■ Networks without time-sensitive traffic

PART THREE

*How to Speed Up:
Wide Area
Solutions*

CHAPTER 13

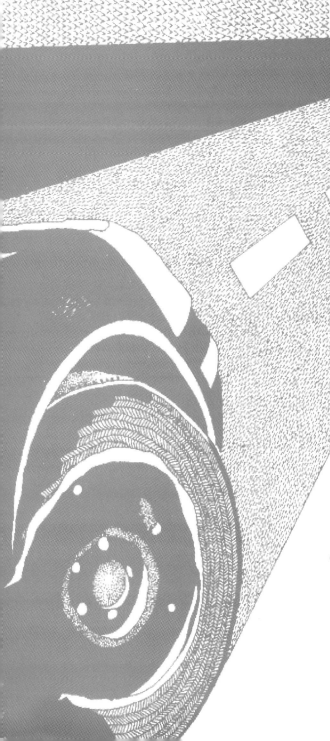

Integrated
Services Digital
Network

The evolution of the ISDN species has been a long and difficult process. You have no doubt been hearing about Integrated Services Digital Network (ISDN) for nearly a decade or more. From its conception, it was proclaimed by the telecommunications pandits as the public telephone and telecommunications interface of the future. But for years no practical, productive, or cost-effective implementations materialized. As a result, both users and providers began attributing new definitions to the acronym ISDN, the kindest of which was probably "I Still Don't [K]Now."

Today, however, ISDN is finally booming. It is available in most large metropolitan areas now, and the service providers there report a backlog of installation requests—mostly to residences. Because ISDN integrates data, voice, and video signals into a digital (as opposed to analog) telephone line, it can provide an efficient and cost-effective way to connect office LANs with high-bandwidth digital services, and to provide home "telecommuters" with the same digital services they are accustomed to having at their offices. Furthermore, ISDN has developed international standards for providing many digital services, making it easier for data networks to span countries and continents.

The Primordial Mire

The origin of the ISDN species is the narrowband ISDN standard. The first ISDN standards defining end-to-end digital interfaces appeared in 1984, handed down by the Consultative Committee for International Telegraph and Telephone (CCITT). The CCITT issued additional defining standards in 1988. ISDN was considered a major advance for a couple of reasons. First, it specified digital network services that would be delivered over the existing integrated digital telephone networks. Second, it offered a top performance of 2Mbps in the local link, and either 64Kbps or 128Kbps over the wide area. At the time narrowband ISDN began to emerge, analog modem speeds topped out at 9,600bps.

While ISDN never became the wide area high-bandwidth digital service of choice for local area network connectivity, it is certainly no dinosaur. It's now considered a cost-effective way to provide:

- Remote access to users who dial into their companies' LANs
- A suitable link for some LAN-to-LAN connections
- High-bandwidth interoffice fax traffic
- High-speed access to the Internet

ISDN is a flexible service that automatically switches among different devices attached to it. For example, it will provide digital services to a phone, a fax machine, or a PC, all of which can be attached to the same ISDN interface. ISDN can also be used as a local access link into frame relay and X.25 networks.

Anatomy of the ISDN Species

ISDN is a service composed of two types of channels: *bearer channels* and *signaling channels*. ISDN providers have combined these two channel types to construct two different types of ISDN service offerings: the *Basic Rate Interface* and the *Primary Rate Interface*. We will define each of these channel types and rate interfaces, then discuss the signaling techniques that they use to make integrated voice and data transmission possible.

Channel Types

As we mentioned, ISDN uses two types of channels, one type for transmitting data, and the other for handling the management signaling and call control. These two types of channels are called bearer channels and signaling channels, respectively.

Bearer Channels

Bearer channels, or B channels, do one thing: they carry data; hence the name "bearer." These channels bear user information across the ISDN network. The B channels are 64Kbps circuit-switched channels of the same type used to handle a regular voice telephone call, although the ISDN B channels are digital channels rather than analog channels like Plain Old Telephone Service (POTS) uses. The B channels are set up, then taken down when the call is complete. They can connect any two ISDN sites.

Signaling Channels

ISDN also specifies a second type of channel, called a signaling channel or D channel. The D channel is separate from the B channels, providing *out-of-band* signaling to set up, control, and tear down calls. Because all this call control signaling is done on a separate channel, the calls are set up much faster than if the signaling information had to share bandwidth with the actual data. For example, the D channel provides the network with the number of the party to call while the data is waiting on the B channels to be transmitted. Therefore, as soon as the call is set up, data transmission can begin. The D channel signaling is a function of the Physical, Datalink, and Network layers relative to the OSI protocol model, as shown in Figure 13-1.

Different operations are performed at each layer of the OSI Reference Model. Here's a brief description of how D channel signaling protocols work within the OSI Reference Model.

Physical Layer Functions

ISDN's Physical Layer protocol sets up a 64Kbps, circuit-switched connection. It also supports the physical interface for the *network terminal adapter*, which will be discussed a little later in this chapter, which supports the connection of multiple devices simultaneously. Finally, this protocol manages circuit testing and monitoring functions.

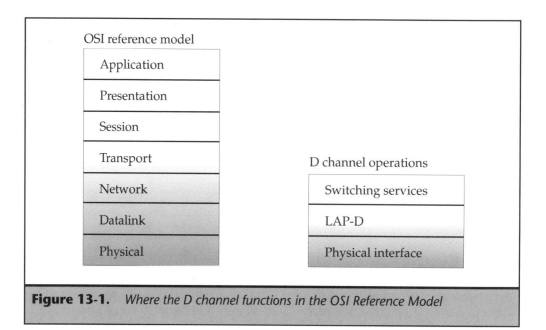

Figure 13-1.   *Where the D channel functions in the OSI Reference Model*

Datalink Layer Functions

ISDN's Datalink Layer protocol sets up the virtual paths through the networks for data frames. This protocol also manages call control and signaling functions via the *Link Access Procedure for D Channel* (LAP-D), which is the procedure that works across the signaling, or "D channel."

Network Layer Functions

ISDN's Network Layer protocol handles all circuit-switching and packet-switching services. The Network Layer creates the addressing and route-determination information that the Datalink Layer uses to set up virtual paths.

It's All in the Packaging

As we mentioned, ISDN carriers have developed two standard service offerings, called *rate interfaces*, that combine the bearer channels and the signaling channel in different densities. These are called the Basic Rate Interface (BRI) and the Primary Rate Interface (PRI).

Basic Rate Interface ISDN

The Basic Rate Interface (BRI) usually consists of two 64Kbps B channels for data transmission, plus one 16Kbps D channel that provides signaling for the B channels.

With the proper equipment, you can bond the two B channels of the BRI together to get a maximum bandwidth of 128Kbps. Therefore, the BRI is appropriate for use in connecting small offices, small-to-medium-sized local area networks, or for telecommuters working from home who want to connect to their company's LAN.

Notice that we said the BRI *usually* consists of two 64Kbps B channels. Some ISDN providers offer BRIs with only one B channel and one D channel, or with only one D channel. In fact, the smallest unit of ISDN that can still be called ISDN is the D channel. The D channel provides the out-of-band signaling that really defines ISDN and makes the service what it is.

Primary Rate Interface ISDN

The Primary Rate Interface (PRI) channels are available to ISDN subscribers who need more bandwidth than a BRI can provide. They are based on the DS1 rate of 1.544Mbps and include 23 B channels and one *64Kbps* D channel to do the signaling. The B channels can be bundled in one of the following configurations, referred to in local exchange carrier terminology as *H services*:

H0 channel:	384Kbps (6 B channels)
H10 channel:	1.472Mbps (24 56Kbps B channels)
H11 channel:	1.536Mbps (24 B channels)
H12 channel:	1.92Mbps (30 B channels)

The lines can be used as a high-speed trunk for transferring large files and other continuous data streams or be subdivided with a multiplexer to provide channels for multiple devices. By providing a range of service options, the PRI can be configured to handle compressed video, video telephones, and teleservices.

ISDN's Function in the Wide Area Food Chain

ISDN is a significant departure from the other wide area data services discussed in this book. ISDN and its attendant equipment actually perform much of the processing and data signaling that used to be the exclusive responsibility of the carrier's central office equipment. Transferring these functions from the central office to your PC is one of the causes of much of the difficulty and confusion in ordering, configuring, and troubleshooting ISDN. Therefore, we should probably spend some time talking about the functions in question: what they are, where they have traditionally been done, and how ISDN changes all of that.

A *Plain Old Telephone Service* (POTS) call, the kind of analog call that we have placed and received nearly every day of our lives since we were able to dial, doesn't require much from the equipment at our houses. As Figure 13-2 shows, all of the processing of voice and data takes place at the local exchange carrier's central office

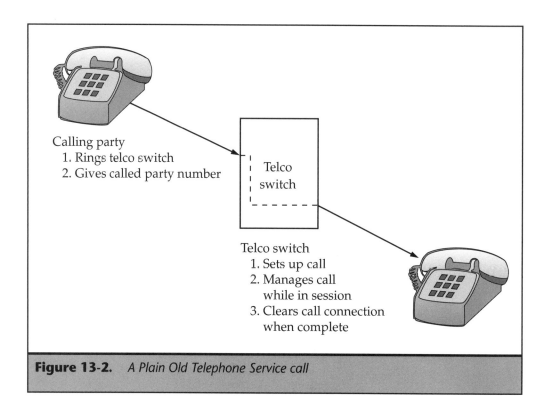

Calling party
   1. Rings telco switch
   2. Gives called party number

Telco switch

Telco switch
   1. Sets up call
   2. Manages call
      while in session
   3. Clears call connection
      when complete

Figure 13-2. *A Plain Old Telephone Service call*

switch. Our analog phones simply contact the telephone company's switch and tell it whom we want to call. The telco's switch does all the rest. In essence, our analog phones are not much more than amplifiers with dials.

An ISDN call, on the other hand, requires that the equipment on the customers' premises be much more sophisticated. ISDN telephones and PC adapters must be able to process information and determine what kind of signal—voice, data, fax, etc.—is being received, and respond by routing the data to the appropriate device.

Figure 13-3 shows the route of an ISDN call from your premises through the public switched network and to its destination. Your call is first set up when your equipment sets up a connection with the central office switch using *Digital Subscriber Signaling System 1* (DSS1).

Once the call is set up between your site and the central office via DSS1, it's time to set up the next leg of its journey. For better or for worse, the signaling needed to route the call within the public switched network is *not* DSS1. Instead, the public telcos use a system called *Signaling System 7* (SS7), which can handle both digital and analog calls, to route calls between central offices. Therefore, at the telco your DSS1 instructions are converted to SS7 signals. SS7 is a packet-mode switch that manages call control, including call setup and teardown.

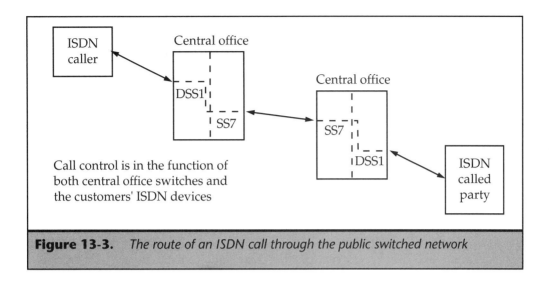

ISDN caller

Central office

DSS1

SS7

Central office

SS7

DSS1

ISDN called party

Call control is in the function of both central office switches and the customers' ISDN devices

Figure 13-3.   *The route of an ISDN call through the public switched network*

When your call reaches the last central office on its route, it is then converted back to DSS1 format for transmission from the last central office to its final destination—the party with whom you wanted to communicate in the first place.

Your ISDN equipment is required to interact with both DSS1 and SS7—something your POTS telephone was never required nor designed to do. It is this interaction with two large and complex external signaling systems that brings about many of the configuration nightmares associated with ordering, installing, and using ISDN.

Great Moments in Evolution: SPID-ing in the Ocean

Although you can probably have a long, happy, and productive career as an ISDN user without knowing the details of DSS1 and SS7, there is one requirement of DSS1 that will affect you immediately and continue to do so for as long as you use ISDN. This requirement is a *Service Profile Identifier* (SPID). SPIDs are identifying numbers assigned to your ISDN line at the time it is set up by the local exchange provider. Be sure to write this number down and keep it in a safe place, because configuring your equipment will undoubtedly require entering a SPID. You see, the SPID identifies the individual logical processes connected to the ISDN interface, and prevents contention among different processes on the ISDN bus in the event that incoming calls are received while a device is actively using the B channel. This is the procedure in DSS1 that lets you connect several devices to one ISDN line. Furthermore, the SPID, together with another parameter required by DSS1, the *terminal identifier* (TEI), identifies the actual ISDN equipment connected to the ISDN interface. A single TEI might have multiple SPIDs associated with it. Negotiating among the SPIDs is difficult and complicated—so much so that some ISDN providers have found it easier to support bus contention, and thus allow you only one SPID per bearer channel.

The Goal of Evolution: What These Services Can Provide

Services provided by ISDN operate at higher protocol levels than simple phone connections. After all that negotiating among your computer's ISDN adapter, DSS1, and SS7, they should. These services use the B channels for transmission and the D channel for signaling. We describe them briefly here.

Bearer Services

In the most basic sense, ISDN bearer services don't really do anything that other protocols don't do. These are the services that carry data from end to end. They come in two types:

- Circuit mode
- Packet mode

Circuit Mode versus Packet Mode

Circuit mode is pretty much the same as the circuit switching we have discussed in various chapters throughout this book. In circuit mode, a connection is established between the caller and the called party, and the circuit remains dedicated to that conversation until one of the parties disconnects. The two parties are the only ones who can use the connection for as long as they maintain the call. Even if no data is being transmitted, while the call is in session, all the bandwidth associated with that circuit is dedicated to that call. This can be very wasteful, since many conversations are largely "dead air." See Figure 13-4.

Packet mode solves the problem of unused, dedicated bandwidth. Packet mode breaks a single conversation up into small pieces, gives each of these pieces an address and a sequence number, and sends them on their way over the wire—along with packets from many other conversations. Because each packet has its own address, it can share bandwidth with other packets without scrambling data transmissions. Furthermore, each packet could take a different route to the called party, as shown in Figure 13-5.

Packet mode transmission isn't nearly as wasteful as circuit mode transmission, because several conversations are using the same connection. Therefore, when one conversation isn't transmitting anything, the other conversations sharing the connection can use that idle bandwidth to transmit more of their data. Ultimately this means that the carrier needs less packet switching equipment than circuit switching equipment to support the same number of conversations.

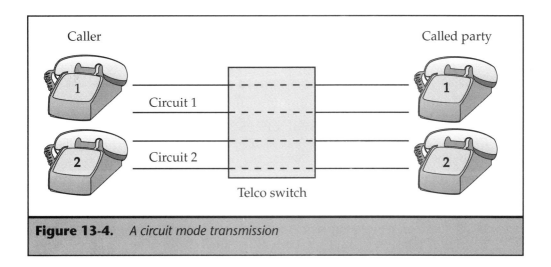

Figure 13-4.   *A circuit mode transmission*

ISDN bearer services offer both circuit mode and packet mode services. Circuit mode uses B channels to transmit data and the D channel to control the call. Packet mode can use both the B and the D channels to transmit data.

Generally, circuit mode services are best for voice traffic and packet mode services are best for data traffic, but this isn't always the case. ISDN packet mode bearer services offer a virtual circuit service that can handle analog traffic, such as voice, quite well.

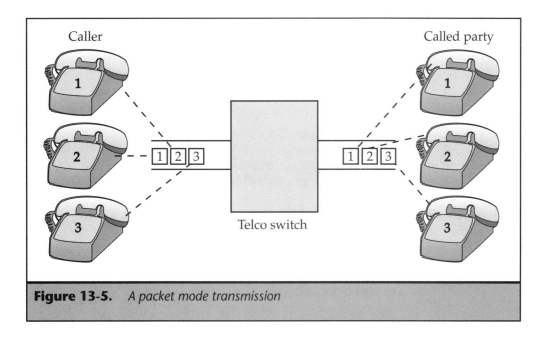

Figure 13-5.   *A packet mode transmission*

Supplementary Services

These supplementary services are exactly that: services *in addition* to the bearer services that provide added functionality. Supplementary services vary from ISDN provider to ISDN provider, so this is just a representative list of the types of services you may find available.

- **CALLING LINE IDENTIFICATION PRESENTATION** This is similar to Caller ID that is becoming widely available for incoming calls on most public telephone systems. It identifies the number of the incoming caller.

- **MULTIPLE SUBSCRIBER NUMBER** This service assigns a different telephone number to each device attached to your ISDN interface. For example, suppose you have a telephone, a modem, and a fax device all on one ISDN interface. With Multiple Subscriber Number service, each of these would have its own telephone number. Then, when a call comes in for the telephone, the telephone rings. When a call comes in for the fax, the fax answers—you get the idea.

NOTE: In the ISDN world, telephone numbers are known as directory numbers, *or* DNs.

Call Offering

These are services such as call transfer and call forwarding that let you control where the call goes after it rings your number.

- **CALL TRANSFER** Anyone who has worked in an office with a PBX is familiar with this one. When you answer a call, then find the call needs to be sent to someone else, you can transfer it to the right person.

- **CALL FORWARDING BUSY** This service lets your calls be directed to another number if they come in while you are on your phone.

- **LINE HUNTING** Known in the PBX world as a *hunt group*, call hunting defines a group of telephones that can answer any call coming in to any telephone in the group. This enables an incoming call to ring—one phone at a time—at each telephone in the group until it is answered.

Call Waiting and Call Hold

Thanks to the out-of-band signaling of the D channel, ISDN adds a new dimension to these familiar services.

- **CALL WAITING** Unlike the familiar POTS, when a call comes in on your ISDN line, your conversation isn't interrupted. This is because signaling is done on the separate D channel ("so *that's* why the D channel is so cool"). This is especially handy when you're using your modem—incoming calls won't break your data connection. That's right—you can keep Call Waiting on while using your modem.

- **CALL HOLD**   ISDN lets you put multiple calls on hold simultaneously without tying up a separate connection for each call. That means you'll have a tough time "busying out" your phones.

Multiparty Services

ISDN also offers a variety of multiparty services such as conference calling.

Teleservices

Teleservices are sophisticated services that ISDN can provide because ISDN operates at higher levels in the OSI Reference Model than POTS. Although currently not widely used in this country, they are often considered the future direction—and the real value—of ISDN. Some of these teleservices are

- **Telefax**   Group 4 fax capability that uses digital information at 64Kbps.
- **Teletex**   Provides end-to-end messaging between two devices using standard character sets.
- **Videotext**   Enhances Teletex services by adding a text and graphics mailbox.
- **Videotelephy**   Provides television transmission service over ISDN.

Making ISDN Happen

Now that you know what ISDN is and what it can provide, how do you get it? Acquiring and configuring the equipment and services for ISDN is far from simple. Here's a roadmap and checklist for making sure you and your local exchange carrier have all the right stuff for ISDN.

The Local Exchange Carrier's Part

The first, most critical, and least controllable issue in getting ISDN service is whether your Local Exchange Carrier (LEC) is able and willing to provide it. Here's what you need to find out.

The LEC's ISDN Switch

Does your carrier offer ISDN? If your carrier doesn't have an ISDN-ready switch in your area, it doesn't offer ISDN. If it does offer ISDN, you'll need to find out how ISDN is implemented on the switch so you can configure your devices to communicate with it. The key to how ISDN is implemented on the LEC's switch is contained in two pieces of information you must get from your LEC:

1. Which ISDN protocol (NI-1 or NI-2) they use
2. What type of ISDN switch they have

When you configure your ISDN equipment, you will need to enter either or both of these pieces of information.

NATIONAL ISDN-1 (NI-1) AND ISDN-2 (NI-2) PROTOCOLS   The NI-1 protocol is the BRI protocol used by the Regional Bell Operating Companies (RBOCs). It is the first step in establishing a consistent ISDN definition for the US. As such, it enables all NI-1 compliant devices to connect to any switch that supports the NI-1 protocol. A newer version of the protocol, NI-2, is emerging.

If your ISDN device and your providers' switch support either the NI-1 or NI-2 protocols, then that's all the compatibility information you'll need. However, it usually isn't that simple. Note that NI-1 is used mostly by the Regional Bell Operating Companies. Other LECs may not use this protocol, and so in order to configure your ISDN device to communicate with their switch, you'll need to know the manufacturer of the switch.

Media

The next issue is the wiring from the LEC's ISDN switch to your premises. If you're lucky, your local access is fiber-optic cable, and you can skip to the next section. However, it's more than likely that your local access loop is copper. In this case, your twisted-pair local access wire must be no more than 18 kilofeet (a little under 3.5 miles) in length. If it exceeds this length, your telephone company may be able to install a *mid-span repeater* between the central office and your premises. A mid-span repeater regenerates the ISDN signal and doubles the distance allowed between the central office and your premises.

Even though your local access loop meets these specifications, it may not be ready for ISDN. That's because your local cable pair may have connections running off it. These connections are called *bridge taps*—and they aren't supposed to be there—but sometimes when the telephone company is installing a new customer, they run a line from the new customer's premises and join, or *tap*, into an existing, unused local loop left behind by a former customer, as shown in Figure 13-6. The former customer's tap is disconnected at the former customer's site, but still joined to what is now your local loop. Such taps can cause signal distortion that doesn't usually affect analog signals, but wreaks havoc with ISDN. Therefore, any bridge taps must be removed.

Next, the LEC will have to check your line to remove any devices that were installed to *condition* analog lines. Conditioning means adjusting lines to reduce signal distortion. Unfortunately, techniques that reduce signal distortion for analog signals can actually *cause* distortion in digital signals.

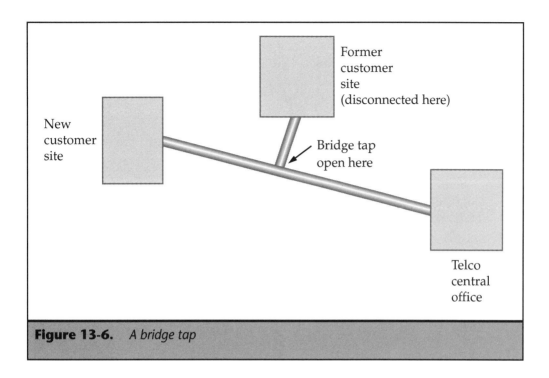

New
customer
site

Former
customer
site
(disconnected here)

Bridge tap
open here

Telco
central
office

Figure 13-6. *A bridge tap*

Finally, your LEC will test your line to see if it meets ISDN specifications. If it does, you're good to go. If it doesn't, the phone company will have to install another line.

The Home Front

Assuming your LEC is able to provide ISDN service to your premises, the next step is to select the proper equipment to use that service. There are two major pieces of equipment you will require: a network terminal adapter (NTA) and either an ISDN adapter or bridge.

Network Terminal Adapter

An NTA is a device that connects your data or telephone equipment to the local exchange carrier's ISDN line. In the United States, the NTA is purchased and installed by the customer, while in other countries it is owned and maintained by the local exchange carrier.

The NTA connects both *terminal equipment* (TE) and *terminal adapter* (TA) equipment to the local loop. TE devices are equipment: telephones and computers that are ISDN compliant. TAs are interfaces: adapters that connect non-ISDN equipment to the ISDN service.

In the United States, the NTA is connected to the local exchange carrier's ISDN service via the *U interface* that is described next. The customer's equipment is connected to the NTA via an *S/T interface*, also described later in this section, that allows up to eight devices to connect with and be addressed by the NTA device.

Figure 13-7 illustrates the NTA device and the eight possible connection points for TE and TA devices. Note that not all NTA devices are the same. Some may have only two connectors, one for data equipment and one for a phone. Additional devices are then daisy-chained together.

INTERFACES   Your NTA equipment provides three different types of interfaces to support connected devices. These are described here:

- **U interface**. This interface transmits full-duplex information on a single wire pair. This means information travels in both directions simultaneously. The U interface supports only one device.

- **S/T interface**. This interface breaks the ISDN signal into two paths: transmit and receive. Each signal is now carried on a separate pair, and you are allowed to connect multiple devices.

- **R interface**. This interface allows you to connect a POTS telephone to your ISDN service. The telephone will function, but it won't provide all the features that an ISDN telephone connected to an S/T interface would.

ISDN Adapters

ISDN terminal adapters, also commonly known as *ISDN modems*, come in internal and external models just as analog modems do. And these two models have the same benefits and liabilities as their analog cousins: internal modems support higher internal data transfer rates, while external modems provide more diagnostic information and control.

SERIAL PORT CONNECTIVITY   If you select an ISDN terminal adapter that connects to your computer through a serial port, you will need to be sure to install a serial port driver that supports ISDN's higher bandwidth. Otherwise, the serial port will become a serious bottleneck, and all that extra bandwidth for which you are

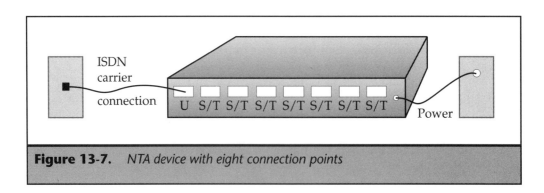

Figure 13-7.   *NTA device with eight connection points*

paying will be useless. For example, the highest serial port data rate supported by Microsoft Windows for Workgroups 3.11 is 19,200bps—considerably below ISDN's common 64Kbps. There are several high-speed drivers for serial ports available both as freeware and on the commercial market, including TurboCom/2 from Pacific CommWare.

INTEGRATED NETWORK TERMINAL ADAPTERS   Some ISDN terminal adapters have integrated NTA devices. This may save you a little expense as well as time and trouble when configuring your ISDN devices for the first time. However, it can also limit the number of devices you can connect to your ISDN line to the number of S/T ports the adapter vendor supplies—usually much fewer than provided by external NTAs.

MULTIPLE B CHANNELS   Not all ISDN terminal adapters support more than one B channel. If you plan to pay for more than one B channel, be sure your network terminal adapter supports it. As well, be sure the equipment you select can bond multiple B channels if you hope to take advantage of the 128Kbps or higher bandwidth possible by combining bearer channels.

ISDN and Telephones

Your ISDN service will require ISDN telephones unless your terminal adapter has an *R interface*. The R interface supports analog equipment-like standard telephones. You can also buy separate adapters that will convert existing analog telephones to ISDN telephones. However, keep in mind that standard analog telephones can't take advantage of some special ISDN services such as Caller ID.

ISDN Equipment for LANs

Installing ISDN equipment for LANs requires a bridge or router with an ISDN interface, as shown in Figure 13-8. Among the router vendors currently offering ISDN interfaces are Cisco and Ascend. The ISDN router is connected directly to the ISDN wire, so it must be configured not only to route traffic to the appropriate segments, but also to interoperate with the ISDN network. This involves many of the same tasks as configuring a standalone PC, including entering the correct SPIDs and DNs.

 NOTE: *Routers and bridges are covered in detail in Chapter 17, "Alternatives to High-Speed Networking."*

Configuration and Installation

Now that ISDN connectivity is becoming cheap and readily available, organizations of all sizes are flocking to install it for the increased bandwidth and therefore increased functionality it offers over garden-variety 56Kbps lines. However, as you have probably surmised from reading this chapter, implementing ISDN isn't nearly as

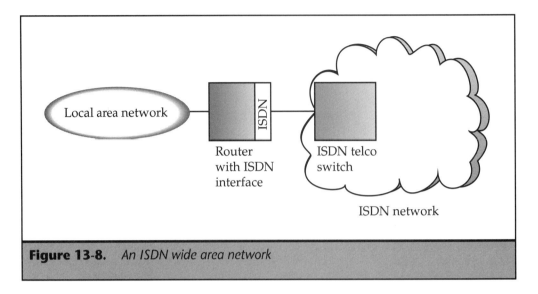

Figure 13-8. *An ISDN wide area network*

simple as installing those 56Kbps lines was. It takes a lot more than a mere telephone call to the local exchange carrier. In fact, it's fairly safe to say that right now, to be a sane, successful ISDN user, you must also be an ISDN expert.

You'll have to make yourself understand what's involved in implementing ISDN *before* you commit to a full-scale installation. To help you do this, I've put together a cheat sheet of issues that you must address before, during, and after the installation of ISDN.

First: Ordering What You Want

Ordering ISDN from your local exchange carrier (LEC) is like walking into an ice cream parlor and ordering *gelato*. Even if somebody behind the counter understands what you said, they may never have heard of it before. And even if the clerk has heard of gelato, he or she may not really know what it is, much less that he or she can provide what you want. Even if you find a clerk who understands that gelato is ice cream, and that he or she can sell it to you, you may still not be any closer to getting the flavor you want than when you walked in the door.

Not every local exchange carrier offers ISDN, and not every company that does can offer the type of ISDN that you need. Different switches are *provisioned*, or configured, to provide different types of ISDN service. Therefore, the first thing you have to determine is which ISDN features you want, then ensure that your local exchange carrier can provide them.

What Are You Hungry for?

What is the real reason you need more bandwidth? Do you want to do videoconferencing? Do you want to send more faxes faster? Or do you simply want to speed up file transfers? Do you want to use ISDN to transmit voice? Data? Both? What's the maximum bandwidth you will need: 64Kbps? 128Kbps? More?

Make a list of all the bandwidth-gobbling applications you may want to implement over the next year or so. This will be absolutely vital to selecting the ISDN service you need.

What's on the Menu?

As we mentioned, ISDN comes in two packages, or *rate interfaces*. The Basic Rate Interface (BRI) provides two 64Kbps B channels that carry transmission signals and one 16Kbps D channel that carries signals that control the calls on the B channels. The Primary Rate Interface (PRI) provides 23 64Kbps B channels and one 16Kbps D channel. The rate interface you choose depends entirely upon the number of connections and amount of bandwidth you need.

How Many Channels?

Many veteran ISDN users think that the smallest ISDN component that still retains the properties of ISDN is the BRI: two B channels and one D channel. This isn't true. The real molecule of ISDN is a single D channel. So for a BRI, you could have two B channels and one D channel, or one D channel and one B channel, or simply one D channel. This gives you some ability to scale your ISDN connection to meet your needs. Furthermore, as we mentioned, the PRI comes in several different bandwidths, as shown here:

384Kbps (6 B channels)
1.472Mbps (24 56Kbps B channels)
1.536Mbps (24 B channels)
1.92Mbps (30 B channels)

ISDN à la Mode

Once you have decided how many channels you want to order, you need to find out which *mode* of data transmission you will be using on each channel. As we described earlier in this chapter, ISDN services are either circuit mode or packet mode. At this writing, ISDN offered ten different circuit mode services and three different packet mode services (and counting), each designed for transmitting a different type of data. Generally, circuit mode services are preferred for voice and other analog transmissions, while packet mode services are better suited for data.

 TIP: New services are being added to ISDN all the time, so ask your ISDN order taker to explain in detail each type of bearer service they offer so you can select the most appropriate for each channel.

If There's Room for Dessert. . .

Additional services are available for ISDN, just as they are for regular telephone services. As we described earlier in this chapter, some of the additional services available are Videotext, Teleconference, Caller ID, Call Waiting, and Call Forwarding.

 TIP: Don't forget your long distance carrier and Internet access provider. If you can't find a long distance carrier in your area that can handle ISDN, there's really no point in implementing it for long distance, now is there? Ditto for your Internet access provider, if you were planning to use ISDN primarily as a high-speed access service.

Confusion Sets In

Now—and only now—it is time to call your Local Exchange Carrier to order ISDN. Be prepared for "IS what?" or other expressions of confusion and/or disbelief from your LEC. You may be told to call a variety of different numbers, and be switched to many different operators before finding the appropriate department. If you are told that ISDN is not available, be sure to ask them:

1. Why, and
2. When it will be available.

The reason for asking why is because LEC order takers have been known to tell callers that ISDN isn't available rather than admit they have no idea what ISDN is. So if you get an answer like, "It's a proprietary technology," or "The standards haven't been finalized," or even "ISDN is another company—you'll have to contact them," you'll know you haven't found the right person.

When you finally find the right person, and when that person tells you that ISDN is available in your area, you can start describing the type of ISDN service you need.

56/64KBPS   Your order taker may tell you that the ISDN service available is 56Kbps. While this isn't really ISDN, it isn't necessarily bad. This 56Kbps service is ISDN, adapted to work on an LEC's existing T1 systems, and it's frequently offered in places where full 64Kbps ISDN isn't yet available. The popular ISDN protocols can accommodate 56Kbps service until full 64Kbps ISDN service is available, so there's no need to avoid it simply because it's not "the real thing."

LINE SETS   Furthermore, while you're talking to your order taker at the LEC, he or she may use a term such as *line sets*. A line set is a term used by the National ISDN Users' Forum (NIUF) to describe the different combinations of B (from 0 to 2) channels with the D channel and the kinds of information (circuit mode data, packet mode data, and/or voice) that you want to transmit on these channels. For example, Line Set 1 has no B channels and one D channel on which you can transmit packet mode data. Line Set 6 has one B channel on which you can transmit voice and one D channel on which you can transmit packet mode data. The various combinations of channels and call types are identified by number, currently Line Set 1 through Line Set 29. To avoid having to memorize all the line set numbers and their corresponding descriptions, just tell the order taker how many B and D channels you want, and what kind of information you want to transmit on them. Then the order taker can find the correct line set number that describes this configuration.

The order taker should also ask you about *feature sets.* As we mentioned earlier, a feature set is another NIUF term that describes a combination of either circuit mode or packet mode data services and/or call management services. There are at least ten different feature sets, detailing everything from data throughput rate to call forwarding options. Have your order taker provide you with the latest information on available feature sets, then choose them after you've had a chance to study them.

Finally, after you have selected the number of channels, call type(s) supported on those channels, and the features and interfaces you want, you will have completed the ordering process. Your LEC should send you a letter or form confirming your order and specifying the services contained in it. This letter should also include the telephone number(s) of your new ISDN connection(s) (which are known as *directory numbers* or *DNs* in the ISDN world), as well as something called your Service Profile Identification number, or SPID. *Write both of these down and keep them in a safe place!* You will need them when configuring your ISDN equipment.

Exhausting process, isn't it? And we've only finished the ordering stage! Therefore, if you're short of time and staff, ISDN implementation may not be a good project for you right now. However, as the LECs move up the learning curve in ISDN implementation, the job of ordering it will get easier.

Cabling Considerations

ISDN cabling uses eight pins, as shown in Figure 13-9, and therefore requires RJ-45 connectors. Furthermore, ISDN cabling is straight-through, not crossed the way standard POTS cabling is. Therefore, it will require special ISDN cables to connect your ISDN adapters and/or bridges to the ISDN jack.

Performance

ISDN isn't really such a high-speed performer. The maximum bandwidth available from an ISDN BRI is 128Kbps, and that's only providing that your BRI includes two B channels and your equipment and service providers all support bonding the two channels together. The maximum bandwidth available through a PRI is 1.92Mbps, through what is called an *H12 channel* that consists of 30 B channels and one 64Kbps D channel. Again the equipment and all the parties—the local exchange carrier, the access software provider, and the called party—must support the bonding of the B channels.

The Broadband ISDN standard, an emerging standard which we will discuss later, will support data transmission rates of up to 622Mbps. However, this standard is not yet finalized, so the cap on ISDN remains at the Narrowband ISDN rate of 1.92Mbps.

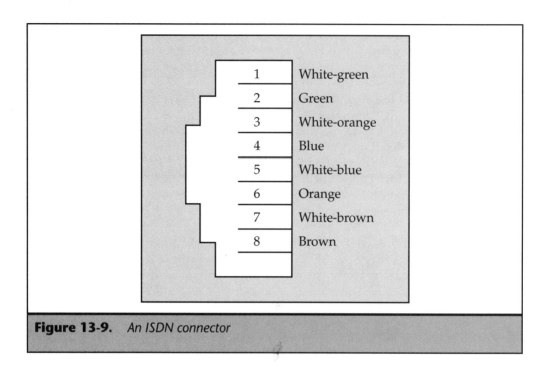

Figure 13-9. *An ISDN connector*

Management and Fault Tolerance

While ISDN by its very nature provides you with many different call management and control services—some of which were described earlier in this chapter in the section entitled "The Goal of Evolution"—management of the ISDN service itself is wholly in the hands of the local exchange carrier. Optimizing and troubleshooting ISDN service is therefore a tedious and often fruitless exercise involving multiple telephone calls to a service provider and long waits for repair people to respond.

As for fault tolerance, remember that your ISDN provider may have only one ISDN-ready switch per area. If so, when something goes wrong with that switch, you're out of service until it is repaired.

Scalability

ISDN is probably the most scalable wide area high-speed protocol available. With the proper equipment and services, it can be scaled from a simple 14.4Kbps modem connection to 1.92Mbps. However, as we've described earlier in this chapter, configuring your equipment and services to support this scalability is no simple matter, and sometimes it's simply not possible to get the needed cooperation among vendors to make it a reality.

Availability and Pricing

As we mentioned, ISDN is currently available in most major metropolitan areas, and its availability is spreading rapidly. As ISDN becomes more readily available, prices for ISDN PC cards are falling sharply. You can now get an ISDN modem with a built-in NT-1 for around $200.

Pricing for ISDN services varies widely. In certain areas, during special promotions conducted by the local exchange carrier, ISDN installation rates are free. In other areas during peak pricing times, ISDN installation can be as much as $400 per line. Monthly rates vary just as much, ranging from $30 per line per month to over $100.

TIP: *In the past few months, several LECs across the country have begun to raise their ISDN rates from the bargain basement to the outlandishly expensive. The reason given is that the demand for ISDN far exceeded initial projections, and that the market isn't nearly as price sensitive as they had first thought.*

The Future: Broadband ISDN

The ITU-T is currently working on specifications for the Broadband ISDN model, shown in Figure 13-10, which will deliver up to 622.08Mbps full-duplex data transmission. These high data rates will support sophisticated two-way interactive transmissions, store-and-forward multimedia broadcasts, and multimedia messaging and retrieval services.

The B-ISDN standard is also the basis for Asynchronous Transfer Mode (ATM), which we'll discuss in Chapter 16. ATM and B-ISDN appear to be the direction in which the whole voice and data networking are going.

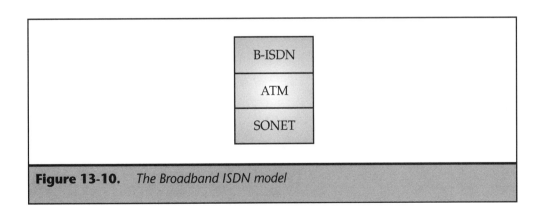

Figure 13-10.   *The Broadband ISDN model*

Advantages

ISDN is an affordable, scalable high-speed protocol. In areas where it is available, it can be fairly inexpensive to implement and expand.

Disadvantages

ISDN has some major disadvantages to overcome. As we described in painful detail earlier in the "Configuration and Installation" section, simply *ordering* ISDN services requires a level of expertise most busy network managers don't have time to develop. Becoming an expert on the installation and configuration of ISDN devices, especially in different LEC areas, is usually out of the question for most network managers. That means hiring integrators and consultants, and that means a lot of extra expense.

Furthermore, gaining the cooperation of the various vendors and providers can be difficult. For all its fairly long history, ISDN is still unfamiliar to the technical staffs of many providers. It may be some time before the local exchange carriers can train their employees to provide the level of service in ordering, selection, installation, and troubleshooting that most network managers require.

Narrowband ISDN's maximum bandwidth is also limited well below that of other promising high-speed wide area protocols, so it may only be a stopgap measure on the way to protocols such as ATM.

Recommended for:

- Internet access
- Multimedia
- Combined voice and data traffic

Not Recommended for:

- Voice-only traffic (there are simpler, cheaper options)
- Data-only traffic (again, simpler and cheaper options)

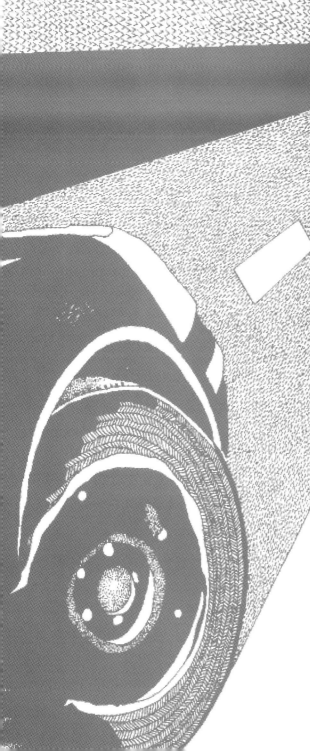

CHAPTER 14

Switched
Multimegabit
Data Service

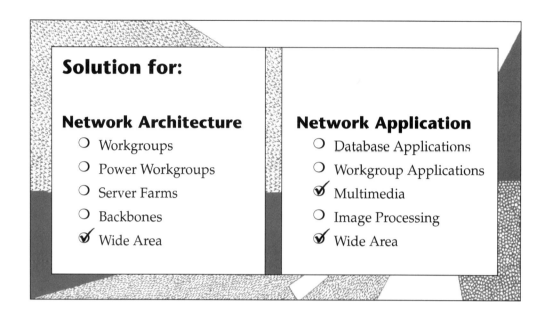

Solution for:

Network Architecture
- ○ Workgroups
- ○ Power Workgroups
- ○ Server Farms
- ○ Backbones
- ☑ Wide Area

Network Application
- ○ Database Applications
- ○ Workgroup Applications
- ☑ Multimedia
- ○ Image Processing
- ☑ Wide Area

Switched multimegabit data service (SMDS) is not actually a protocol, but rather a "metropolitan area service." In essence, it is a method of transmitting ATM cells over a shared bus. First deployed in 1992, SMDS gained momentum when the Regional Bell Operating Companies (RBOCs) and other local exchange carriers began feeling the heat of competition from interexchange carriers (IXCs) in local markets, and felt the best defense against that competition was a high-speed data transmission facility. As a relatively low-cost and definitely high-speed switched data service, SMDS seemed the perfect solution, and many local exchange carriers (LECs) in large metropolitan areas began offering the service.

Today SMDS is currently offered only by local exchange carriers (although whether and how the Telecommunications Act of 1996 affects this remains to be seen). SMDS provides transmission rates in the T1–T3 range on demand, so customers pay only for the bandwidth they use. Obviously this can be more efficient and cost-effective than leasing dedicated, point-to-point lines if those lines are not fully utilized.

What Is . . .?

Switched multimegabit data service is a marriage of the features of a shared-medium LAN and ATM. It is based on the IEEE 802.6 protocol, which defines the transmission of ATM cells over a shared bus. However, SMDS cells aren't identical to ATM cells: they use an 8-bit Access Control field, while ATM uses a 4-bit generic Flow Control field. This is due to the fact that SMDS is a shared-medium, connectionless service, and therefore requires a more detailed address than the switched, connection-oriented ATM (which we will discuss in detail in a later chapter).

SMDS was developed by Bellcore and is based on the IEEE 802.6 metropolitan area network standard. It is a cell-based, connectionless, packet-switched network that focuses on transmitting data—and data only. SMDS cells are switched from source to destination through one or more SMDS switches. These switches are connected by high-speed trunks, such as DS1 or SONET transmission systems, as shown in Figure 14-1.

NOTE: *Although SMDS supports shared media, Bellcore's adaptation concentrated on point-to-point implementation. You can understand this when you consider that nearly all of the transmission facilities handled by the LECs to that time were **exclusively** point-to-point in nature, not shared media or rings.*

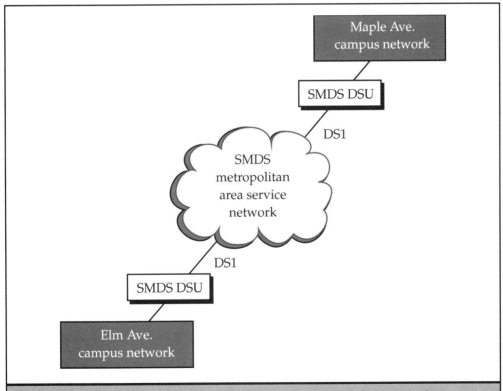

Figure 14-1. *A switched multimegabit data service metropolitan network*

Cell-Based?

Cell-based means that the basic unit of data transfer is a fixed-length cell rather than a variable-length packet. Packet switching, which utilizes bandwidth only when data traffic is present, was developed to handle bursty data traffic. However, packet-switching systems don't perform adequately for real-time, two-way traffic such as interactive video. Cell switching overcomes this limitation because it employs *cells*, which are fixed-length packets rather than variable-length packets. Each SMDS cell consists of a 48-byte payload and a 5-byte header, as shown in Figure 14-2. Because these packets are identical to ATM packets (in fact, they *are* ATM packets), SMDS is considered by many to be a stepping-stone to ATM connectivity.

Switched?

SMDS is not a shared bandwidth service. Rather, each port on an SMDS switch is dedicated to one user. An SMDS switch sets up a virtual connection between a transmitting node and a receiving node. This connection is made on the basis of the destination address of each cell, and it lasts only as long as it takes to transfer one cell. These data transfers can take place in parallel and at full network speed. Because the cell is transmitted only to the port associated with that specific destination address, no other port receives the cell, which provides both low traffic and, as an extra bonus, high security.

Connectionless?

Like ATM, SMDS defines a service at the user-network interface. But, unlike ATM, which is a connection-oriented service, SMDS is a connectionless service. *Connectionless* means that no connection is established between the transmitting and receiving computers before data is transferred. Packets are simply transmitted on the medium as soon as the SMDS interface receives them. Therefore, there is no delay for call setup or teardown.

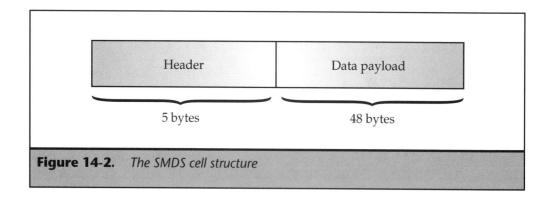

Figure 14-2. *The SMDS cell structure*

In SMDS, the switch takes essentially connectionless data cells and maps them into a virtual circuit for transit through the network. The station's network adapter substitutes an 8-byte SMDS address for the 6-byte address used by legacy LAN protocols. The transfer may be in cells or in packets, as we will see shortly, but it always appears connectionless to the end user.

The Architecture

As we mentioned, SMDS is based on the IEEE 802.6 metropolitan area network (MAN) standard. This standard specifies a high-speed network protocol that runs on a shared dual fiber-optic bus. The SMDS network is a dual bus design that forms an open ring, as shown in Figure 14-3. Physically, it looks like a star, and in this respect it is somewhat similar to Token Ring, which is a logical ring topology that forms a physical star because all cables are connected at a central hub. If the SMDS bus is cut, the open portion is automatically closed to "heal" the ring, which makes it something like FDDI.

Standards Compliance

SMDS is not only compatible with the IEEE 802.6 MAN standard on which it is based, but also with the broadband ISDN (B-ISDN) model, illustrated in Figure 14-4. As a

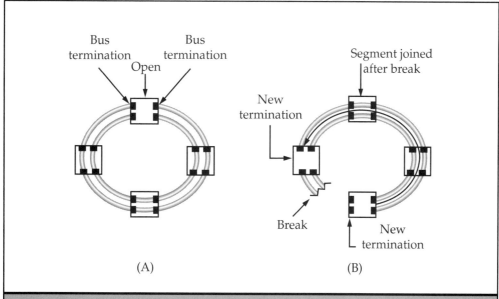

Figure 14-3. *The SMDS dual fiber-optic bus architecture*

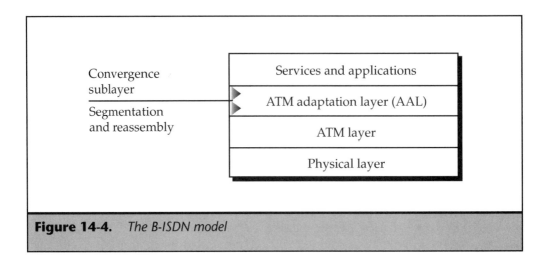

Convergence sublayer

Segmentation and reassembly

Services and applications

ATM adaptation layer (AAL)

ATM layer

Physical layer

Figure 14-4. *The B-ISDN model*

result, SMDS supports a fixed-length cell size of 53 bytes, as well as the ATM adaptation layer protocols 3 and 4. SMDS also provides some services that aren't described in the MAN standard, such as management and billing, which we will discuss later in this chapter.

Data Exchange Interface

Because SMDS supports the transmission of data only, most of the data sent on the SMDS network is received from legacy LANs in the form of packets. To avoid having to convert these packets into cells on every segment, the SMDS data exchange interface (SMDS-DXI) was developed. SMDS-DXI supports routing over SMDS services. SMDS-DXI is based on packets rather than cells. It uses standard high-level data link control (HDLC) framing, so unlike cell-based interfaces, it needs no additional hardware to transmit packet-based traffic.

SMDS-DXI makes implementing SMDS easy and inexpensive, because the HDLC hardware necessary to support SMDS-DXI is easy to obtain, relatively inexpensive, and time-tested. SMDS-DXI also supports the low-speed access of legacy protocols, giving network managers more flexibility over bandwidth choices, and thus more control over costs (remember, in SMDS, users pay only for the bandwidth they use).

Where . . .?

Switched multimegabit data service is a metropolitan area service. Therefore, it is currently available only from LECs. As discussed earlier in this book, *local exchange carriers* are companies such as the RBOCs, GTE, and others that handle local telephone and telecommunications connections. Until recently, these companies were restricted by federal law to handling local communications, providing *point-of-presence* (POP) facilities for long-distance carriers, and offering wide area communications services only within their local service areas, known as *local access and transport areas* (LATAs). However, recent legislation has permitted them to compete with long-distance carriers and eventually to discontinue providing POP facilities to their competitors in this.

As carriers prepare for ATM, some are installing SMDS as a stepping-stone to ATM. MCI and GTE, for example, are offering SMDS. AT&T, on the other hand, seems to be a proponent of the "pure" ATM network. Because SMDS uses the same cell-switching technology as ATM, carriers can offer SMDS service running on ATM switches. In fact, many carriers are installing ATM switches that implement all of the fast-packet technologies, including not only SMDS, but also frame relay, and X.25 interfaces.

How . . .?

SMDS is a *fast-packet* technology, meaning that the protocol doesn't handle error-checking and flow control itself. Instead, it leaves these procedures up to the end nodes. The belief is that current telecommunications transmission technologies and facilities transmit data with very few errors, so the complex and sophisticated error-checking mechanisms of earlier protocols are no longer necessary. If a packet is missing, the receiving node is responsible for requesting a retransmission. Asynchronous transfer mode and frame relay are also fast-packet protocols that do not include error-checking as a network function.

Access Method

The IEEE 802.6 Metropolitan Area Network Standard specifies access to the shared-media dual fiber-optic bus via the *distributed queue dual bus* (DQDB). DQDB divides the bus into vacant time slots that any connected station can fill with data cells for transmission. All attached stations can access the bus at any time until the bus is saturated. Theoretically, the DQDB access method supports up to 512 nodes and operates at 150Mbps on a network that can span up to 160km. The DQDB transmitting node can transmit packets of up to 9,188 bytes. These packets are disassembled into smaller 53-byte cells (48-byte data payload with 5-byte header) to fit into the SMDS slots. After transmission, they are reassembled at the receiving end.

Why . . .?

As a switching technology, SMDS has advantages over building private networks with dedicated digital lines such as T1 or even ATM. These advantages include ease of installation and configuration, scalability, and cost.

Installation and Configuration

As shown in Figure 14-5, customers installing an SMDS network only have to set up one line into the LEC's SMDS network. In a T1 environment, users would have to set up lines between all the sites that need interconnection. Its connectionless nature provides any-to-any connections between a variety of sites without the delays involved in

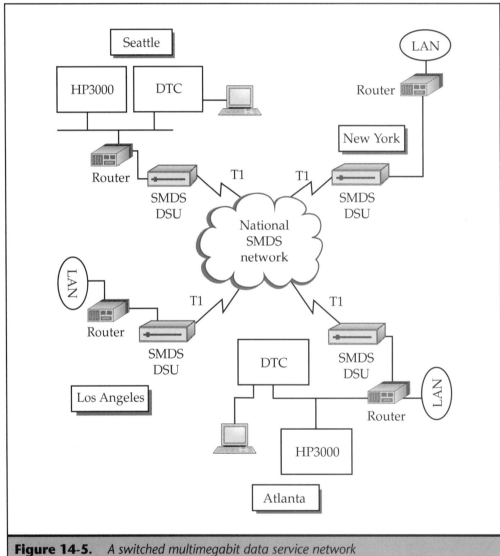

Figure 14-5.   *A switched multimegabit data service network*

call setup and teardown procedures. Therefore, SMDS offers LAN-type communication over metropolitan areas. Once information reaches the SMDS network, it can be switched to any site or sites.

Furthermore, the connectionless nature of SMDS makes it easy to add and drop sites in just minutes. Adding or dropping sites in an ATM network, with its connection-oriented protocol, would require reconfiguring address tables over the entire network.

Manageability

SMDS offers some nice management features that many other protocols, such as ATM, don't. For example, SMDS provides usage-based billing as well as a feature that controls network access to prevent nodes from monopolizing the network. It also has an address screening facility that heightens security by limiting communication to a group of addresses, and lets you build a private logical network over the public SMDS network. SMDS also provides usage statistics and other network management data directly to the end users. Finally, SMDS lets you construct data packets on top of the basic ATM cell structure, letting you take advantage of both packet features and fast cell switching.

Scalability

Switched multimegabit data service is widely and easily scalable. Because it is easy to add and drop connections—and because you only pay for the bandwidth you use—SMDS can provide flexibility and connection options to accommodate quickly changing needs.

Furthermore, SMDS isn't just a MAN service. Despite its emphasis on the metropolitan area, SMDS is also a WAN service that can span long distances. This means that it's theoretically easy to expand an SMDS network to span the city or the nation. However, at the time of this writing, MCI is the only long-distance carrier offering SMDS, and the availability varies among LECs.

SMDS also has a wide range of access speeds, from 56Kbps to 45Mbps, which gives you many options for building high-speed segments. For example, you could build a 45Mbps backbone, then link lower traffic sites to the backbone at 56Kbps. And remember, you're only paying for the bandwidth you use.

Interoperability

Switched multimegabit data service provides a fairly high level of interoperability with existing network infrastructures. It supports most existing network environments, including TCP/IP, Novell's IPX, AppleTalk, DECnet, SNA, and OSI. Furthermore, as we mentioned in our discussion of the DQDB access method, it allows a data unit of up to 9,188 bytes. Thus, SMDS can encapsulate entire packets from most LANs.

Perhaps most significantly, the SMDS Interest Group and the ATM Forum working together have developed specifications for SMDS and ATM service internetworking. However, if you are considering using SMDS as a means to migrate to ATM, you should note that SMDS supports the ATM adaptation layer-3/4. As you will discover in Chapter 16, most LAN emulation is based on ATM adapter layer-5. This means that when it comes time to integrate your existing local area networks into your high-speed backbone, you may have to convert to ATM to take advantage of LAN emulation. There is a complete discussion of LAN emulation and the issues surrounding it in Chapter 16, "Asynchronous Transfer Mode."

Performance

As we mentioned, SMDS supports a wide range of network and access speeds. It currently provides for user access at DS1 (1.544Mbps) and DS3 (45Mbps) rates. Network access requires a dedicated line running at a DS1 or DS3 rate.

Cost

Over the metropolitan and wide area, in which transmission media are relatively expensive to purchase, install, and maintain, the economics of shared media, which SMDS offers, are compelling. The cost of the service is usually a flat monthly fee based on the bandwidth of the links. Furthermore, SMDS offers easy expansion abilities by simply paying for another port connection charge and the related usage fees.

However, the buyer should beware: because the local exchange carriers are the primary providers of SMDS, there is usually no competition for the service in any given area. Therefore, you may want to weigh the cost of SMDS against other services.

 TIP: *It's hard to predict network usage. Therefore, to keep SMDS usage fees from playing havoc with your budget, try to find a carrier that offers a flat monthly usage fee or a monthly cap on SMDS usage charges.*

Support Group

The SMDS Interest Group (SIG) is the biggest promoter of switched multimegabit data service. It is an association of SMDS product vendors, service providers, carriers, and end users. The SIG has not only user groups, but also working groups that promote SMDS and work on specifications. The *technical working group* works on improvements to the IEEE 802.6 standard, while the *intercarrier working group* suggests enhancements to the standards that dictate the interconnection and management of intercarrier SMDS. They also sponsor a user group and, of course, have a public relations group that organizes seminars and disseminates information about SMDS and its availability.

For additional information, contact SMDS Interest Group Incorporated, 303 Vintage Park Drive, Foster City, CA 94404-1138, (415) 578-6979, fax (415) 525-0182, http://www.sbexpos.com.

Disadvantages

While SMDS seems like an easy-care, cost-effective solution for the "waitin' on ATM blues," it does have some significant disadvantages. Weigh these carefully before taking the plunge.

Limited Multimedia Support

As we mentioned at the beginning of this chapter, the LECs began implementing SMDS to help them compete in the long-haul data transmission market. Therefore, they didn't spend much time developing voice and video support for the service. As a result, SMDS can only transfer data. It doesn't offer deterministic transmission like frame relay or guaranteed, sequenced-packet delivery like ATM.

Limited Usage

Currently, there are just a couple hundred or so companies in the United States that are actively implementing SMDS. Even though the SMDS market is expanding very rapidly, such a small market may not be able to guarantee sufficient revenue to keep a lot of vendors in the market, which ultimately limits your choices in SMDS equipment and services, as well as increasing your costs. Although many SMDS vendors and industry analysts are predicting that this number will grow substantially, there are just as many naysayers who believe that SMDS has missed its opportunity as ATM products become cheaper and more plentiful.

Limited Vendor Support

As we mentioned, SMDS is far from universally available. It isn't offered by some LECs. Furthermore, as of this writing, MCI is the only long-distance carrier offering nationwide SMDS.

The Future

To be perfectly candid, SMDS has an uncertain future. While it is a relatively cost-effective means to transmit data at high rates, its somewhat restricted availability and data-only orientation have limited its usefulness. There is also some confusion over which direction it will go in terms of development. Some users would like to see vendors concentrate on enhancing DXI, making it more of a support service to connection-oriented protocols. Others would like to see vendors and carriers put more energy into developing multimedia support, making SMDS a direct *competitor* with connection-oriented services. However, in both areas, SMDS has more than enough well-established competition to challenge its widespread adoption.

Recommended for:

- ■ Customers who need to switch among many sites
- ■ Linking LANs within a single metropolitan area
- ■ Metropolitan area networks that plan to implement ATM in the future

Not Recommended for:

- ■ Real-time terminal-to-host applications
- ■ Wide area networks, because of currently severely limited wide area support

CHAPTER 15

Frame Relay

Frame relay is a spawn of Integrated Services Digital Network (ISDN). It is the packet-switching data service portion of ISDN, which has been unbundled and offered as a separate service. While relatively low-speed, frame relay's improved packet-switching architecture offers some features that may appeal to the network manager seeking to speed up a wide area data connection.

Son of ISDN

Before frame relay emerged as a protocol in 1989, it was actually part of the ISDN standards. As the packet-switching component of ISDN, frame relay was designed to provide a very high-speed packet-switching data transmission service to provide connectivity between devices such as routers that required high throughput for short durations. Then the developers of frame relay realized that the principles behind the protocol could be applied outside the realm of ISDN. As a result, frame relay was developed as an independent protocol for standalone use.

What It Is

Much like X.25, frame relay is a packet-switching protocol that connects two local area networks (LANs) over a public packet-switched network. In essence, a frame from one LAN is placed in, or *encapsulated* in, a frame relay frame. It is then transmitted through the frame relay network to the destination LAN. Frame relay uses statistical multiplexing techniques to load data from multiple sources at the customer site on a single line to the frame relay network. Statistical multiplexing essentially provides the LAN with *bandwidth on demand*, meaning that the network can get the bandwidth it needs when it needs it without having to reserve the bandwidth in advance and hold it unused until it is needed.

Each frame relay packet contains addressing information that the network uses to route through the telephone carrier's switches. Frame relay can be implemented using either private networks or a public carrier service. By placing responsibility for managing the network infrastructure in the hands of the frame relay service provider, using a public data network lets frame relay subscribers minimize service and equipment costs.

Frame relay offers improved performance over X.25 because it has very limited error detection and correction routines, which we will describe in detail later in this chapter. The result of the streamlined packet delivery mechanism is data transmission speeds of up to 45Mbps.

How It Works

Like the X.25 protocol, frame relay divides the user data stream into packets that are transmitted over the carrier network and reassembled at their destination. However, frame relay does it much faster than X.25. What follows are the nuts and bolts of how frame relay transmits data—and transmits it so quickly.

Frame Relay vs. Packet Switching

Like X.25, frame relay is based upon the principle of packet switching, which makes it well-suited to data applications. In frame relay, data is divided into variable length frames that contain destination addresses. These frames are then forwarded into the frame relay network, which delivers them. On its surface, this looks exactly like packet switching. In fact, the real difference between frame relay and packet switching lies under the hood: packet switching operates at Layer 3 of the OSI reference model, shown in Figure 15-1, while frame relay operates at Layer 2—and even then it doesn't implement all of the Layer 2 functions. This means that frame relay is a simpler protocol than X.25 and other packet-switching protocols, implementing less error checking and correction, but offering more speed.

To understand frame relay's advantages and how it achieves them, let's take a look at how X.25 and other Layer 3 packet-switching protocols work, then compare them to frame relay's simpler operation.

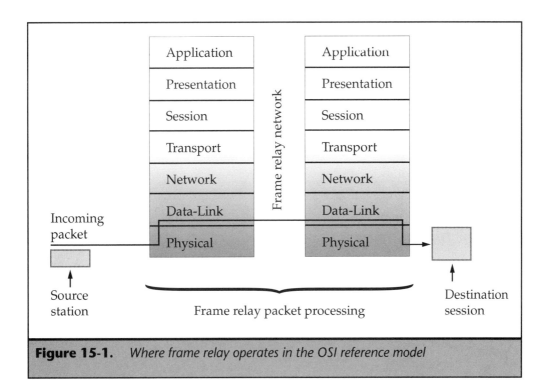

Figure 15-1. *Where frame relay operates in the OSI reference model*

Packet Switching and How Little It Means to You

Figure 15-2 shows a sample X.25 packet. As you can see, the packet includes a field containing network layer information. A packet contains six major components:

- **Start of Frame Delimiter.** This is an 8-bit sequence that signals the beginning of a packet. The Start of Frame Delimiter and End of Frame Delimiter are crucial to determining when a packet begins and ends, because X.25 packets are not fixed in length.

- **Link Layer Field.** This field contains information to handle packet errors and flow control. The link layer functions manage error correction and recovery as well as detecting whether there are sufficient buffers in the destination packet switch to receive the packet.

- **Network Layer Field.** This field contains all the information necessary for the packet to establish an end-to-end connection between the transmitting and receiving stations. The network layer is responsible for setting up and tearing down a connection for each packet transmitted, as well as providing some flow control procedures.

- **User Data Field.** This is the data "payload" of the packet. It's usually 4KB or smaller in size.

- **Frame Check Sequence.** This is a 2-byte field containing a checksum to determine whether the packet has been damaged or corrupted during transmission. A checksum is calculated on an arriving frame and compared with the FCS field, which was calculated by the sender. The packet is discarded if there is a mismatch and the end-stations must resolve the missing packet.

As you can see from reviewing the packet structure of an X.25 network, this protocol involves a lot of packet processing. Not only is an end-to-end connection established for each and every packet sent, but the packet is checked for errors by both the link layer protocols and the Frame Check Sequence. As well, both the link layer

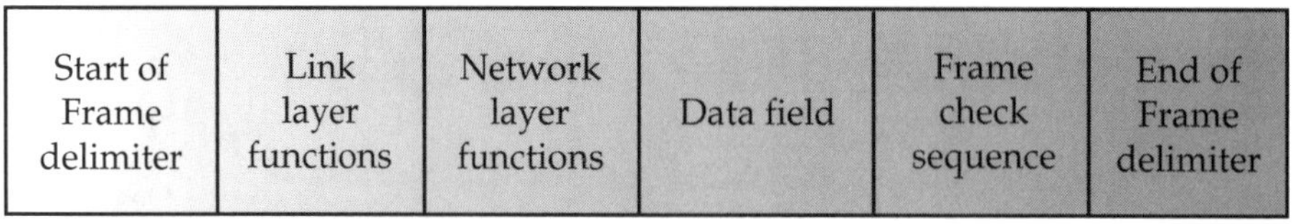

Start of Frame delimiter	Link layer functions	Network layer functions	Data field	Frame check sequence	End of Frame delimiter

Figure 15-2. *A sample data packet*

and the network layer provide extensive flow control, which controls the rate at which devices transmit packets into the X.25 switch. If the receiving switch is unable to accept any packets from the transmitting station because it's congested, the receiving switch won't acknowledge receipt of the packets. Furthermore, it issues a "send no more packets" message to the transmitting device. When the congestion within the receiving switch clears, it will send the relevant "OK to send again" message to the originating device. This guarantees that the receiving switch will never have to discard data for reasons of lack of buffer capacity and offers one more level of data transmission reliability. The protocol's developers considered this level of packet processing necessary because of the relatively unreliable transmission links available at the time.

These extensive error-checking and flow control mechanisms do indeed ensure packet delivery. However, they also slow the transmission of packets and therefore reduce the performance of the network as a whole. Luckily, two things happened that have helped make these mechanisms less important. The first was the advent of much more reliable high-speed transmission systems that delivered packets with much fewer errors and corruption. The second was the development of applications within the end-user stations that were designed to detect and recover packet errors. As a result of these two innovations, network designers were eager and able to do away with these cumbersome—and now unnecessary—error-checking procedures.

Frame Relay to the Rescue

Frame relay was developed on the assumption that the transmission media is reliable and relatively error-free and that the end-user applications can detect and recover from packet errors. Therefore, frame relay discards packets that contain errors. Also, if a frame relay switch's input buffers are full, it discards incoming frames until the congestion clears up. In short, frame relay makes little attempt to detect errors and congestion, and no attempt whatsoever to correct them.

So what *does* it do? A frame relay switch has three core functions:

- Route incoming frames to the correct outgoing port.
- Check the Frame Check Sequence field to determine whether the frame contains an error. If so, it discards the frame.
- Check to see if its buffers are full. If so, it discards incoming frames until the congestion clears up.

That's it. No connections are established, no flow control is maintained—no Level 3 functions are performed at all. If you look at the frame relay frame structure shown in Figure 15-2, you can see that the frame doesn't even contain fields for the information necessary for the switch to perform these functions.

Frame Format

The frame structure for the frame relay packet is pictured in Figure 15-3. Very similar to the X.25 packet, the frame relay packet has the following components:

■ **Start of Frame Delimiter.** This is an 8-bit sequence that signals the beginning of a packet.

■ **Link Layer Field, also called the Frame Relay Header.** This field contains addressing information and what little flow control management frame relay does. The link layer field also detects whether there are sufficient buffers in the destination packet switch to receive the packet. This field has two subfields:

■ **Data link connection identifier (DLCI)** This is the address of the logical connection that is multiplexed into the channel.

■ **Discard eligibility (DE)** This indicates whether the frame can be discarded in the event of network congestion. We'll discuss the use of the DE subfield later in this chapter.

■ **User Data Field.** This is the data "payload" of the packet. It's usually 4KB or smaller in size.

■ **Frame Check Sequence.** This is a 2-byte field containing a checksum to determine whether the packet has been damaged or corrupted during transmission.

Frame Relay Network Devices

So how do these almost-but-not-quite-X.25 frames travel over the frame relay network? A station sends data packets to a router which sends them across the port connections comprised of either permanent virtual circuits or switched virtual circuits to a frame relay switch or router, which reads the destination address contained in the DLCI subfield of the frame relay header. The network device then routes the frame to the proper destination over the frame relay network. At the other end of the network, the frame relay information is stripped off and the data is reassembled in its native packet format, which can then be processed by the receiving station.

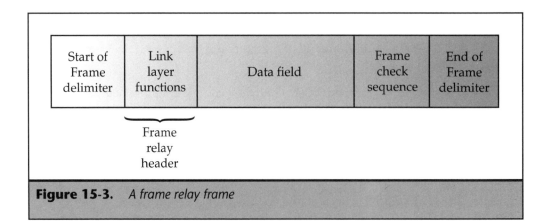

Figure 15-3.   *A frame relay frame*

Frame Relay Connections

Frame relay supports several different types of connections, all of which work together to form the frame relay network mesh.

Port Connections

A *port connection* is a physical access point onto the frame relay network that defines the maximum amount of data sent onto the network across all PVCs at any time. A single network interface can support multiple ports. The port connection is the interface to the public or private frame relay network, and at the time of this writing is generally available at 56/64Kbps, 128Kbps, 256Kbps, 384Kbps, 512Kbps, 768Kbps, 1.024Mbps, and 1.536Mbps. The port connection dynamically allocates data across the permanent virtual circuits.

Frame relay uses a multiplexing technique (which we will discuss later) that allows a large central site to be connected to a public frame relay network with a single router port and a single high-speed connection to the network. Because the circuits are not dedicated to a specific site the way point-to-point services are, multiple transmissions to many different sites can take place simultaneously.

Permanent Virtual Circuits

A *permanent virtual circuit* (PVC) is a path through the frame relay network that connects two points. A PVC is dedicated bandwidth that guarantees a level of service, called a *committed information rate* (which we will discuss later in this chapter), to a particular station. The network manager orders PVCs from a frame relay service provider, who configures them according to the network manager's specifications. Permanent virtual circuits remain active and available to the subscribing network at all times.

Switched Virtual Circuits

Switched virtual circuits (SVC) were added to the frame relay standard in 1993. A switched virtual circuit is a virtual circuit established "on the fly" as needed by the transmitting application, and it adds to the flexibility of the bandwidth for the circuit. However, while SVCs are now a part of the frame relay standard, no carriers are currently offering them—and some carriers don't plan to.

Relief for a Stuffy Network

As we mentioned, the frame relay protocol has no flow control mechanism. Therefore, frame relay networks have no procedure for slowing or stopping data transmission when the network is congested. There is a means of *notifying* stations when the network becomes overburdened, but if the station's application isn't designed to respond to the notification by suspending transmission, the station will just keep sending data onto an already jammed network. Therefore, when a frame relay network gets congested, it starts discarding frames.

The network can select frames to discard in one of two ways:

- Arbitrary selection
- Discard eligibility

In arbitrary selection, the frame relay network simply starts discarding packets when it gets congested. This is certainly effective, but it doesn't distinguish between packets that were sent under the auspices of the customer's committed information rate (CIR) and packets that were sent as part of a burst over and above the CIR. What's worse, though, is that it doesn't distinguish between vital data transmissions and transmissions that contain idle chit-chat. That's why many frame relay users prefer the second method of selecting frames to discard.

End users designate the *discard eligibility* of frames within transmissions by configuring their routers or switches to set flags within the frame relay data frames. For example, a customer may configure its router to flag all administrative traffic DE ("discard eligible"), but not flag all manufacturing related transmissions. Then, should the network become congested, frames from the administrative traffic would be discarded—to be retransmitted by the application later when the network is not so busy—while all manufacturing traffic would continue. Using the DE flag lets you determine which information is most important to you and ensure that it receives a higher transmission priority than less important data. It is entirely the responsibility of the receiving workstation to determine whether packets have been discarded and to take steps to initiate a retransmission.

Getting What You Pay for . . .

As we mentioned, frame relay has no flow control mechanism. Therefore, users can theoretically send as much data as they want over the frame relay network. This means that the protocol has no means of preventing a single bandwidth-hungry station from monopolizing the entire bandwidth for the same flat fee. This is why frame relay carrier services have developed the CIR.

When you order frame relay service and its attendant virtual circuits from a frame relay provider, you will be asked to specify a committed information rate. The CIR is the minimum bandwidth that your carrier will guarantee to be available to your PVC 24 hours a day, 7 days a week. The committed information rate is not tied in any way to the speed of your physical connection. Therefore, you could have a 1.544Mbps physical connection but only a 64Kbps CIR. You determine what your CIR should be by estimating your normal network traffic (or your budget—the higher the CIR, the higher the cost of the frame relay PVC).

And Getting More

If your network traffic exceeds your committed information rate, you're not necessarily out of luck. Frame relay can theoretically accommodate bursts in excess of the allocated bandwidth. Therefore, if the frame relay network receives a transmission from your network that bursts beyond your CIR, the frame relay network will attempt to open additional circuits to complete the transmission. When the network is not congested, sometimes you can send data bursts as large as twice your CIR.

Don't count on being able to exceed your CIR on a regular basis, however. Bursting above the CIR can occur only when the network isn't congested. We'll explain why later in the section on statistical multiplexing. Still, you should be able to plan on sending *some* traffic bursts, which means that frame relay network designers must build networks with sufficient capacity to handle the CIR plus a reasonable amount of bursts in excess of the CIR.

To provide some guidelines to frame relay network designers, most frame relay carrier services have adopted two additional guaranteed rates. These are the *committed burst rate* (CBR) and the *excess burst rate* (EBR). The CBR is the maximum amount of data rate that the network provider agrees to transfer under normal network conditions. The EBR is the maximum data rate *over and above* the CBR that the carrier's network will *try* to sustain. EBR data is automatically flagged DE.

Management and How Little There Is of It

The frame relay protocol really has no integrated management. Therefore, what little management information the network devices require to control the connections between end stations and the network mesh is provided *out of band*, meaning this information travels over a separate virtual circuit. The management system that provides this information is known as the *local management interface* (LMI).

The LMI is very much a "bare bones" management system, providing only four basic functions:

- Establishing a link between the end user and the network interface
- Monitoring the availability of frame relay circuits
- Notifying network stations of new PVCs
- Notifying network stations of deleted or missing PVCs

Statistical Multiplexing and Bandwidth on Demand

As we mentioned, frame relay was designed to handle bursty traffic efficiently and even elegantly. Therefore, much of the traffic you see on a frame relay networks is bursty in nature, which means that much of the time these devices are transmitting little if any data at all. Rather than waste money on idle bandwidth for a large number of bursty connections, frame relay gives network managers the ability to connect multiple bursty connections to the same segment. The strategy is that on only a very few occasions will two or more connections send a burst of traffic at the same time, and when some of them do, there is enough buffer capacity in the frame relay switch to capture the frames and transmit them as bandwidth frees up.

Statistical multiplexing is the technique for interleaving of data from several devices onto a single transmission line. Figure 15-4 is a simplified illustration of how statistical multiplexing works. Each device with data to transmit is allowed a transmission slot on the network. If the device has nothing to transmit, however, its slice of bandwidth is allocated to a station that *does* have data to transmit. This is how frame relay

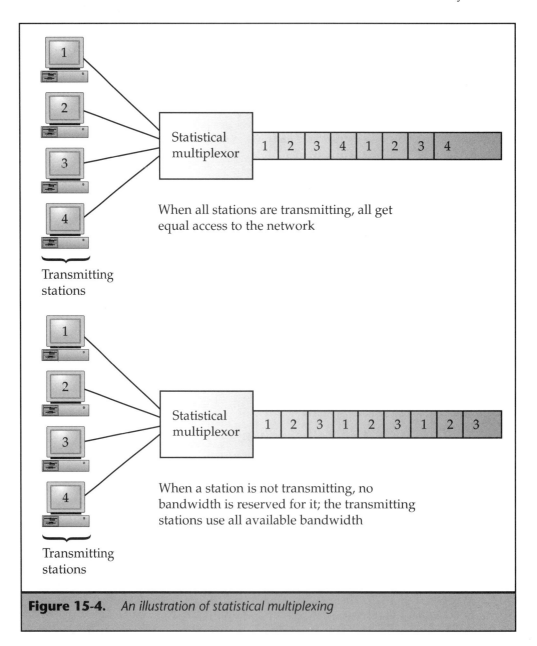

Figure 15-4.   *An illustration of statistical multiplexing*

accommodates bursting in excess of a subscriber's committed information rate—it makes use of bandwidth currently unused by other stations on the network.

Installation and Configuration

When you are preparing your order for frame relay service, there are a few issues you need to work out before placing the call to the carrier service. These are

- **Access method.** This is the speed of the connection between your site and the carrier's frame relay network. You have several options, and the speed you select will determine the type of access line required:
  - 56/64Kbps over switched 56 or ISDN lines
  - 128Kbps over ISDN lines
  - 384Kbps to 1.544Mbps over fractional T1 or T1 lines
- **Physical location** of the frame relay devices at your site. As we mentioned earlier, you'll need a router with a frame relay WAN port. Furthermore, your carrier will need to install a frame relay assembler/disassembler on your premises, as shown in Figure 15-5.

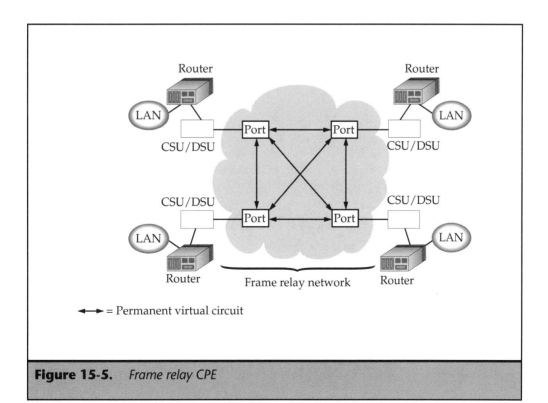

Figure 15-5. *Frame relay CPE*

■ **Committed Information Rate, Committed Burst Rate, and Excess Burst Rate.** You will need to determine your network's traffic requirements—or your budget limitations—before you begin ordering the service.

To configure your router for frame relay, all you have to do is enter the data link connection identifier (DLCI) information furnished by the frame relay service provider in your router's configuration tables. While you will be responsible for the LAN-to-router connection and router-to-FRAD connections, your local telephone company will be responsible for the FRAD-to-central-office connection. Furthermore, your local telephone company and your frame relay carrier together will be responsible for the central-office-to-frame-relay-network connection. Clearly this leaves a lot of room for finger pointing, so be sure you're comfortable with the expertise of the carriers—and be patient.

Availability and Pricing

Most wide area carriers in major metropolitan areas offer some flavor of frame relay service. However, destination cities and pricing vary a great deal, so make sure you verify that the carrier you are considering indeed offers frame relay services to all the locations you want to connect.

As we mentioned, frame relay can be very cost-effective, especially when compared with leasing multiple point-to-point connections. Generally, frame relay is very cost-effective for companies that have multiple sites in multiple geographically distant locations. Most leased-line connectivity is priced through federally regulated tariffing, which provides a fixed monthly fee plus an additional mileage fee. Frame relay, on the other hand, is usually priced on a flat fee, based on the port access speed and committed information rate. The monthly rates for frame relay service are in the neighborhood of $125 for 56Kbps service up to around $650 for 1.544Mbps service. However, you should be aware that these services come with a fairly hefty one-time installation fee of around $1,500 per port. If these rates are significantly lower than the costs involved in establishing a point-to-point dedicated line network to connect the same locations, then you should definitely consider implementing frame relay.

Management and Fault Tolerance

One of the beauties of using frame relay is that, if you are using the services of a public frame relay carrier, your physical management responsibilities are very limited. Adds and changes to your services require nothing more from you than a call to your carrier. Fault tolerance is also the responsibility of the carrier, and frame relay offers automatic rerouting of PVCs when a connection fails.

On the other hand, as we have already mentioned, frame relay as a protocol isn't known for its manageability. There are only a few management features offered with frame relay, and those are implemented via out-of-band signaling. However, here are a few *optional* services available that may make your life easier:

- **Simple flow control** provides XON/XOFF flow control for those network devices that require flow control.
- **Multicasting** allows stations to send frames to multiple destinations.
- **Global addressing** lets applications emulate LAN addressing.

Frame relay also offers the security benefit of having only private lines access the frame relay mesh. There are also some optional security features you can implement from your carrier, such as password protection and a feature that logs stations off the network after a predefined period of inactivity.

Interoperability

Frame relay offers good interoperability now, and also holds the promise of quicker and easier interoperability when switched virtual circuits (SVCs) are supported by the public carriers. SVCs could connect ISDN to frame relay networks, and they may eventually give users the ability to dial-up frame relay connections.

You may want to consider routing nonlocal area network protocols over frame relay as well. It may seem a bit strange at first, but frame relay is often much more cost-effective than other wide area transmission protocols, so it's worth a look. To route non-LAN protocols over the wide area, you'll need a device called a *frame relay assembler/disassembler* (FRAD). A FRAD takes data packets from other protocols—such as SNA, asynchronous, and even X.25—and breaks them into pieces, encapsulates the packet pieces in a frame relay frame, and sends them over the frame relay WAN to its destination. At the other end, the frame relay headers are stripped off the packets, and they are reassembled as packets in their original protocol, where they can be processed by the receiving stations. Figure 15-6 illustrates this.

A FUNI Way of Interconnecting

Most ATM switch manufacturers have announced support—or at least an intention to support—frame relay and ATM connectivity. The ATM Forum has offered a proposal, known as *Frame-to-User Network Interface* (FUNI), designed to set standards for connecting 56Kbps to 1.544Mbps circuits to ATM networks using a frame structure much like frame relay's. However, we've yet to see any actual FUNI installations, so the success of this proposal is yet to be seen.

Interconnecting the Carriers

Different frame relay carriers implement the service in different ways, and as a result many of them are unable to interoperate. Not only do they often use different switches, but they also may implement different congestion control and signaling methods. The Frame Relay Forum has set about to resolve some of these inter-operability issues by developing a set of interconnection specifications called the Network-to-Network Interface (NNI) standards. Theoretically, if all carriers use frame

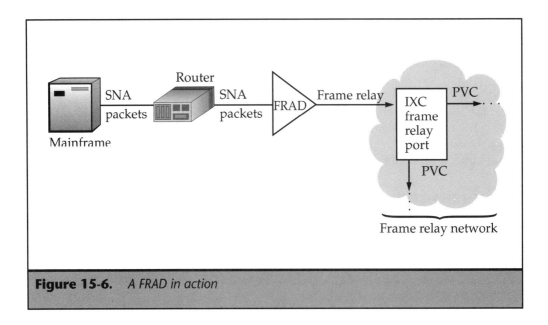

Figure 15-6. *A FRAD in action*

relay equipment that adheres to these standards, the interoperability problems will cease to exist.

Performance

Frame relay is generally available at CIRs from 56Kbps to 1.544Mbps. As well, it supports much higher burst rates—up to 45Mbps. Furthermore, frame relay has low network latency of about 20ms.

Scalability

Scalability is the hallmark of frame relay. The ease of adding more bandwidth via the committed information rate, along with the ability to send bursts of traffic well over the CIR, make frame relay one of the most flexible wide area protocols around. At the same time, thanks to frame relay's use of statistical multiplexing, providing this flexibility doesn't result in wasted idle bandwidth.

Can Your Vendor Do This?

Whether you're selecting a vendor to implement a frame relay WAN from scratch, or to provide a specific device for your existing frame relay WAN, there are certain questions to answer fully. Although every frame relay network is different, and every expansion and upgrade within each network is unique, there are basic questions that are relevant to every frame relay project. To help you get started with the vendor selection process, we've provided a sample list of five questions to put to each prospective vendor. We've divided these questions into issues of experience, interoperability, performance, and management. Please note: for those of you implementing a frame relay network for the first time, we've assumed you have done your homework and are CERTAIN that frame relay is the correct protocol choice given the traffic, type of data, speed, transmission reliability, and internetworking characteristics of your network.

The Experience Question

Has your vendor ever done this before? Are the technicians who have done it still on staff? This may seem silly, but it could be the most important question of all. You don't want to subsidize on-the-job training for your vendor's technical staff. Get references and check them thoroughly. Ask for the names of the technicians who performed the work. Make sure that those technicians are still employed by the vendor. Ask to interview them. Consider writing the name(s) of the experienced technician(s) into your bid acceptance.

The Interoperability Question

Are you a member of the Frame Relay Forum? If not, does your equipment meet the frame relay standards? This is really relevant to equipment vendors. Ask them to provide examples—complete with references—of other vendors' equipment with which they have successfully internetworked. Be sure to check the references thoroughly. The last thing you need is to be bound to a single vendor because their frame relay implementation is "almost" in compliance with the standards set by the Frame Relay Forum.

The Performance Question

What is the maximum line speed supported now—and 12 months from now? Obviously, 2.048Mbps should be the minimum. And for now it can be the maximum. Your vendor should have—or at least have plans for—support for speeds up to 45Mbps. And it wouldn't hurt to check the cost of upgrading to these higher speeds.

What are the switching speeds, expressed in frames per second, between: a) trunk ports; b) access ports; c) access and trunk ports? Get speeds for frame sizes varying from 128 bytes to 2,048 bytes. This question helps you ensure that the equipment can switch frames as quickly as it can receive them. For example, connected to a 2.048Mbps line, your router will receive about 2,000 128-byte frames per second. So if you have a device that can be configured to support more than one 2.048 line, yet can switch at a maximum of 2,000 frames per second, the router is actually a bottleneck.

TIP: *You can expect the best performance on the trunk-to-trunk ports, so make them quote their access port-to-trunk port switching speed, too.*

The Management Questions

How does the router handle congestion management? How does it handle recovery? Congestion and overflow comprise the number one management issue for frame relay, so this is a key question. Ask whether the equipment complies with the CCITT and/or ANSI standards for congestion management, and if so, how. Explore whether the vendor's implementation uses the discard eligibility bit to let the equipment or the user set the discard priority of frames. What management facilities do they offer? Frame relay is not famous for its inherent manageability. Therefore, it pays to spend some quality time learning the management facilities offered by the proposed system or equipment. The number one feature you should require is congestion notification, since—as we noted above—congestion management will be your overriding concern with frame relay.

Another critical management issue is routing. The system should provide both manual and automatic routing, because although you will prefer manual routing for priority traffic, it would be silly to try to define manual routes for every frame of every priority. And, as with most systems, your frame relay system should provide useful troubleshooting and diagnostics utilities. You should also expect the system to provide comprehensive statistics on traffic levels, speeds, and discarded frames. You can use this information not only for network administration purposes, but also for billing information if your network has a chargeback system. Finally, if security is an issue, have the vendor describe security features in detail to see whether they meet your needs.

Searching for a frame relay vendor can be like a treasure hunt without clues. It can be frustrating and tedious. However, the stakes are high, so it's well worth the effort it requires. Although this list is by no means comprehensive, these questions will give you a map to follow while hunting for the right vendor for the job.

The Good News

Frame relay services require less hardware than dedicated circuits. With dedicated circuits like 56Kbps and T1, because of their point-to-point orientation, you need two channel service units (CSUs) and two routers for each circuit—one per connection. So, for a configuration like the one shown in Figure 15-7, you will need five CSUs and five routers at each site.

With frame relay, on the other hand, you will need only one router and one CSU at each site, as shown in Figure 15-8.

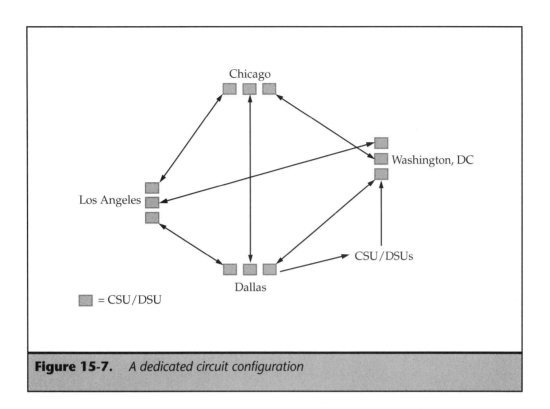

Figure 15-7.   *A dedicated circuit configuration*

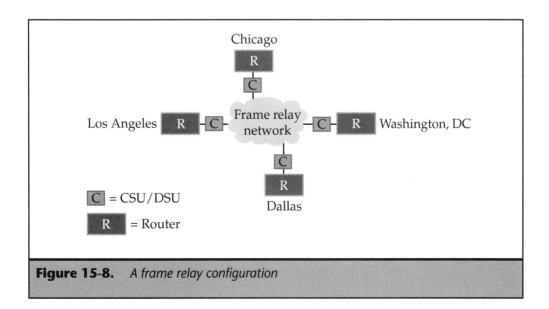

Figure 15-8.   *A frame relay configuration*

Frame relay services typically cost less, yet give you more bandwidth. A dedicated circuit gives you the stated amount of bandwidth and no more. However, a frame relay circuit can support bursts of bandwidth well above your CIR.

It's faster and easier to reconfigure a frame relay network than a dedicated circuit network. Adding a new location to a dedicated circuit network requires that the end user purchase new equipment and order new lines, which can take anywhere from a few days to a few weeks to organize. Adding a new location to a frame relay network is simply a matter of adding an access port and configuring new PVCs, both of which are done by the carrier and can often be completed in a couple of days.

The Bad News

When frame relay was proposed to the standards committees in 1988, it was quickly defined and approved. It was subsequently implemented and supported by many local and interexchange communications carriers. By late 1991, frame relay was both widely available and widely implemented by users. At the time, the Federal Communications Commission didn't consider frame relay a basic service, and therefore it wasn't tariffed—that is, the FCC didn't require carriers to publish and abide by a set rate for frame relay service. Instead, the price of frame relay services was negotiated privately and separately between the carrier and each frame relay customer. This negotiated price was then written into a contract between the two parties. Shrewd customers were sometimes able to negotiate very favorable pricing through this procedure.

In October 1995, however, the FCC changed its mind. It now feels that frame relay is so widely used that it now constitutes a basic service. As such, the FCC is requiring frame relay carriers to tariff the service. Although this may be more equitable, it also eliminates the possibility of getting a bargain, because prices of tariffed services are much less flexible than those of untariffed services.

Voice and Frame Relay

Originally, people didn't think voice (or video) could run over frame relay due to the protocol's variable-length frames. However, many vendors, including Micom Communications, are now offering mutliplexors that put both voice and data on frame relay bandwidth with very acceptable performance.

Frame Relay Forum

The Frame Relay Forum is an association of Frame Relay users, vendors, and service providers based in Mountain View, California (415-962-2579). The organization is made up of committees that create implementation specifications and agreements for the purpose of developing frame relay standards.

Recommended for:

■ Connecting LANs over the wide area

■ Database applications and other applications that generate bursty data traffic

Not Recommended for:

■ Video traffic, because of frame relay's variable-length frames

■ Voice traffic, because of frame relay's variable-length frames

■ Delay sensitive applications

CHAPTER 16

Asynchronous
Transfer Mode

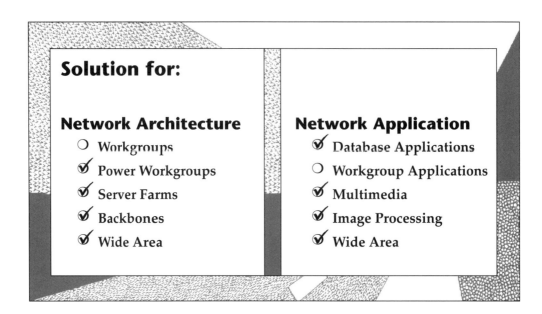

Solution for:

Network Architecture
- ○ Workgroups
- ✓ Power Workgroups
- ✓ Server Farms
- ✓ Backbones
- ✓ Wide Area

Network Application
- ✓ Database Applications
- ○ Workgroup Applications
- ✓ Multimedia
- ✓ Image Processing
- ✓ Wide Area

Anyone who has read a network trade magazine or attended a technical conference in the last three years has heard about ATM. Asynchronous transfer mode seems to be the great networking hope of both the near and distant future; some vendors have even called ATM this decade's most significant networking technology. ATM promises to integrate LAN functions, WAN functions, voice, video, and data into a single uniform protocol and design. It also promises uniformity and scalability that will ultimately simplify network design and management. Therefore, nearly all complementary technologies are engineering "ATM readiness" into their own development.

All the hype notwithstanding, ATM offers some benefits that no other networking protocol has offered:

- **Speed:** ATM supports transmission rates of up to 622Mbps.

- **Scalability:** ATM allows increased bandwidth and port density within existing architectures.

- **Dedicated bandwidth:** This guarantees an application's consistency of service, which is not available in shared technologies.

- **Universal deployment:** ATM offers the potential of an end-to-end solution, meaning it can be used from desktop to local segment to backbone to WAN.

So, if ATM is so significant, what exactly *is* it? How will it improve your network? How much will it cost? When should you implement it? Because ATM will no doubt have an important role in your network before the end of the century, we will spend a great deal of time exploring exactly what ATM is, why it is so significant, where it is now in its development, where it is going, and the issues surrounding its implementation both in its current form and in the future.

How It Started

ATM began as part of the Broadband-Integrated Services Digital Network (B-ISDN) standard developed in 1988 by the Consultative Committee for International Telegraph and Telephone (CCITT). An extension of narrowband Integrated Services Digital Network (which defined public digital telecommunications networks), B-ISDN provides more bandwidth and enables more data throughput than narrowband ISDN. The B-ISDN reference model is shown in Figure 16-1.

As you can see, ATM lies directly on top of the physical layer of the B-ISDN reference model. However, it doesn't require the use of any specific physical layer protocol. Therefore, the physical layer could be FDDI, DS3, SONET, or others. We'll talk more about the reference model and its implications for ATM later in this chapter.

Who Started It

As mentioned earlier, asynchronous transfer mode was originally defined by the Consultative Committee for International Telegraph and Telephone, a part of the United Nations charged with developing and recommending international standards for telecommunications technology and operations. This body is now more commonly known as the International Telecommunications Union, of which the CCITT is a committee. The ITU is currently formalizing standards for ATM.

In 1991, the ATM Forum, a consortium of vendors, carriers, and users, was formed to expedite industry agreement on ATM interfaces in North America. The ATM Forum is a driving force in the establishment of industry-wide ATM standards.

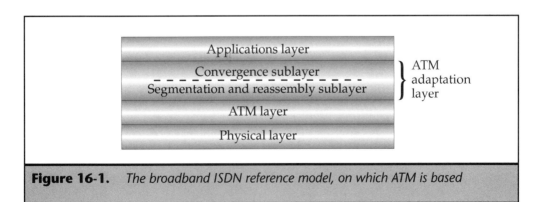

Figure 16-1. *The broadband ISDN reference model, on which ATM is based*

ATM: The Short Answer

In brief, ATM is a cell-switched, connection-oriented, full-duplex, point-to-point protocol that dedicates bandwidth to each station. It uses asynchronous time division multiplexing to control the flow of information over the network. ATM operates at bandwidths ranging from 25Mbps to 622Mbps, although most of the development time (and marketing fanfare) is going into 155Mbps ATM.

Among the benefits offered by ATM are

- Excellent scalability
- Legacy network integration
- Bandwidth on demand
- Ability to handle the entire range of network traffic—voice, data, image, video, graphics, and multimedia
- Adaptability to both LAN and WAN environments

If ATM Is the Answer, What Were the Questions?

Like all the high-speed protocols discussed in this book, ATM was developed as an alternative to existing transport protocols such as Ethernet and Token Ring that were obviously limited in bandwidth and scalability. However, ATM was also designed to handle multiple types of data simultaneously and with increased efficiency. Therefore, ATM had to be able to transmit a wide variety of bit rates and support bursty communications, since voice, data, and video traffic all exhibit bursty behavior.

NOTE: Most people don't think of circuit-switched voice traffic as bursty, but it is. In fact, a circuit-switched voice conversation utilizes far less than half of the available bandwidth.

What Is a Cell?

Packet switching, which utilizes bandwidth only when data traffic is present, was developed to handle bursty data traffic. However, packet-switching systems don't perform adequately for real-time, two-way traffic such as interactive video. ATM overcomes this limitation because it employs *cells*, which are fixed-length packets, rather than variable-length packets. Each ATM cell consists of a 48-byte payload and a 5-byte header, as shown in Figure 16-2.

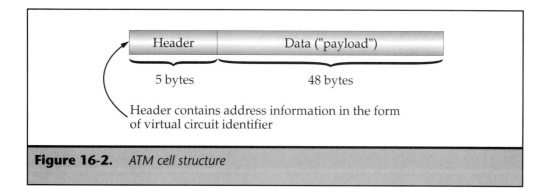

Figure 16-2. *ATM cell structure*

Fixed-length ATM cells offer many advantages over variable-length packets:

- **Hardware switching capability:** Because it is simple, predictable, and reliable to process fixed-length cells, ATM switching can be done at the hardware level, rather than requiring expensive and processing-intensive software to manage flow control, buffers, and other management schemes.

- **Guaranteed levels of service:** Networking and switching queuing delays are more predictable with fixed-length data cells. Therefore, switches can be designed to provide guaranteed levels of service for all types of traffic, even for delay-sensitive services such as voice and video.

- **Parallel processing:** Fixed-length cells allow cell-relay switches to process cells in parallel, for speeds that far exceed the limitations of bus-based switch architectures.

- **Voice-processing capability.** Although ATM cells require bandwidth only when traffic is present, they can still provide the equivalent of a time division multiplexer time slot for continuous traffic. As a result, ATM can handle real-time continuous traffic, such as digitized voice, and bursty traffic, such as LAN transmissions, equally well.

The ATM cell is used to carry data transmitted between switches. A 48-byte segment of the user data payload is placed in a cell along with a 5-byte header forming the 53-byte ATM cell. The cell header carries the information necessary for switch operation.

What is Switched?

ATM does not employ shared bandwidth. Rather, each port on an ATM switch is dedicated to one user. An ATM switch sets up a virtual connection between a transmitting node and a receiving node. This connection is made on the basis of the destination address of each cell, and it lasts only as long as it takes to transfer one cell. These data transfers can take place in parallel and at full network speed. Because the cell is transmitted only to the port associated with that specific destination address, no other port receives the cell, thereby providing both low traffic and, as an extra bonus, high security.

ATM Switching and Virtual Connections

To communicate over the ATM network, applications must first establish a *virtual connection (VC)* among switches. A VC is a transmission path for an ATM data cell. The VC extends through one or more switches, establishing an end-to-end connection for the transmission of application data via ATM cells. VCs can be established in two ways. First, a *permanent virtual circuit (PVC)* can be manually configured by a network manager. A PVC is dedicated bandwidth that guarantees a level of service to a particular station. Network managers would configure PVCs for mission-critical applications that must always receive high priority or for permanent connections such as among routers and bridges. The second means of establishing a VC is the *switched virtual circuit (SVC)*. An SVC is a VC set up "on the fly" as it is needed by the application.

VIRTUAL CIRCUIT IDENTIFIER   The cell header also contains two address fields, the *virtual path identifier (VPI)* and the *virtual channel identifier (VCI)* that together total 3.5 bytes and define the *virtual circuit identifier,* which is the route of the cell to a particular switch. These fields are updated by each switch in the path.

Virtual circuit identifiers tag the cells for a particular connection, then the switches transfer the data in a VC by hardware-based switching, triggering the VC connection tag in the cell header.

The problems of congestion and "VC routing" among multiple switches are still outstanding in the standards process. Congestion management is important because a small level of cell loss (e.g., 0.1 percent) gets magnified to a dramatically large frame loss (e.g., 20 percent). This is unacceptable, and several alternative congestion management policies are under active study and evaluation.

All ATM cells are the same size, unlike frame relay systems and local area networks, which have variable packet sizes. Using same-size cells allows:

- **Guaranteed bandwidth:** Variable-length packets can cause traffic delays at switches in the same way that cars must wait for long trucks to make turns at busy intersections.

- **High performance:** Large volumes of data can flow concurrently over a single physical connection.

- **Hardware Switching:** In the short term this yields higher throughput, and over time the technology can continue to exploit improved price/performance as processor power increases and incremental costs decrease.

■ **Data Prioritization:** ATM can deliver a deterministic response, which is essential to carry "latency-sensitive" communications, such as motion video and audio, or mission-critical, interactive data traffic.

What Is Connection-Oriented?

Connection-oriented means that a connection must be established between the transmitting and receiving computers before data is transferred. Each intermediate switching point must be identified and informed of the existence of the connection. Each packet is routed independently, and therefore each must carry a complete address of the ultimate destination.

What Is Full-Duplex?

Full-duplex allows transmission over one pair of wires and receipt over the other pair simultaneously, which provides nearly full utilization of both pairs and sustainable high data rates. By supporting full-duplex operation, ATM doubles the effective bandwidth of ordinary half-duplex transmission that is employed by most network protocols.

What Is Point-to-Point?

As mentioned earlier, ATM networks must establish a connection between the sending and receiving stations before transmitting a cell. This connection between two stations is the only concern of the ATM switch. Unlike a router, an ATM switch doesn't try to define this one-to-one connection in the context of all possible connections on the network. Instead, the ATM switch selects the route between the sending station and the receiving station, then informs the intermediate switches along this route to ensure that the resources for transmitting the cell are allocated through the network.

Once a cell's transmission route is established, the ATM switch then assigns a connection number to each point-to-point link along this route. Connection numbers are chosen independently for each of the point-to-point links in the transmission path. A path may be formed from a number of such links, with the links joined by switches. This means that a single cell carries a potentially different connection number on each different link of the connection path. A switch changes the connection numbers of each cell as it transfers the cell from one link to another. This change of connection numbers at the junction of two links means that the Connection Number fields only need to be big enough to distinguish the connections carried by a single link.

This point-to-point connection orientation of ATM and the changing of the connection numbers at each switch hop let ATM use small connection numbers rather than the large addresses required by most protocols. This makes ATM more efficient, because small connection numbers conserve space in cells and thus bandwidth, and also faster, because it makes for small lookup tables in switches.

What Is Dedicated Bandwidth?

Efficient bandwidth use is not the only issue addressed by ATM technology. In fact, different traffic types require different delay behavior, delay variation, and loss characteristics. ATM provides different qualities of services to accommodate these differences. ATM allocates bandwidth to each active station. The station requests the appropriate amount of bandwidth for each connection, and the network automatically assigns this bandwidth to the user. In reality, the bandwidth isn't actually dedicated per se. It is shared by other users, but the network ensures the requested level of service. The network can do this because it controls the number of simultaneous conversations on the network.

To access the network, a station requests a virtual circuit between the transmitting and receiving ends. During connection setup, the end station can request the quality of service it needs to suit transmission requirements, and ATM switches will grant the request if sufficient network resources are available. The guaranteed level of service of cell-based switched access is particularly useful for transporting real-time, interactive communication such as voice or video. ATM uses a protocol called *user-to-network interface (UNI)* to establish dedicated levels of bandwidth to stations and applications.

User-to-Network Interfaces (UNI)

ATM's UNI protocol provides multiple service classes and bandwidth reservation established during call setup of a switched virtual connection. The UNI defines the interoperability between the user equipment and the ATM switch port. A public UNI defines the interface between a public service ATM network, and usually supports a SONET or DS3 interface. A private UNI, on the other hand, defines an ATM interface between an end-user and a private ATM switch, and would most likely have a copper or fiber-optic cable interface.

While the ATM Forum has successfully stabilized the UNI protocol, there are a couple of key issues that network managers should consider when choosing products. The UNI protocol in the products they select must coordinate the bandwidth allocated locally among other switches and internetworked LAN segments. It must also support a variety of network operating systems to guarantee multiple classes of service. Both of these issues affect the interoperability of the ATM network, and so the network managers should select products that support the network's current design and equipment.

How It All Works Together

The combination of cell switching and point-to-point connections with their resulting small connection numbers, lets ATM break the core networking task into two separate components—route determination and data forwarding (better known as routing and switching)—and handle each with a different technology. To illustrate this separation of functions fully, let's first look at how a cell is transmitted across an ATM network.

Route Determination

Route determination is a computer-intensive function, typically software-based, that requires dynamic knowledge of the global network topology. Route determination in ATM is performed by establishing virtual connections, and the route determination occurs only once per data transfer session. ATM chooses a path for the cells of the connection (routes the connection) during establishment of the connection; all cells of the connection follow the same path. After connection establishment, only simple cell transfer operations are performed—operations that implement routing decisions made at connection establishment time. This keeps data transfer simple and efficient, but it requires a separate system for connection setup. The connection setup part of ATM is, and must be, based on connectionless protocols. The main difference between ATM and traditional networking solutions is that traditional networking must solve both components of the networking problem simultaneously. Thus, every packet in a traditional network carries the globally significant routing information, and every packet must be processed by routers before the data can be forwarded. This continual evocation of the route determination function is a very wasteful use of an expensive resource and becomes the network bottleneck due to the expense of wire-speed capable routers.

To illustrate the routing problem that the ATM architecture solves, let's consider a network backup. Suppose you must back up 2 gigabytes of data residing on a server on a routed network. The backup program will probably create ten million 200-byte packets, because 200 bytes is the most common transfer unit size permitted in routed networks. Each of these ten million packets will be assigned a network-wide routing address, and each router along the path processes these ten million packets separately—even though they are streaming continuously along the same route. This means that *each* router along the path must examine the network layer header of *each* packet, then compute the route again for *each* packet separately, despite the fact that the route is identical for all ten million packets. What a waste of processing power!

The scenario is very different with ATM. The ATM switch establishes the route only once with a virtual connection (VC). The switch then assigns a connection identifier to tag the route. Switches on the route are informed of the bandwidth requirements of the VC and are instructed to interpret the connection identifier appropriately. After that, all cells with that connection identifier are hardware-switched along the route, permitting the route determination function to service new requests rather than continually servicing the request of an established session. Thus, cells don't contain complex routing addresses. Instead, they are tagged with a small temporary connection identifier, which the ATM switches are instructed to map onto the route defined by the VC.

Data Forwarding

Data forwarding, on the other hand, is a hardware-intensive function requiring gigabits of switching capacity. ATM's cell-based switching allows simple switching which, like Ethernet switching, can be performed entirely in hardware. It is performed by ATM switches operating on ATM cells, and the ATM cell definition has been optimized for implementing a gigabit-capable, hardware-based switching capability. Therefore, cells are hardware-switched along the path previously established by the VC for the session.

ATM is primarily a format for use by switches and includes no access arbitration protocol. Each port on a switch behaves in many ways like a station. The cell header information in a received cell is used to look up forwarding information needed to route the cell within the switch. Error checking is performed in the cell header, and cells with errors are discarded. This cell header address information is changed at each switch to represent the route at the next switch. Addressing in the ATM cell is of local significance to a switch, in contrast to the MAC address, which identifies individual users either with locally or globally unique values.

ATM Switches

ATM switches allow one desktop connection per port. Some ATM switches are nonblocking, meaning they have the capacity to support a backbone link equivalent to the sum of the input port speeds. In addition, a nonblocking switch transfers traffic directly from input to output without a store-and-forward process. Buffering is used only if multiple inputs attempt to access the same output simultaneously. In spite of occasional buffering, ATM is still superior to the slow, store-and-forward operation of traditional routers.

Scalable hardware-switching elements are the basis for the gigabit-speed backbone networks that can be built with ATM. Although gigabit switching seems far beyond the needs of today's 10Mbps desktops, nonblocking LANs are constrained to small numbers of ports without a gigabit switch in the backbone.

ATM Switch Control Point

The ATM switching function really consists of two parts: the switch hardware, which performs the actual switching, and the switch control point, which manages the switching fabric. The ATM switch control point maintains the switch fabric by

- Managing requests for virtual connections (VCs)
- Learning the ATM network topology
- Maintaining the forwarding databases
- Enabling SNMP-based ATM network management

Cabling Considerations

ATM's topology is a mesh of switches. This means that any point in the network can be reached from any other point via multiple routes involving independent connections among switches. ATM doesn't require any specific physical layer protocols to accomplish this. ATM also has no distance limitations other than those imposed by the attenuation characteristics of the media used. This simplifies the building of the cable plant, because there really aren't any rules to constrain the design. However, it makes documentation all the more important, because with no rules as guidelines, it would be nearly impossible to decipher an undocumented cable plant.

ATM Media Support

Media independence is a driving principle of ATM. Many physical layers are specified, starting at 25Mbps, including several for 100 to 155Mbps, and going all the way up to 622Mbps. ATM at 155Mbps will include support for Category 3, 4, 5 UTP, Type-1 STP, fiber-optic cable, multimode fiber, and single-mode fiber local area networks.

Wide Area Network Physical Interface

The 155Mbps WAN interface to the public network carriers will be based on the Synchronous Optical Network (SONET). As we mentioned earlier, SONET is an internationally supported physical layer transport scheme developed in the early 1980s.

Setup and Configuration

ATM is different from any LAN protocol you have ever managed. While its installation and configuration isn't physically difficult, it is complex. It requires a detailed level of knowledge about ATM as well as a great deal of careful planning. Therefore, be prepared to spend both money and time training, planning, and consulting before undertaking an ATM implementation.

Scalability

ATM can add scalability to legacy protocol networks. For example, in Figure 16-3, the network is connected by three 24-port Ethernet switches, each having two 100Base-TX uplinks connected to the other two switches to form a mesh. Such a network could provide nonblocking service for 60 Ethernet users—less than currently connected. Furthermore, as the number of users and switches grows, more switch capacity must be dedicated to backbone links than to desktop interfaces.

Using a 1.55Gbps ATM switch in the backbone adds ten ATM ports, each at 155Mbps, as shown in Figure 16-4. Only one ATM port is required from each Ethernet switch to provide connectivity among all ports. Whereas the network in Figure 16-3 could support only 60 users, the network in Figure 16-4 can provide nonblocking service for 240 dedicated Ethernet users with room to grow.

Scalable ATM LAN switches on the market today can support as many as 100 155Mbps ports in nonblocking configuration. In conjunction with dedicated Ethernet access devices, these switches provide the foundation for a nonblocking network of 1,000 dedicated Ethernet users. As the ATM market matures, nonblocking networks with 1,000 155Mbps ports—or 10,000 Ethernet ports—will be achievable.

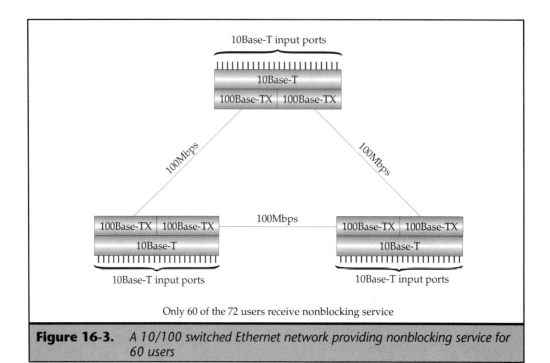

10Base-T input ports

10Base-T

100Base-TX | 100Base-TX

100Mbps

100Mbps

100Base-TX | 100Base-TX

100Mbps

100Base-TX | 100Base-TX

10Base-T

10Base-T

10Base-T input ports

10Base-T input ports

Only 60 of the 72 users receive nonblocking service

Figure 16-3. *A 10/100 switched Ethernet network providing nonblocking service for 60 users*

10Base-T

ATM

155Mbps

10Base-T | ATM   155Mbps   ATM switch   155Mbps   ATM | 10Base-T

Support 240 dedicated 10Base-T users with nonblocking service

Figure 16-4. *An Ethernet network with an ATM backbone*

A need for nonblocking networks or high-speed desktop connections isn't necessary to justify ATM. Although ATM is most beneficial when used in a nonblocking LAN configuration, it can also be deployed in a blocking configuration to maximize bandwidth usage.

In a blocking configuration, the sum of the user port bandwidths exceeds the backbone link bandwidth, and contention for backbone links can occur. Constructing a network with potential blocking can be a cost-effective solution for customers in the early stages of migrating to ATM. For customers who are installing ATM to the desktop, current workstation processing loads may not yet require full use of the available bandwidth. In this case, more users can be added to the network than the backbone can support in a nonblocking configuration. When bandwidth-hungry workstation applications are deployed, bandwidth and switching capacity can be adjusted to produce a nonblocking configuration.

When combined with proper traffic management techniques, a blocking ATM network is capable of exceeding the performance of a shared-media LAN. Traffic management allows conventional LANs with relatively low-speed users to benefit from ATM with cost-effective blocking configurations.

Manageability

ATM backbones are easier to manage than those in most routed networks, because ATM eliminates a lot of the complexity required to configure large internetworks that have different addressing schemes and routing procedures. ATM hubs provide connections between any two ports on the hub, independent of the type of device attached to it. The addresses of these devices are premapped, making it easy to send a message for example, from one node to another, regardless of the network type the nodes are connected to. In fact, simplified network management may be the primary reason for many users to migrate to an ATM-based solution, even prior to performance requirements dictating the transition.

Virtual LANs

Setting up filters or constraints between different groups of users is awkward and time-consuming with conventional bridges and routers. Network managers think in terms of workgroups, not the physical location of users. Therefore, they shouldn't have to set up a series of filtering statements based on physical ports. The connection-oriented nature of ATM and performance of hardware cell switching enables the creation of virtual networks.

Rather than configuring and reconfiguring routers every time end stations move, network managers can implement *virtual LANs*. A virtual LAN is a list of device media access control (MAC) or network addresses that are independent of a physical port, much like an access list used by some router vendors. However, virtual LANs have network-wide significance. A device can access any other device on the same virtual LAN. Virtual LANs can define filters among themselves, just like routers can.

Devices on different media can be members of the same virtual LAN. Furthermore, users can move end stations onto any segment within the virtual subnet without requiring address reconfiguration.

Virtual LANs enable network managers to group devices logically regardless of physical location and provide dedicated bandwidth and services to each, as shown in Figure 16-5. Users can plug into any port in the network, and the virtual LAN handles the rest.

In addition to address filtering, virtual LANs also provide

- Simplified moves, adds, and changes
- Bandwidth allocation
- Security features

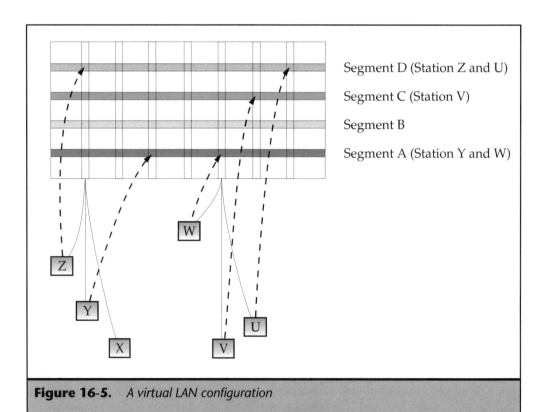

Figure 16-5. *A virtual LAN configuration*

Simplified Moves, Adds, and Changes

One of the major problems network managers have in large, routed networks is the big administrative effort required to perform moves, adds, and changes. This is particularly true of Internet protocol (IP) networks, where each physical LAN is associated with a logical subnet, as shown in Figure 16-6. If a user needs to move from one floor of a building to another, the workstation typically has to be reconfigured with a valid IP address on the new subnet.

To handle such moves, managers of legacy networks have to reconfigure routers manually. Virtual LANs, however, eliminate all of the manual address resolution and reconfiguration. Virtual LANs enable network managers to group devices logically regardless of physical location and provide dedicated bandwidth and services to each, as shown in Figure 16-7.

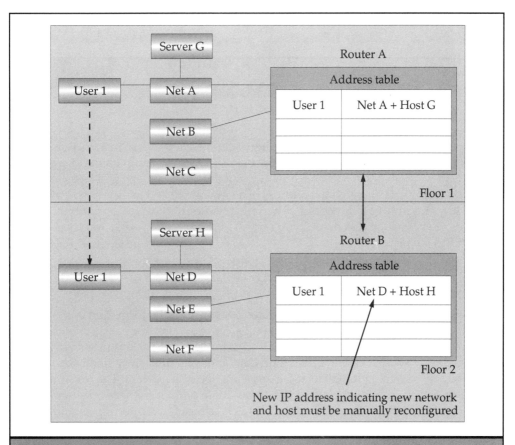

Figure 16-6.   *Affect of a physical move on Internet protocol addressing*

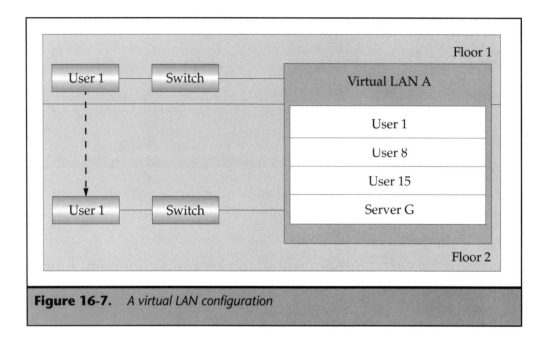

Figure 16-7. *A virtual LAN configuration*

While networks obviously require routing capability, network managers would like to avoid having to manually reconfigure network address assignments every time users move from one network segment to another. Virtual networks let them do just that by identifying the physical address of a new device and associating it with a network layer address based on prior assignment without human intervention to the system or the end station. Users can plug into any port in the network, and the virtual LAN handles the rest.

Performance

ATM switches provide high-performance data forwarding: all information is converted to the common format of 53-byte cells. Unlike routers or packet switches, which are forced to process relatively large and variable-sized packets in software, ATM or cell relay switches always deal with data units of a uniformly small size. This allows key switching functions to be implemented in hardware. The result is very fast cell processing and switching and the capability to build large networks while maintaining acceptable propagation delays. This is critical for supporting multimedia applications such as video or voice where information has time dependency and must be transmitted with consistently low latency.

Fault Tolerance

ATM is a mixed blessing in the area of fault tolerance. ATM allows redundant connections, which increases fault tolerance and consequently reliability. However, to enable a network fast enough to support multimegabit transfer rates, ATM provides no error detection and no retransmission, so let the buyer beware.

Security

As we mentioned earlier, the connection-oriented nature of ATM brings additional potential advantages with respect to security. By using explicit call setup procedures, security can be implemented on a per call basis as opposed to a per packet basis, so users don't automatically have access to other resources. The network could intelligently determine which traffic should be passed based on source and destination identities. Furthermore, user authentication that restricts users from having access to all network resources can be implemented. The connection-oriented nature of ATM also ensures that traffic is only sent to the destination for which it is intended: there is no waste of network resources with unnecessary broadcasts, nor compromise of security. This behavior eliminates the need for broadcast or protocol filters to enhance efficiency.

Security and Virtual LANs

Virtual LANs can increase security on ATM networks. Network managers can use virtual LANs to define filtering restrictions between groups of devices, providing tight security. Furthermore, ATM switches offer port-level security by allowing administrators to restrict virtual subnets to specific physical ports.

Cost of Ownership

ATM is probably the most expensive technology discussed in this book. ATM products are likely to have a higher relative cost due to cell assembly and additional services. However, not only are ATM adapters and switches expensive, they are currently proprietary. This means that training and expertise will be vendor- and product-specific. If you change vendors, therefore, your costs will also likely include hefty training and integration expenses.

The ATM and the OSI Model

ATM reaches farther up the ISO-OSI model than most transport protocols, as shown in Figures 16-8 and 16-9. Therefore, to take full advantage of ATM, as well as to integrate it into existing legacy protocol networks, applications must be developed that support the higher level implications of asynchronous transfer mode.

Application	ATM adaptation layer
Presentation	
Session	ATM adaptation layer
Transport	
Network	ATM layer
Datalink	
Physical	Physical

Figure 16-8. *The relationship among the ISO-OSI, B-ISDN, and ATM reference models*

The ATM Layer

What we have discussed up to this point are actions that take place at the ATM layer, which corresponds somewhat to the data link and network layers of the ISO-OSI model. If ATM were like other protocols, these would be the only layers affected by ATM and we could end our discussion here. However, to ensure service levels by dedicating bandwidth to stations or applications, as well as to integrate networks of other transport protocols into an ATM network, we must explore the next higher level of the ATM reference model.

The ATM Adaptation Layer (AAL)

The ATM adaptation layer (AAL) sits above the ATM layer. This layer is where ATM translates user traffic from applications into ATM format. It is at this layer that ATM

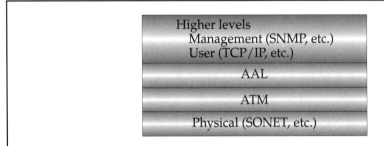

Figure 16-9. *The Broadband-Integrated Services Digital Network reference model*

provides support for connection-oriented and connectionless applications, variable bit rate applications (like X.25 and local area network traffic, respectively), and constant bit rate applications (like video and multimedia).

Actually, the AAL is composed of two sublayers, the *convergence sublayer (CS)* and the *segmentation and reassembly (SAR)*. Here's how they work.

Convergence Sublayer (CS)

The convergence sublayer permits the relaying of voice, video, and data traffic through the same switching fabric. It interprets the data coming in from the higher level application and prepares it for processing by the segmentation and reassembly sublayer. Obviously, the operations and functions performed by the convergence sublayer vary depending upon the type and format of incoming data.

The Segmentation and Reassembly Sublayer (SAR)

Before an application transmits data over an ATM network, the SAR sublayer *segments* data into 48-byte ATM data cells. Once the ATM cells reach their destination, the SAR sublayer *reassembles* them into higher level data and transmits them to the appropriate local devices.

AAL-5   Because ATM can carry multiple traffic types, several adaptation protocols, each operating simultaneously, exist at the adaptation layer. For example, local area networks often employ the AAL-5 adaptation protocol, designed specifically to handle this type of variable rate data traffic. In the AAL-5 convergence sublayer, an 8-byte field, including data length and an error-detection checksum, is appended to a frame (or block) of user information (up to 64KB in length) coming from the higher layer application. The AAL-5 frame is then separated into a stream of 48-byte data cells by the segmentation and reassembly sublayer, then sent along its way. At the receiving station, the SAR reassembles the cells into frames, and the CS processes, then removes the 8-byte Data Length and Error-Detection Checksum field. The frame is then passed to the higher level protocol.

AAL-5 is the foundation for LAN emulation, a key technology in ATM integration and migration. We will discuss LAN emulation in detail later in this chapter.

ATM Migration Issues

Installing ATM will probably require some dramatic changes in the design and equipment of your network. The concepts and rules of ATM are very different from those used in most local and wide area network protocols. For example, most LAN protocols are connectionless in nature, and therefore conflict on a very basic level with the connection-oriented ATM protocol. Another example is addressing. Because the ultimate goal of ATM is to be offered as a wide area public network, large addresses are going to be required to accommodate the millions of potential devices on a public ATM network. As a result, a scheme will have to be developed to resolve the smaller local area network addresses with the large ATM addresses. There is also a problem with standards and interoperability: ATM products from different vendors do not interoperate, and ATM LANs have only limited capability to interoperate with other LAN protocols. Connection setup and other issues stand in the way of internetworking between ATM and existing LANs. Knowing what issues to consider and what questions to ask will help ensure you make the right decisions both for the present and the future. Therefore, any integration and/or migration from legacy protocol networks to ATM's connection-oriented, dedicated, switched environment will require careful planning and execution.

Incomplete Interface Specifications

While the user-to-network interface (UNI) is a fairly well-established and stable specification, the ATM Forum must describe and standardize several other interfaces to ensure interoperability of ATM networks. The network-to-network interface for private networks, or P-NNI, is one such critical interface. The P-NNI, still unstable and largely proprietary, handles

- Virtual connection arbitration
- Congestion control
- Topology management

Without a stable P-NNI, vendors can't develop interoperable ATM equipment.

LAN Emulation

A major obstacle for the widespread acceptance of ATM in mainstream LANs is the integration of existing protocols such as Ethernet, Token Ring, and FDDI. As a point-to-point, connection-oriented protocol, ATM doesn't natively support the way legacy LAN protocols work.

The installed base of Ethernet isn't going to disappear soon. In fact, it will continue to grow for some time, particularly given its very low cost, standardization, new technology extensions such as switched Ethernet products, and huge installed base. Obviously, therefore, without providing an integration scheme for this large installed base, ATM will remain a niche technology for isolated pockets of high-end users.

NOTE: *There are approximately 40 million Ethernet nodes installed today, and about ten million new ones being shipped every year.*

LAN emulation for ATM is the migration technology that allows end stations running existing applications—even those that require features unique to the legacy protocol—to be adapted to ATM services. LAN emulation is a program that emulates conventional local area network operation. It provides a sort of bridge between legacy

LAN protocols and ATM segments. LAN emulation is tricky, because ATM is vastly different in many ways from the familiar LAN transport protocols of Ethernet and Token Ring. For example, as we mentioned, ATM is connection-oriented, while Ethernet and Token Ring are connectionless, meaning that packets go to all stations on the network and are acknowledged only by the station to which they are addressed. Also, ATM stations will have to provide support for broadcast and multicast operations that are so often used in Ethernet and Token Ring. Also, ATM uses a 20-byte addressing scheme, while Token Ring and Ethernet both use 48-bit MAC addresses. Therefore, LAN emulation has to resolve the differing MAC and ATM addresses.

What Makes LAN Emulation Tricky

There are many issues that make LAN emulation difficult to implement. Among these issues are

- Address resolution
- Broadcast and multicast support
- Speed
- Connection setup

SPEED   To provide the performance necessary for successful bridging between legacy and ATM networks, LAN emulation devices have to have full wire-speed conversion and switching.

CONNECTION SETUP   As we mentioned earlier in this chapter, ATM is a connection-oriented transport service. Legacy LAN protocols, on the other hand, are connectionless, meaning they send packets containing the full station address over the media without first establishing a connection with the receiving station. The receiving station monitors all the packets on the media and accepts those that are addressed to it. With only 5 bytes of header, an ATM cell cannot carry the full destination address for each cell. Therefore, adapting existing network layer protocols that require the full destination address to ATM's connection-oriented cell-switching is a major challenge.

One interface that has been developed to address this interoperability issue is the LAN emulation user-to-network interface (LUNI). LUNI protocols allow the ATM network and its edge devices to control the virtual connections required for transmission and to emulate the connectionless nature of a LAN.

ATM Edge-Routing Devices

An ATM *edge-routing device* is a device that converts packets from an Ethernet or Token Ring LAN to the cell structure of an ATM network and vice versa. To move traffic through the ATM network, devices at the boundary or *edge* of the network convert non-ATM traffic streams into cells. The addition of new traffic types requires only a new edge device, deployed where the demand for such traffic exists.

The ATM edge router is a radical departure from conventional routers. Conventional routers are symmetrical multiprocessor products designed to handle a balanced load of incoming and outgoing traffic. Each CPU is dedicated to one function, either route calculation and management, ATM connection setup and management, or data forwarding. Edge routers, on the other hand, are asymmetrical in design to create a switched fabric of small, modular routers that scale indefinitely by exploiting the enormous bandwidth and redundancy of a highly meshed ATM backbone.

Edge routers are also designed to overcome a problem in conventional routers: latency. The latency of the average multiprotocol router is relatively large (ranging from hundreds to thousands of microseconds). Furthermore, this latency is also unpredictable. However, edge routers are designed for deterministic latencies of 50 microseconds per device. This performance is a good match for ATM latencies, which are typically measured in tens of microseconds, which in turn are a good match for delay-sensitive data such as voice and video.

An Overview of LAN Emulation

LAN emulation is a collection of services that translate between the higher level protocols of connectionless protocol services and the lower level, connection-oriented ATM protocols, as shown in Figure 16-10.

As we mentioned earlier, the ATM adaptation layer (AAL) sits above the ATM layer. The AAL formats data into the 48-byte ATM cell payload, a process known as segmentation. Once the ATM cells reach their destination, they are reconstructed into higher level data and transmitted to the respective local devices in a process referred to as reassembly. Because ATM can carry multiple traffic types, several adaptation protocols, each operating simultaneously, exist at the adaptation layer. AAL-5 is the adaptation protocol on which LAN emulation is based.

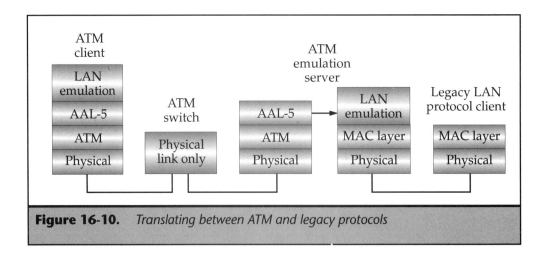

Figure 16-10. *Translating between ATM and legacy protocols*

LAN emulation sits above AAL-5 in the protocol hierarchy. In the ATM-to-LAN converter at the network edge, LAN emulation solves data networking problems for all protocols—routable and nonroutable—by resolving LAN and ATM addresses at the MAC layer. LAN emulation is completely independent of upper layer protocols, services, and applications.

Because LAN emulation occurs in edge devices and end systems, it is entirely transparent to the ATM network and to Ethernet and Token Ring host devices.

How LAN Emulation Works

Figure 16-11 shows how LAN emulation works in a legacy LAN. Low-end PCs in an Ethernet environment access high-end servers with native ATM interfaces through a LAN/ATM switch. Because LAN emulation makes ATM look like a classical LAN, standard bridging techniques allow the LAN/ATM switch to provide protocol-independent connectivity. No change is required in the legacy PCs, yet they experience improved performance because of the high input/output capacity of the server, made possible through the high-speed ATM interface. In addition, they benefit from the dedicated bandwidth provided by the switched LAN implementation.

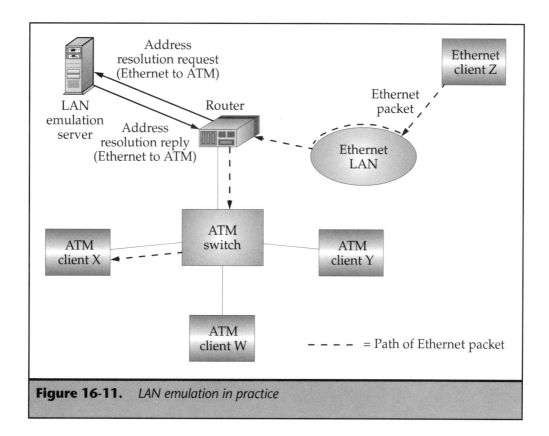

Figure 16-11. *LAN emulation in practice*

Multiple Emulated LANs

The ATM Forum LAN emulation standard also supports the implementation of multiple emulated LANs within a single ATM network. LAN emulation is implemented through a client-server model. It works like this: a LAN emulation client, such as workstation software, resolves MAC addresses into ATM addresses. Each client connects to the server by a virtual connection. Only those clients connected to the same server can learn about each other and communicate directly. Logically segmenting the network across multiple server functions—which can be standalone devices, software in end systems, or ATM switch modules—allows multiple emulated LANs to exist simultaneously on the same physical network.

Figure 16-12 shows the physical and logical view of multiple emulated LANs. In the physical view, the router runs two LAN emulation clients—A2 for the accounting department and M2 for the manufacturing department. Each departmental server keeps track of its clients through a resident database. When accounting user A1 sends a packet to manufacturing user M1, the accounting server checks its database for a match. Finding none, it maps the MAC address to the router (A2/M2), which then forwards the packet to the manufacturing department server for delivery to M1.

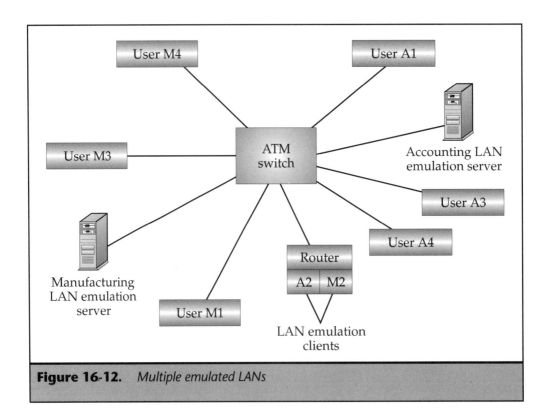

Figure 16-12.   *Multiple emulated LANs*

The logical view looks like the physical layout of today's LANs and is consistent with the goal of LAN emulation. Departmental clients communicate directly with each other, directly with servers, and indirectly with other departments through a network router.

LAN Emulation and Switched Virtual LANs

There are now products available, such as 3Com's Transcend suite of network management applications, that allow network managers to define multiple emulated LANs. When several different emulated local area networks communicate through one or more switches on an ATM network, the result is a *switched virtual LAN*, as shown in Figure 16-13. Managing virtual LANs can be difficult because managing physical connectivity isn't enough. You will have to be able to monitor and manage the logical interconnection across the LAN. With switched virtual LANs, routing is no longer a physical bottleneck, but a logical processing function that can be handled efficiently by the ATM switches.

Virtual switched emulated LANs offer the same benefits as garden variety virtual LANs:

- Simplified moves, adds, and changes
- Secure workgroups
- Firewalls against broadcast storms
- Flow control to better utilize network bandwidth

It offers all of these benefits without requiring the purchase of new equipment or the recabling of network segments. Network administrators can manage segments just by redefining groups in the network management system and/or reconfiguring software in the end device and/or ATM switch.

Routing Issues

Although ATM LAN emulation greatly simplifies the creation of virtual workgroups, it doesn't change the role of routers on virtual LANs. Routers are still required to manage broadcasts and address resolution, as shown in Figure 16-14. As the network scales to higher speed backbone links, the router must process traffic from these links at wire-speeds in order to avoid creating a bottleneck.

ATM and Conventional Routers

Even though some high-end routers now have ATM interfaces designed to forward packets at ATM speeds of 155Mbps, conventional routers just aren't designed to take full advantage of ATM's performance capabilities. Today's routers are optimized for a balanced load of incoming and outgoing traffic across a number of interfaces, unlike the ATM edge routers that we described earlier.

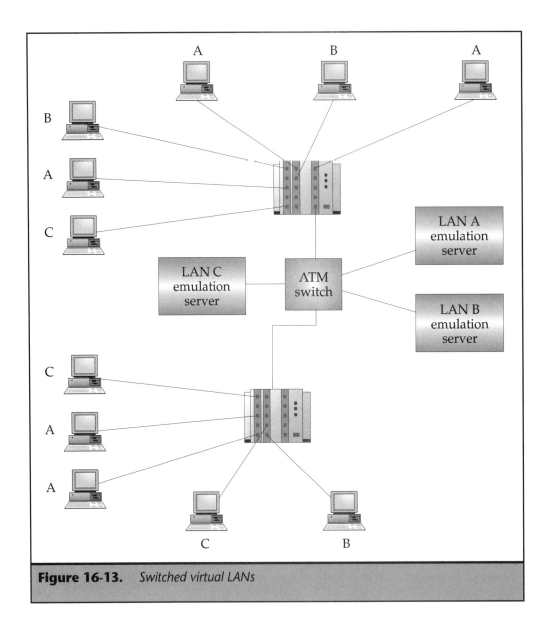

Figure 16-13. *Switched virtual LANs*

A scalable ATM LAN architecture uses all of the functions of a router in a distributed manner. This enables the routing function to scale economically with the ATM network. A distributed router architecture separates the packet-forwarding functions from the routing functions. Routing functions are processor-intensive, but are performed on a relatively infrequent basis. Packet-forwarding functions, on the other hand,

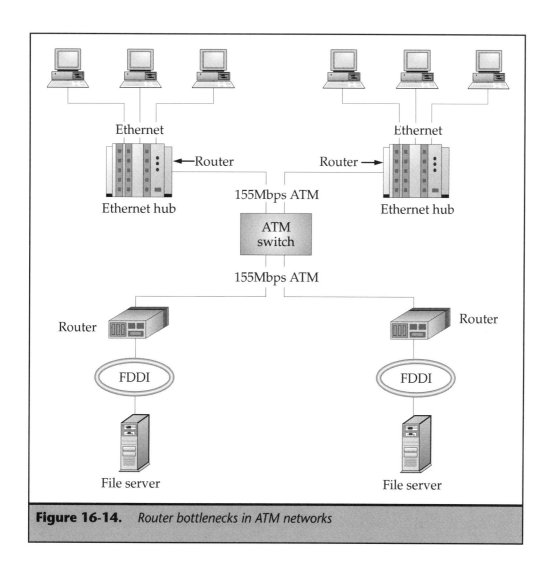

Figure 16-14.   *Router bottlenecks in ATM networks*

require little processing, but high performance. In a distributed router, the packet-forwarding functions are performed by network access devices, as shown in Figure 16-15.

ATM switches are designed to perform many of the functions routers perform—to select an optimal network path, provide an efficient LAN and WAN interface, and provide internal security, flow control, and bandwidth management. As a result, routers are evolving into edge devices with the principal function of connecting multiple LANs to the ATM switch.

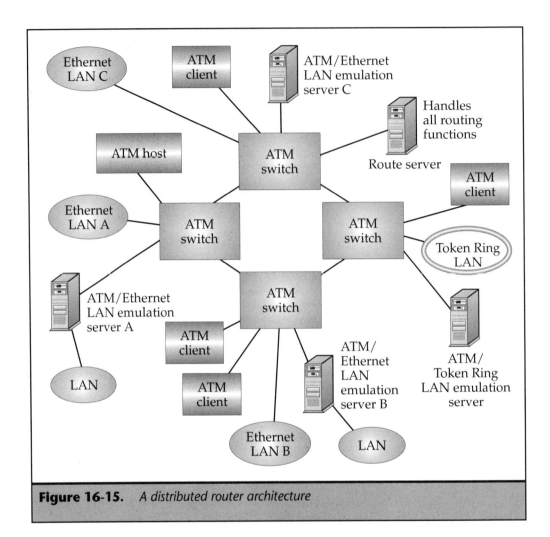

Figure 16-15.   *A distributed router architecture*

The easiest way for a router to use ATM is to use PVCs through the switched fabric. But this negates two of ATM's greatest strengths: dynamic connection and bandwidth allocation.

ATM Virtual Routers

Although edge routers are the router of choice among ATM vendors these days, much of the industry is buzzing with talk of a new kind of ATM router called a *virtual router*. A virtual router works very differently from an edge router. It combines a central *route server* and a number of *multilayer switches*—hardware-based devices that are nearly as fast as a conventional switch that work on the MAC layer, but much smarter—that link existing LANs. The thinking behind this virtual architecture recognizes that conventional routers are a bottleneck because, as we mentioned earlier, they calculate routes on a packet-by-packet basis. In a virtual router, on the other hand, LAN interconnection is achieved by the multilayer switch.

The multilayer switch forwards on the basis of MAC or network layer packet fields. But it doesn't handle the route discovery and topology updates. These functions are managed by the route server. Each port on the multilayer switch can be assigned its own subnet address, just as with a conventional router. As well, just as with an edge router, multiple ports can share the same subnet address. The route server runs the routing protocols and maintains a picture of the ATM and internetwork topologies. The route server can even act as a broadcast server and resolve address queries. As far as the end stations are concerned, the virtual router performs all the functions of a physical router: protocol processing, bridging, routing, and filtering.

Incomplete Product Lines

Incomplete product lines is probably the biggest, scariest problem associated with migrating to an ATM network. Many vendors have an ATM product line, but very few vendors offer everything from network adapters to backbone switches. Currently, few vendors can offer you a complete end-to-end working ATM network today, so you'll have to mix and match products from different vendors. Given the proprietary nature of ATM and the resulting lack of compatibility among ATM products, this makes interoperability essentially impossible. The lack of a solid, well-planned blueprint for an ATM architecture from any vendor is a major obstacle.

Training Holes

Many vendors' ATM strategies are highly complex and require users to be experts in the product lines of multiple vendors. Because these products are proprietary, however, training in one vendor's ATM switch or LAN emulation technology doesn't guarantee any knowledge applicable to another vendor's ATM products. Furthermore, the ATM Forum is still in the process of developing many of the specifications necessary to implement interoperable ATM networks, so solid training on these interfaces is not available because the information simply isn't available.

Expect to Phase it In

ATM is currently a very costly technology, so widespread deployment throughout your network is probably prohibitively expensive. As well, most of your segments don't require its 155Mbps to 622Mbps bandwidth. Therefore, migration to a switched network should be considered a process, a series of evolutionary steps as new technologies are phased in. So, plan to implement it in phases: first the backbones (especially campus backbones), video-intensive segments, and even trunked voice traffic from the PBX switches.

A transition to ATM will require consideration of the protocol suites at both specific sites and the overall enterprise. In some cases, ATM will initially be limited to a few directly connected workstations, while the rest take advantage of ATM in the backbone, enabling high-speed access to shared resources such as servers. This means that legacy network access to ATM will be important.

An incremental approach to ATM migration combines the best of the various technologies by enhancing existing network investments in three ways:

■ ATM deployment extends the life of the installed base of network equipment by boosting performance.

■ Combined with such capabilities as LAN emulation, ATM enhances network management and operations by allowing virtual network configurations.

■ Incremental upgrades keep investment and technical risks low while ATM technology matures.

Figures 16-16 through 16-18 show one way to phase in ATM. It begins with implementing an ATM backbone.

Next, the network plan progresses to add ATM workgroup segments, employing LAN emulation to enable all network users to communicate with one another.

Finally, a collapsed router backbone—a single, high-performance router connects multiple segments into a logical network.

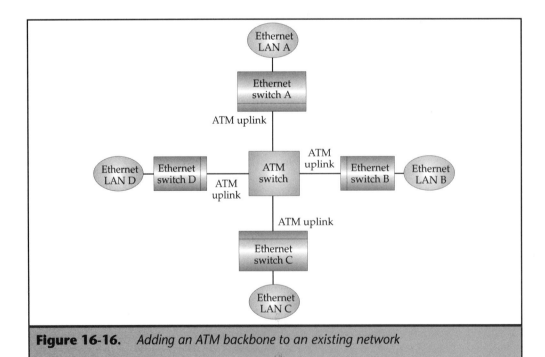

Figure 16-16. *Adding an ATM backbone to an existing network*

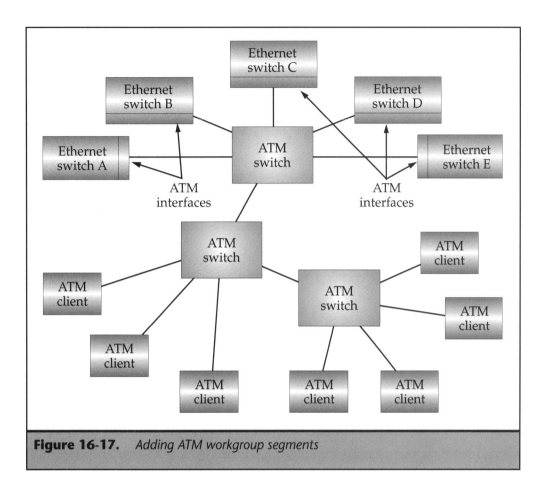

Figure 16-17. *Adding ATM workgroup segments*

Desktop Migration Issues

Although ATM is usually considered primarily a backbone solution, most ATM networks are currently workgroups in which workstations and servers are connected directly to an ATM switch. Though ATM workgroups are usually small in size and centralized geographically, thus simplifying implementation, there are still several issues to consider.

Media Support

Review your existing network infrastructure. Most ATM products currently run over multimode fiber and unshielded twisted-pair Category 5 copper at rates ranging from 25Mbps to 155Mbps. Due to the attenuation characteristics of copper, the maximum distance for Category 5 cable runs is typically 100 meters. Multimode fiber, on the other hand, has a maximum cable length of 2,000 meters. Be sure your cable plan meets these requirements.

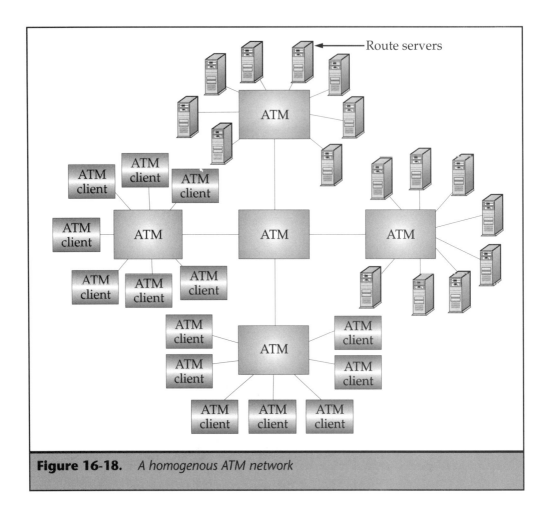

Figure 16-18. *A homogenous ATM network*

Application Support

Can your existing applications run over an ATM network? Because ATM is a lower
level protocol, this is usually not a problem. Most commonly, these applications are
TCP/IP-based or based on PCs, Novell NetWare, or Microsoft Windows. However, are
the applications you plan to use optimized to take advantage of ATM's dedicated
bandwidth and data prioritization capabilities? To get the full benefit of ATM,
whenever possible, choose applications that support these features.

Computer Compatibility

In an ATM workgroup, each workstation must have an ATM network interface card.
The NIC must be compatible with the bus type of the workstation, as well as with both
the workstation and network operating systems. It is important that the NIC has been
tested with both the type of workstation and the type of ATM switches you are using.

WAN Integration Issues

Although you can often integrate ATM into wide area networks without *replacing* any equipment, you *will* need some additional equipment, a thorough knowledge of applicable ATM interfaces, and a lot of careful planning.

There are four primary protocols required for successful internetworking over the wide area. They are

- Public user-to-network interface (UNI)
- Public network-to-network interface (NNI)
- Intercarrier interface (ICI)
- Data exchange interface (DXI)

Public User-to-Network Interface (UNI)

As we discussed earlier, ATM's UNI protocol provides multiple service classes and bandwidth reservation established during call setup of a switched virtual connection. The UNI defines the interoperability between the user equipment and the ATM switch port. A public UNI defines the interface between a public service ATM network, and usually supports a SONET or DS3 interface. It is the link between the ATM user and the ATM switch on the public ATM carrier's network.

Public Network-to-Network Interface (NNI)

As we also mentioned earlier, the NNI protocol provides virtual connection arbitration, congestion control, and topology management for private or public ATM network connections. It is the link between ATM switches within a public ATM carrier service.

Intercarrier Interface (ICI)

The ICI defines internetworking mechanisms on wide area ATM networks. It lets you link between two ATM carriers' nets.

Data Exchange Interface (DXI)

The DXI provides a standard ATM interface for legacy equipment. The DXI supports routing over ATM because it is based on packets rather than cells. It uses standard high-level data link control (HDLC) framing, so unlike cell-based interfaces, it needs no additional hardware to transmit packet-based traffic. Therefore, it is the protocol that allows you to connect existing equipment to an ATM network.

To illustrate how each of these interfaces will affect the implementation of an ATM network, look at the network in Figure 16-19. This shows how a wide area ATM backbone might be integrated into an existing FDDI and 10Base-T network.

FDDI has an aggregate backbone bandwidth of 100Mbps, shared by all attached devices. The wide area ATM switch in this illustration has eight ports, each 155Mbps.

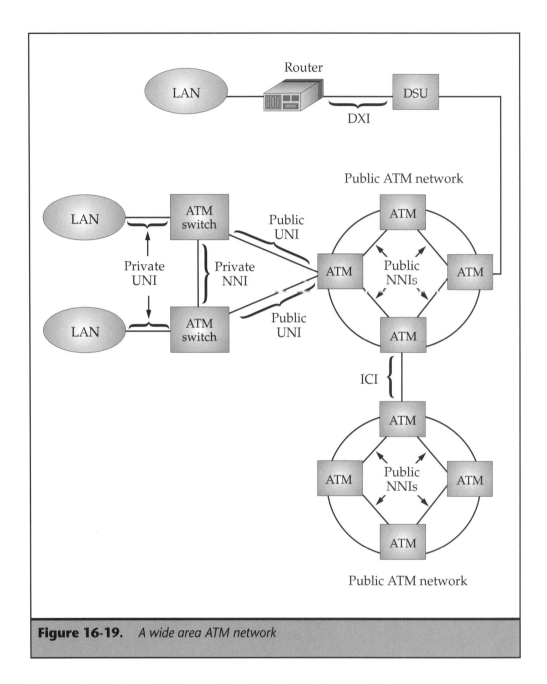

Figure 16-19. *A wide area ATM network*

Because those 155Mbps are dedicated to each attached device, the aggregate bandwidth is 8 multiplied by 155Mbps, or approximately 1.2Gbps.

NOTE: The actual aggregate bandwidth of this example will fall somewhere between 155Mbps and 1.2Gbps, depending on the traffic patterns and usage.

An ATM UNI was installed in both the FDDI router and the 10Base-T switch so both devices could be connected to the ATM switch. The WAN connection to the ATM switch is through a data exchange interface (DXI) to a service multiplexer, typically a special CSU/DSU. Thanks to its DXI, in addition to multiplexing traffic onto the wide area link, the service multiplexer performs AAL segmentation and reassembly, allowing non-ATM-capable devices to access the ATM network replacing hardware.

Other Issues to Consider

Implementing a backbone with ATM involves many of the same issues and concerns as with any other protocol. Some of these are

- Security
- Fault tolerance
- Bandwidth requirements
- Management systems

Availability of ATM Carrier Services

One of the big challenges you may face when implementing a wide area ATM network is finding a carrier service that both offers ATM and is reasonably priced. Although most digital service providers offer ATM, it isn't widely available yet because of lack of strong, widespread demand. Contracts may be available from service providers to ensure both availability and pricing, but obtaining one may require some persistence and negotiating skill.

Common carrier service providers acknowledge that ATM is definitely the future of wide area network communication. They understand that it erases the barriers between LANs and WANs, which are

- The drop in throughput between local area network protocols and public networks protocols, and
- Delays caused by store-and-forward WAN connection devices like routers.

However, not all local exchange carriers (LECs) and interexchange carriers (IXCs) have installed integrated ATM/SONET digital networks to offer economical virtual private data network services. When they do, you can assume they will pass the heavy expense of installing these new networks on to the consumer. The good news is that ATM carries more traffic at reduced cost, which will *eventually* result in savings for the consumer. But that may be quite far off in the future, so be prepared for large ATM carrier service expenses for the wide area.

ATM and Voice

Although proponents of ATM point to the fact that it is suitable for carrying voice traffic, very little progress has been made in developing ATM technology for voice. Currently ATM doesn't have an ATM adaptation layer protocol that is optimized for handling voice traffic. The AAL protocols that exist handle voice traffic very inefficiently, so inefficiently, in fact, that standard time division multiplexing T1/T3 networks can often carry much more voice connections than ATM T1/T3 networks. Therefore, unless an expensive SONET upgrade is in your budget (and once you have SONET, conventional voice interfaces provide so much bandwidth you probably won't need to consider ATM), it's best to hold off on implementing ATM for voice.

The Promised LAN

Overall, ATM holds excellent promise for nearly every network. It provides performance and functions never before available for:

- Electronic funds transfer
- Voice annotation of memos
- Interactive training videos
- Design and manufacturing development in which collaborative efforts involve complex data objects residing on a variety of different, geographically dispersed processors

ATM probably *is* the future of transport protocols and networking in general. However, *the future is not now*. As we mentioned earlier, many vendors have been quick to announce plans for ATM products and systems, but as of this writing, there simply aren't any end-to-end open, viable, interoperable ATM systems available.

Recommended for:

- Multimedia and video applications because of its ability to dedicate allocated bandwidth to applications and its data prioritization capability
- Backbones because of its scalability, high performance, and security
- Wide area networks because of its seamless, high-performance integration of WANs and LANs
- Widely dispersed networks because of its lack of distance limitations

Not Recommended for:

- Small networks, because of its high cost
- Networks that must retain an installed base of different legacy network protocols, due to ATM's current lack of standard interfaces for integrating various protocols

Strengths:

- High performance
- Scalability
- Dedicated bandwidth
- Potential for universal deployment
- Security

Weaknesses:

- Interoperability (currently)
- High cost
- Moderate fault tolerance

PART FOUR

Caution: Network Construction Ahead

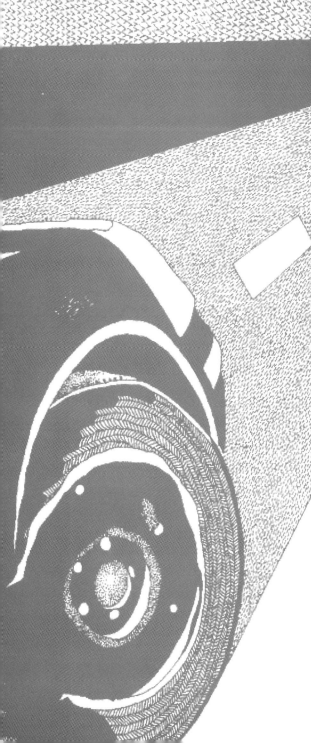

CHAPTER 17

Alternatives to High-Speed Networking

Now that you've had a chance to evaluate the available high-speed networking options, you may be wondering whether you're ready for all that. After all, many of the options are either nearly outdated or not yet quite ready for prime time. So you may be asking yourself whether there might be some way to make your current networking protocol last another year until some of the high-speed protocols mature a bit, and hopefully the market shakes out. Or maybe your network isn't quite ready for some of these big-muscle (and often big-money) protocols, but it still needs a boost.

Well, you don't just have to wait and/or make do with what you have. There are several strategies you may be able to use instead of, and also in combination with, a high-speed network. These are, in order of cost/complexity:

- Network segmentation
- Switching
- Virtual LANs

Network Segmentation

Network segmentation is a relatively easy, quick, and inexpensive means of reducing network congestion. Most network managers know a lot about segmentation. However, you may not have exploited it fully. To make sure that you have left no network segmentation stone unturned, let's start at the beginning and work our way through exactly what network segmentation is and how it can be implemented.

A Segment Defined

The definition of a *network segment*, or *subnetwork*, varies from network to network and protocol to protocol. In classic Ethernet networks, a segment is a cable that is terminated at both ends. In the 10Base-T realm, a segment is a hub or stack of hubs. In a Token Ring environment, a segment is one or more multistation access units (MAUs). The features that all of these configurations, shown in Figure 17-1, have in common is that:

- They all have the same network address.
- They all share the same type of network protocol.
- All the stations connected to them "see" all traffic addressed to all the other connected stations.

This last feature means they must share access to the network with all other stations on the segment, either by waiting their turn (in Token Ring and other deterministic protocols) or by contending with all the other stations on the segment for access (in 10Base-T and similar contention-based protocols).

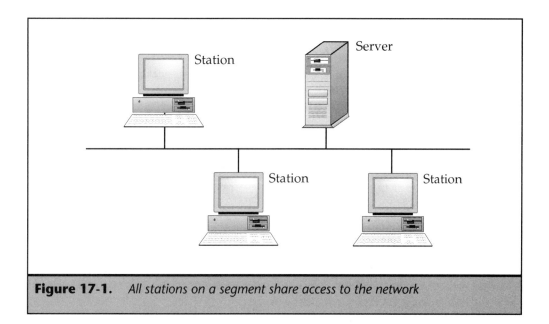

Figure 17-1. *All stations on a segment share access to the network*

Whether you are using a deterministic protocol or a contention-based protocol, the more stations on the segment, the slower the response time. After all, network bandwidth is a finite resource, and the more stations that have to share it, the smaller the bandwidth available to each. One way to improve network performance, therefore, is to reduce the number of stations sharing the bandwidth—in other words, decrease the number of stations on a segment. This is called *network segmentation*.

Creating Internetworks

Clearly, you can't lower the number of stations on a segment simply by disconnecting them (okay, you *could*, but you'd better have your résumé ready). Therefore, the only way to limit the number of stations on each segment is to create more segments. A group of segments that can communicate with one another is known as an *internetwork*. There are three ways to do this:

- Internal bridging
- External bridging
- Routing

Internal Bridging

Internal bridging is a technique in which a server provides bridging between two or more network adapters installed in the server that is running an operating system that supports bridging, such as Novell NetWare or Banyan VINES. In an internal bridging configuration, the server provides all the bridging functionality. While this makes it easy and fairly inexpensive to implement, it also drains server resources that might be better utilized on critical processing tasks.

Internal bridging is a function that takes place in the MAC sublayer of the data link layer in the OSI reference model, as shown in Figure 17-2. We will discuss this functionality in more detail later in this chapter.

External Bridging

Like internal bridging, *external bridging* is also a MAC sublayer function. It occurs when the bridging function is moved away from the server and is handled by another device. This device may be a PC running bridge software or a specialized bridge.

Routing

Routing is a function that takes place at the network layer of the OSI model, as shown in Figure 17-3. Because routers have access to higher level information that bridges don't, they have more intelligence and can make decisions about when, where, and how data packets are to be routed through the network. This ultimately results in more reliable packet delivery.

In case you'd like a refresher course in bridging and routing—just to make sure you've done everything with them you can to relieve your network's congestion—I've included a primer on each of them.

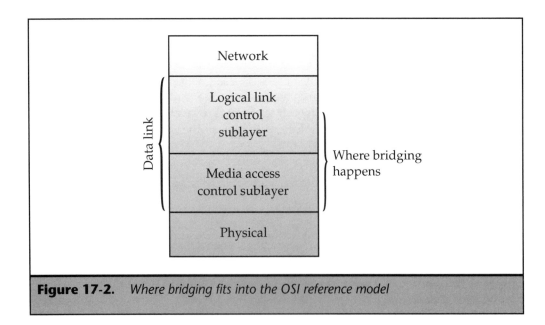

Figure 17-2. *Where bridging fits into the OSI reference model*

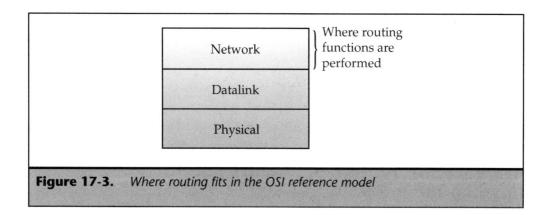

Figure 17-3.   *Where routing fits in the OSI reference model*

The Bridging Primer

A *bridge* is an internetworking device that provides a way for a station on one network segment to send packets to stations on another segment. Bridging takes place at the data link layer (DLL) of the OSI reference model, as shown in Figure 17-2. The DLL is divided into two sublayers: the *logical link control* (LLC) sublayer and the *media access control* (MAC) sublayer. Devices that support the IEEE 802 specification have a standard MAC sublayer that can receive data packets from multiple network transport protocols. Upon receiving a data packet, the MAC sublayer passes the data to the LLC sublayer, translates it to the destination segment's transport protocol, then places it on the destination segment. This process is illustrated in Figure 17-4.

Bridges serve many functions in an internetwork besides creating multiple segments to reduce congestion. Bridges can extend network span by acting as repeaters, regenerating the transmission signal. However, bridges can also perform many functions that repeaters can't. Some of these functions are

■   Joining segments using different network protocols, like 10Base-T and Token Ring. A bridge examines the addresses of packets and places them on the

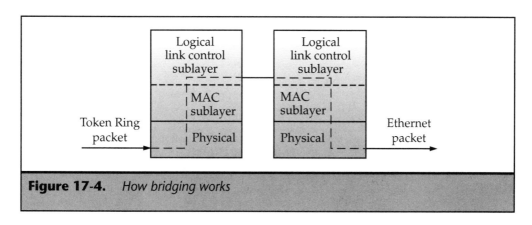

Figure 17-4.   *How bridging works*

network segments where the addressee station or stations are located. Because bridging takes place in the DLL, any device that conforms to the MAC specifications of the IEEE 802 standard—such as 10Base-T and Token Ring—can bridge to other IEEE MAC devices.

■ *Filtering* packets rather than simply forwarding all of them. Without filtering, packets are sent everywhere on a network. When a packet arrives at a bridge, the bridge reads the destination address in the packets and determines whether it should forward the packet across the bridge. Bridges filter packets by reading the MAC layer address in the Ethernet or Token Ring frame, as shown in Figure 17-5, to determine on which segment the receiving station is located. They forward packets only to the segment or segments of the addressee stations.

■ Resolving endless loops. Some bridged networks may inadvertently contain loops that could cause a packet to travel continuously, never reaching its destination address and being taken off the network. There are bridges that will detect such looping packets and remove them. This is done using the IEEE 802.1d spanning tree protocol, which will be discussed later in this chapter.

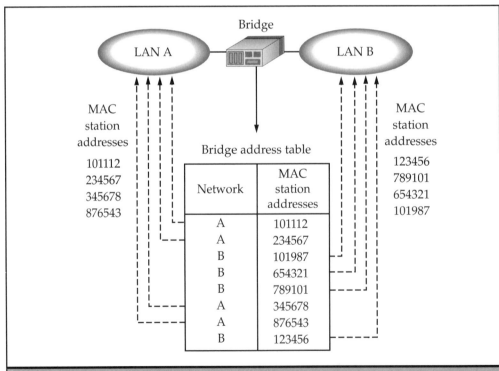

Figure 17-5. *A bridge filters packets on the basis of the MAC address*

- Learning the network and building address tables. This can be accomplished through *source routing* or *transparent bridging*, which are discussed later in this chapter.

- Providing fault tolerance in the form of redundant paths for data packets to reach their destinations.

Bridges Near and Far

Bridges can be either *local* or *remote*. A *local bridge* connects local area networks, which are by definition located within the same geographic area, as shown in Figure 17-6. *Remote bridges*, on the other hand, connect networks that are separated by greater distances. Therefore, remote bridges have interfaces to connect to wide area data carrier services such as ISDN or T1, as shown in Figure 17-7.

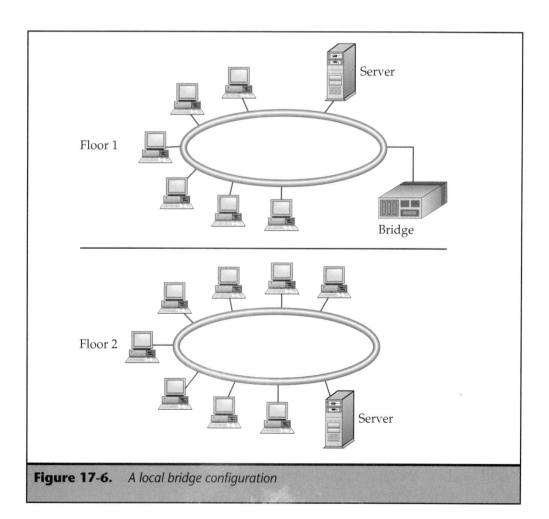

Figure 17-6. *A local bridge configuration*

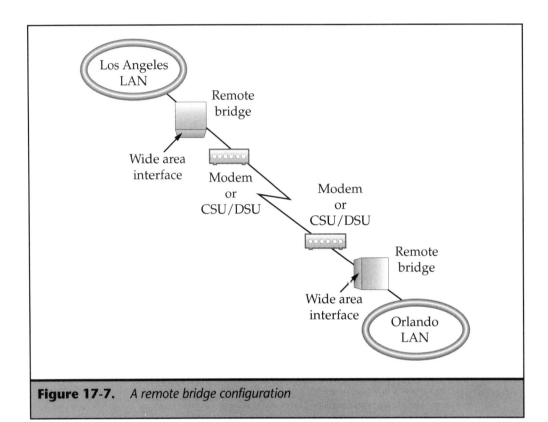

Figure 17-7. *A remote bridge configuration*

Net Learning

When bridges were first introduced, network managers had to configure them manually, typing in the addresses of every segment and station. Every time a station was added or dropped, the network manager had to edit the address table of all the bridges on the network to add or remove the station. As I mentioned earlier, however, bridges can now automatically learn the addresses of every station on the network. By doing this, they can filter traffic that isn't addressed to their segment and thus reduce network congestion. There are two methods a bridge device can use to learn its network: *transparent bridging* and *source routing*.

Looking Through a Transparent Bridge

Transparent bridging is a technique used on IEEE 802.3 (aka 10Base-T) networks. Transparent bridges start learning the network topology as soon as they are connected to the network. When a packet enters a port on a transparent bridge, the bridge notes the address of the network from which it received the packet, then examines the packet's source address and adds that address to a list of addresses of packets that the bridge has received from that network address. The bridge thus builds a table of source addresses located at each network address. As new stations are added or dropped from the network, the bridge updates this address table. The bridge's address table is held in the bridge's memory, and its size is limited by the amount of memory the bridge has allocated to table maintenance. Therefore, when a bridge hasn't received a packet from a particular address for some predefined amount of time, it clears that address from its address table to make room for new, more active source addresses. An example of such a table is shown in Figure 17-8.

The bridge uses its table of addresses to determine whether to forward arriving packets onto another ring or send them on to the next device on the same network. It does this by examining the destination address of an arriving packet, then locating that address in the bridge's address table. If the packet is destined for a network segment attached to the bridge, the bridge channels the packet to that segment. If not, the bridge retransmits the packet to the next bridge on the ring. If a packet arrives with a destination address that isn't in the bridge's address table, the bridge tries to "discover" the unknown address. It sends a special frame to all network segments except the packet's source network. This frame contains a request for the destination address device to respond. If and when the destination responds, the bridge updates its address table with the new address. Through this process, the bridge eventually locates and learns the address of every station on the network.

Obviously, the larger the network, the longer it will take the bridge to learn it—and the more memory the bridge will need to maintain the address table. Therefore, if you are experiencing poor performance on a bridged network, you may want to check to make sure that the bridge has sufficient memory to hold all the addresses. If it doesn't, it will be constantly discovering, recording, and deleting addresses to make use of its limited memory, and it will therefore take more time to forward a packet than if the packet's address were readily at hand in the address table.

Network	MAC station addresses
A	101112
A	234567
B	101987
B	654321
B	789101
A	345678

Figure 17-8. *Bridge address table*

The Catch: Fault Tolerance and Endless Loops

As I mentioned, one of the things that bridges can do that repeaters can't is provide multiple paths for packets. This adds to the fault tolerance of networks, because if a segment of cable is cut or a bridge is down, these redundant paths offer an alternate route between the source station and the destination station, as shown in Figure 17-9.

However, this added fault tolerance is not without its price. On large interconnected networks, multiple bridge paths may form an endless loop, causing packets to circulate through the network never reaching their destination, as shown in Figure 17-10. Not only do these circulating packets take up precious bandwidth, but the packets retransmitted to replace these "lost" packets add to the congestion, ultimately reducing performance and even causing the network to collapse altogether.

SPANNING TREE TO THE RESCUE   The spanning tree protocol, developed by the IEEE 801 committee, solves the problem of endless loops created by multiple paths. It "tricks" the bridge into not seeing the redundant paths unless and until the primary path is not available. The spanning tree protocol is a set of procedures implemented in firmware in the bridge itself. It works like this: The spanning tree protocol gives each bridge a unique address—usually the MAC address of the bridge. Then the algorithm assigns a unique address to each port on each bridge, as shown in Figure 17-11.

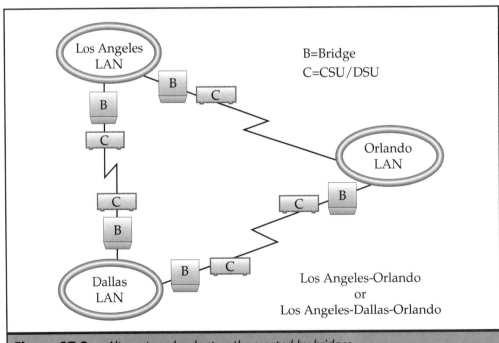

Figure 17-9.   *Alternate redundant paths created by bridges*

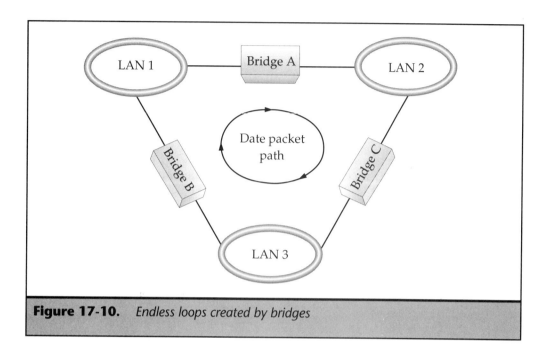

Figure 17-10. *Endless loops created by bridges*

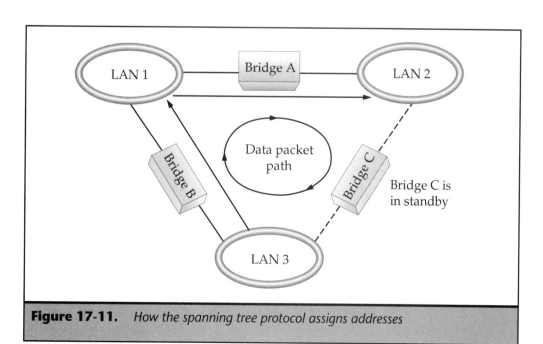

Figure 17-11. *How the spanning tree protocol assigns addresses*

Next, the spanning tree protocol calculates a "cost" for each port on each bridge. These costs are based on distance, cost of any carrier service to which they are attached, preferred path, and other factors that the network manager determines. Some bridging software will automatically calculate a port cost based on vendor-defined criteria, allowing the network manager to change cost values as necessary. Other bridges require that the network manager manually enter all path cost information.

The next procedure for the spanning tree protocol is the selection of a root bridge. The algorithm designates the bridge with the lowest address as the root bridge. Then, all other bridges calculate the cost of a path from each of their ports to the root bridge. The port with the least path cost to the root bridge is designated as the root port of the bridge.

 NOTE: *If more than one port on a bridge has the least cost path to the root bridge, the port that has the fewest bridge-to-bridge hops is designated as the root port.*

Finally, the spanning tree protocol determines which paths will be the primary paths through the network to each destination contained in the bridge's address tables. All alternate paths are then put on *standby*, or temporarily disabled. Should a primary path become unavailable, the spanning tree protocol will enable a standby path for the data being transmitted.

Source Route Bridging

Source route bridging is a routing technique used by Token Ring networks. Source routing is very different from transparent bridging because in source route bridging, the network adapter—as well as the bridge—maintains the address tables. The network adapter discovers all paths from the source station to the destination station using much the same means as a transparent bridge does. Furthermore, the network adapter is the device that makes the path decision. The bridge merely forwards the packet based on the routing information the network adapter has placed in the packet. Therefore, a bridge that supports source routing doesn't have to make route decisions for the packets it receives—the packets come with their routing information contained in them.

Source routing bridges build and maintain address tables just like transparent bridges. However, they don't have to determine the path the packet will take, because that path has already been decided by the network adapter. Source routing bridges use their address tables to locate the device to which they should forward the packet. Therefore, source routing bridges don't have problems with endless loops, so building multiple redundant paths with source routing bridges doesn't require a procedure like the spanning tree protocol.

Bridge Performance Issues

Segmenting your network with bridges isn't an automatic guarantee that your network's performance will improve. In fact, if the bridge you've selected isn't equal to the task, it might even slow things further. Therefore, it's important to evaluate the performance and features of the bridge itself before installing it. Here are the key criteria affecting bridge performance.

Forwarding Rate

Forwarding rate is the rate at which the bridge can transmit traffic from one port to another, expressed in packets per second. 10Base-T, for example, transmits a 64-byte packet at a maximum rate of 14,880 packets per second (pps). This rate is known as *wire speed*.

Memory

As we mentioned earlier, a bridge with insufficient memory will only be able to maintain small address tables. If your network is small as well, this might not be a problem. However, large networks require that bridges maintain large address tables. A bridge without enough memory to maintain a large address table will spend much of its processing power updating its address table with the addresses of the most recently transmitted packets. This can decrease your network's performance far more than the segmentation will increase it.

High-Speed Links

Sometimes a combination of segmentation and high-speed networking is what you need to speed up slow spots in your network, such as a backbone or server farm. Therefore, consider purchasing a bridge that has high-speed networking ports as well as 10Base-T or Token Ring ports. This way you can implement a high-speed segment, then segment other portions of the legacy network.

The Router Primer

Routers, like bridges, provide a way for a station on one network segment to send packets to a station on another network segment. However, whereas bridges function at the DLL of the OSI reference model, routers function at a higher level, as shown in Figure 17-12.

Because routers function at the higher network layer, they have access to information contained in this layer about congested or collapsed network segments. As a result, routers can reroute packets around such failed segments and thus provide better network management, better fault tolerance, and more reliable packet delivery than bridges. Furthermore, routers can automatically route packets over specific paths selected on the basis of distance, cost, or traffic congestion. There are also special routers, called *multiprotocol routers*, that can join networks of many different communications protocols.

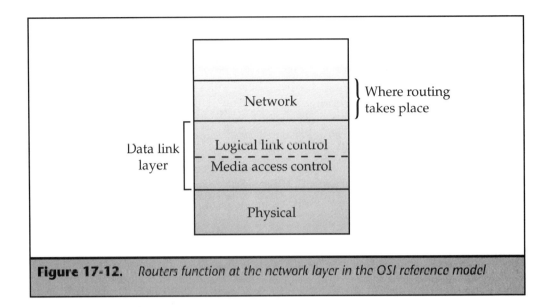

Figure 17-12. *Routers function at the network layer in the OSI reference model*

How Routers Work

Like a bridge, a router examines address information in a packet and sends the packet along a predefined route to its destination. Also like bridges, routers maintain address tables containing the location of other devices on the network. When a router receives a packet, it looks at these tables to see if it can send the packet directly to the destination. If not, it finds the closest router that can forward the packet to its destination and forwards the packet to this router.

And further, like a bridge, a router doesn't have to be an external device. Some network operating systems such as Banyan VINES and Novell NetWare perform routing functions in the server. Just as with a bridge, you implement this by installing two or more network interface cards in the server, and the operating system handles the rest. However, again as in bridging, routing tasks can slow down a server, so many network managers install external routers to free the server's processors for file service functions.

MULTIPROTOCOL ROUTERS   A *multiprotocol router* can route multiple different protocols, such as TCP/IP, IPX, AppleTalk, DECnet, and others. If your network contains platforms running a variety of protocols, be sure to select a router that supports them all. A multiprotocol router has software that processes packets from each of the supported protocols.

Router Functions

As I've pointed out, the functions of a router seem, on the surface at least, very similar to the functions of a bridge. When a router receives a packet, it first error-checks the packet using a checksum value contained within the packet. The router then opens the packet and examines it to determine where the packet should be sent. It does this by examining the network layer protocol information that includes the destination address, and for some source-routing communications protocols, a predetermined path for the packet to take. If the packet's destination address is on the same network as the router, the router forwards the packet. If the destination address is not on the same network, the router locates the next router to which the packet should be delivered and sends the packet on to that router. Unlike a bridge, however, a router discards packets if it doesn't know or can't find the destination of a packet in its routing table. The router may also return an error message to the packet's source address. A router also discards packets that have exceeded the allowed number of router hops for its protocol type, assuming that the packet is in a loop. This is just the first of several differences that sometimes make routers a better choice for segmentation than bridges.

What Makes It Different Is What Makes It Special

Because routing takes place at the network layer, routers employ protocols that are capable not only of creating redundant data paths, but also of managing them for the greatest efficiency of data delivery. Routing protocols select data paths based on cost, speed, distance, or network manager preference. These protocols can also reroute data paths around failed and congested network links. They can also prioritize traffic, making sure that high-priority packets go over the fastest network paths, for example, while low-priority packets are sent over the least costly packets. As the network manager, you can define high-priority and low-priority data paths, or even let the router define these for you based on your criteria.

An example of a wide area routed network is shown in Figure 17-13. If Houston wants to send a message to New York, the router can use either the 56Kbps direct-connect line or the T1 lines that connect through Chicago and Philadelphia. The router can determine the path based on the following:

- Packet priority
- Speed
- Cost
- Hop count

If these are high-priority packets, then the router must determine the fastest route, which in turn will depend upon the amount of traffic already on each of these two routes. If cost is the criteria for route selection, then the router will probably choose the 56Kbps line. On the other hand, if hop count is the criteria, the direct 56Kbps line will be the best path.

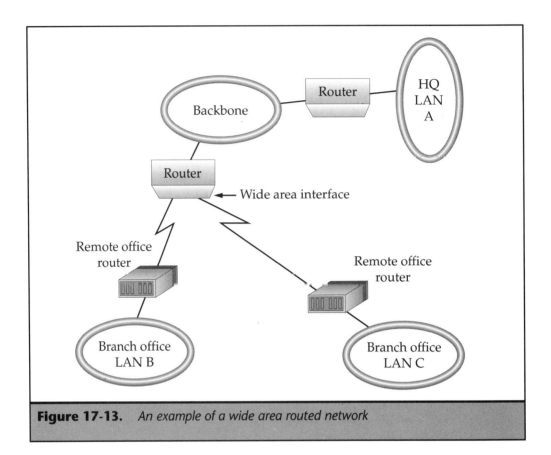

Figure 17-13. *An example of a wide area routed network*

Distant Routes

Like bridges, routers can be either local or remote. A *local router* has interfaces for local area network protocols such as Token Ring and 10Base-T. A *remote router*, on the other hand, has wide area network interfaces for services such as T1 and frame relay.

The Router Shopping Guide

Because routers are inherently more complex devices than bridges, there is a lot more to consider when evaluating and buying routers. Therefore, I've put together a list of criteria to help you make your router selection.

Compatibility and Interoperability

All the routers in your network should support the same protocols and routing methods. Small differences in implementation of routing protocols and compression methods can cause big interoperability problems. Therefore, you may even need to use the same brand and model of routers throughout your network.

Ease of Installation and Configuration

Router setup is not a job for the weak-spirited. Therefore, be sure to purchase a router that offers

- A streamlined installation program, or
- Free training, or
- Professional installation and configuration, or
- All of the above

Fault Tolerance

Your router is more than an internetworking device. It is also an integral part of your network management and cost control. Therefore, a failed router is a very expensive proposition. Be sure your router includes fault tolerance features, such as redundant power supplies and "hot swappable" modules.

Planning Segmented Networks

Creating multiple segments with a small number of stations on each one will limit traffic, but it may not improve performance. If a user regularly has to access a server that is on another segment, it will take longer for the request to be transmitted to the other segment, and longer for the reply to be received, than if the server were on the same segment as the user.

- Put users as close as possible to the resources they use the most.
- Limit internetwork traffic.
- Make sure stations that need to can communicate with each other no matter what segment they are on.

When you create more segments, if the segment is interconnected to another segment with a bridge or router, it is possible to send packets between those segments. Network segments joined with bridges or routers form internetworks. Each segment has its own internetwork address.

Microsegmentation

Microsegmentation is exactly what it sounds like: creating many very small network segments. Limiting the traffic on a segment to that of only a handful of users can often increase performance dramatically by reducing collisions and dividing more bandwidth among fewer users. On a microsegment, stations don't often have to contend for access to the network, and they rarely have to wait for another station to finish transmitting before they begin their transmissions.

Microsegmentation can be done with common household objects—lots of hubs and patch cables. However, over the last three years a new, efficient, very manageable, and increasingly cost-effective way to microsegment your network has become available. This means of microsegmentation is known as *LAN switching*, and it has a lot to recommend it. Read on.

Switching

When bridging doesn't quite cut it, but routing is overkill, it's time to consider a switch. After all, a switch is really a specialized bridge that creates a segment of one. Here's how switches evolved from bridges. When your network first begins to slow down, you segment it. All the nodes on the segment still have to share the same 10Mbps bandwidth—with segmentation; however, there are fewer nodes to share that 10Mbps. Pretty soon, high-traffic users simply can't be segmented enough to keep response time acceptably low. Unless, of course, there is only one user per segment.

Enter switching, which creates a virtual segment containing one node. Switches make a virtual connection between a transmitting node and a receiving node. This connection is made on the basis of the destination address of each packet, and it lasts only as long as it takes to transfer one packet, in essence creating a private segment for the user. Because the packet is transmitted only to the port associated with that specific destination address, no other port receives the packet, which provides both low traffic and, as an extra bonus, high security. In a switch, data transfers can take place in parallel and at full network speed.

Making the Switch

There are a couple of ways to implement switching, which we'll refer to as *static* and *dynamic*. *Static switching*, illustrated in Figure 17-14, can be accomplished through either module switching or port switching. In module switching, an entire hub module is assigned to a specific Ethernet segment so that all devices attached to the ports on that module are connected to the specified segment. Port switching, on the other hand, assigns devices to a segment on a port-by-port basis. Both module and port switching maintain segment assignments until they are manually changed by the network administrator, hence they are classified as static switching methods.

Dynamic switching, illustrated in Figure 17-15, is implemented by a switching method similar to that used in a telephone central office. Just as a telephone switch connects two callers only for the duration of their telephone call, the dynamic switch connects two ports long enough to transmit a single packet and then clears down the connection. For its duration, the connection has the full 10Mbps bandwidth, rather than sharing the bandwidth with all of the devices on the segment. The switch can support several of these port-to-port connections simultaneously.

To illustrate dynamic switching, think of a packet traveling along shared medium, shown in Figure 17-16, as something like an old-fashioned hotel bellboy meandering through the lobby with his message board. Not only is the message delivery painfully slow, but you've also got a security problem—anyone in the lobby can read the sign. A packet traveling along a switched network, shown in Figure 17-17, is like having a bellboy who knows you and knows where you're sitting in the lobby (you probably

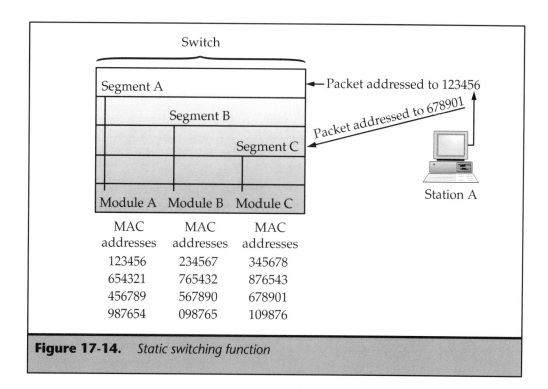

Figure 17-14. *Static switching function*

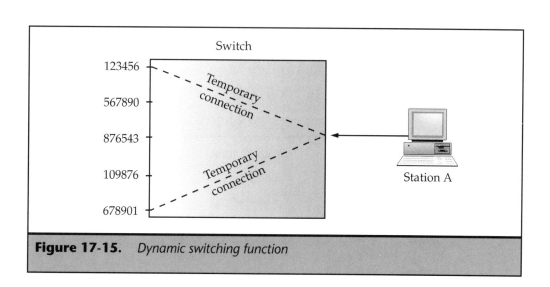

Figure 17-15. *Dynamic switching function*

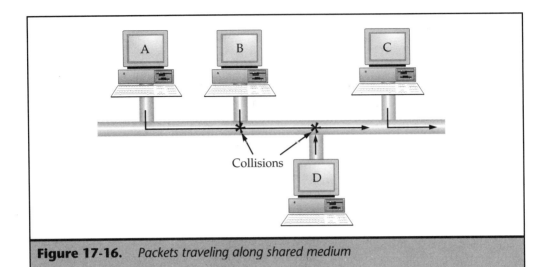

Collisions

Figure 17-16. *Packets traveling along shared medium*

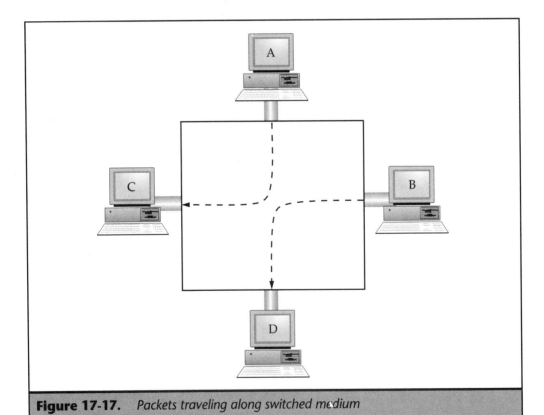

Figure 17-17. *Packets traveling along switched medium*

tipped him very well). Actually, a switched network is more like having one bellboy assigned to each guest in the lobby. Messages can be delivered to all guests simultaneously, and a switched network is therefore much faster.

There are two main types of switches: *workgroup* switches and *network* switches. The bellboy delivering a message to a single guest is an illustration of workgroup switching. A workgroup switch transfers data between pairs of end stations or nodes, as shown in Figure 17-18. A workgroup switch gives each node a dedicated 10Mbps connection. Each port on the switch is associated with one Ethernet address of the attached device.

A network switch, on the other hand, is better illustrated by a team of bellboys delivering messages between two conference rooms. They have to search from person to person to find the addressees. Although this takes more time than if they each knew the exact location of the addressees, it's still faster than having to go to each room in the hotel looking for the addressee. In much the same way, network switches support multiple Ethernet addresses per switch port, which provides wire-speed transfers between pairs of Ethernet segments attached to those ports, as shown in Figure 17-19.

Blocking Versus Nonblocking

An important aspect of how a switch operates is whether it is *nonblocking*. A nonblocking switch is one in which the number of output lines equals the number of input lines, so therefore data packets don't have to wait in the switch before being sent to their destination. A switch that isn't nonblocking can cause delays in packet transmission while the packet waits in a queue for access to one of the output ports.

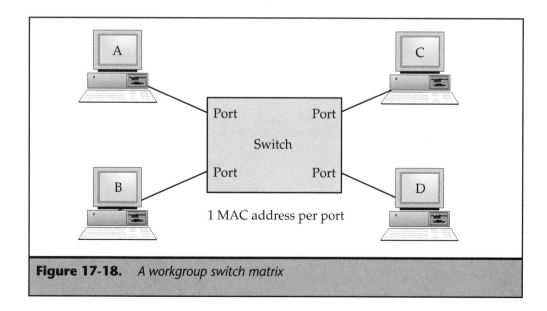

Figure 17-18. *A workgroup switch matrix*

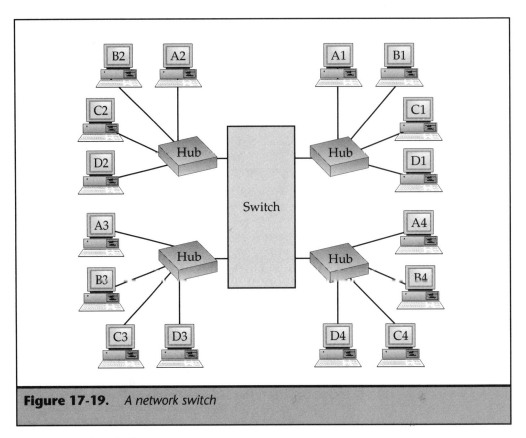

Figure 17-19. *A network switch*

Which Switch?

With at least 40 Ethernet and 15 Token Ring switches on the market—and more coming—selecting the right one for your network can be an arduous task. Obviously, you want the device that delivers the best cost of ownership/performance. But price lists, raw performance numbers, and features specifications reveal only half of the story. The other half—determining what it will take to configure, optimize, and manage the devices—is difficult to extract. It may seem as though you are doomed to evaluate every switch on the market. Fortunately, there's a much easier way.

Every LAN switch employs one of three basic architectures:

- Shared memory/CPU
- Matrix
- Bus

The design you use generally determines the overall manageability, functionality, and scalability the device will provide. By understanding the benefits and limitations of each, you can get an idea which switch will meet the needs of your particular network and what it will cost to own it.

Hardware Versus Software

All switches manufactured to date are based on either software or hardware implementations. Hardware switching breaks down further into matrix and bus switching. The hardware switches generally offer faster performance; software switches usually offer greater manageability. Keep in mind, however, that this generalization doesn't hold true in every case.

Software switching, which is implemented in switches such as Alantec Corp.'s PowerHub and 3Com Corp.'s LANplex, works like this: A packet enters the software switch, where it is synchronized, converted from serial to parallel, and examined for address information. Once in parallel format, it is written cyclicly to fast memory. The switch searches its address table to find the destination address and establish the switched connection. Once the switched connection has been established, the packet is read from memory, reconverted from parallel to serial format, and transmitted via the switched connection, as shown in Figure 17-20.

If this sounds familiar, it should: Software switches are actually based on router technology, as we discussed earlier in this chapter, that has been optimized for frame switching.

One of the main benefits of this legacy is that software switches are founded on tried-and-true technology. One of the main drawbacks is that—just as with many routers—there may be considerable up-front configuration work. But if you and your staff are versed in router configuration, you'll probably find software switch setup a snap.

Because of its roots in routing, software switching is also a very flexible architecture—it can ease the integration of switching and routing for networks that need both functions. But software switching does have its caveats. Because all the switching is handled by the CPU and memory, software switching often doesn't scale

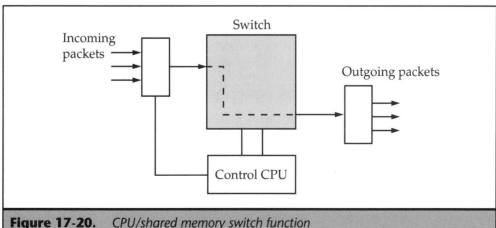

Figure 17-20. *CPU/shared memory switch function*

well, and performance can drop significantly as you add stations and management features.

Buyer Beware

It's easy to understand why the CPU gets bogged down. It handles not only switching, but also all the garden-variety processor activities such as servicing interrupt requests and performing packet housekeeping tasks. In addition, every feature you add will pull CPU cycles, so the more you ask software-based switches to do, the more inconsistent their performance will be.

If you have a multiprotocol network or are interested in implementing virtual LANs, for example, software-based switching will get expensive in terms of performance, management, and help-desk calls. Both protocol translation and virtual networking weigh heavily on a software switch.

Software switching also tends to have difficulty handling broadcasts. This is because broadcast frames have to be placed in all output buffers, not just in one central location, which puts an additional strain on the CPU. And because a CPU can't multitask, broadcasts are not handled simultaneously.

Finally, the software-based switch offers a single point of failure in both the CPU and the shared memory.

The Hard Facts

Hardware-based switches, on the other hand, resemble bridges, operating primarily on the MAC layer. Unlike software switches, they receive, buffer, and transmit packets without involving the CPU. However, the two types of hardware switches, matrix and bus, accomplish this function by very different means.

Matrix switches, also called "crossbar" switches, are based on a point-to-point matrix. This straightforward, hardware-based switch fabric sets up connections between MAC addresses in very much the same way as old electromagnetic voice switches set up connections between telephones.

In essence, a frame enters the input port, travels down the matrix until it finds the "intersection" for the correct output address, then proceeds through that output port. Such switches, like Kalpana Inc.'s Etherswitch and NetWiz Ltd.'s TurboSwitch, are fast and easy to implement because the switching function requires no software configuration, as shown in Figure 17-21.

Matrix switching is implemented in one of three architectures:

- A concentrator, which has more input lines than output lines, so outgoing packets are queued

- An expansion switch, which has more output lines than input lines, so incoming packets may be queued for access to output ports

- A nonblocking switch, in which the number of incoming lines equals the number of outgoing lines

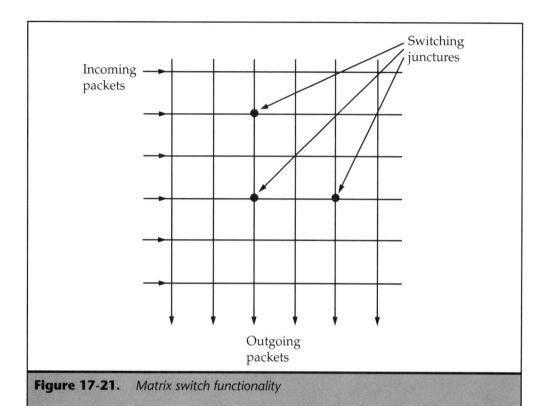

Figure 17-21. *Matrix switch functionality*

The biggest drawback of a matrix switch is that its effective size is limited. It can only support a static configuration of the number of incoming ports multiplied by the number of outgoing ports, and nonblocking service is limited to the number of incoming ports squared.

A variation of the matrix switch, known as the *knockout switch*, is shown in Figure 17-22. A knockout switch works just like any other matrix switch, with input ports being connected to output ports in standard crossbar fashion. However, a knockout switch also has a mechanism on each port for handling switch congestion. This mechanism places outgoing packets in a queue. Ordinarily, the packets leave the switch in the order in which they arrive. However, the knockout switch's congestion management mechanism can place high-priority packets at the beginning of the queue.

The performance of matrix switches is very consistent because they are not depending on a shared CPU to nail up and clear down the connections. Instead, each connection is made separately—and usually buffered separately—on the hardware matrix.

Matrix switches lend themselves to dynamic switching, whereby the switch connects two ports long enough to transmit a single packet and then clears down the

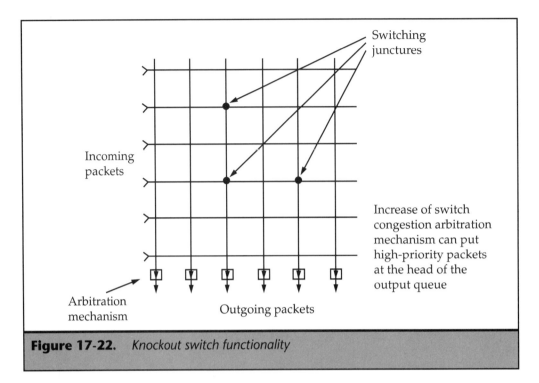

Figure 17-22.   *Knockout switch functionality*

connection. For its duration, the connection has the full 10Mbps bandwidth, rather than having to share the bandwidth with the rest of the devices on the segment. The switch can support several such port-to-port connections simultaneously.

Matrix switches are also usually very fast because, if properly buffered, they tend to be nonblocking as a result of their one-to-one nature of input frames to output frames.

The difficulties with matrix switches, however, can also be attributed to their one-to-one design. Adding ports, for instance, can be complicated. Inputs must equal outputs, which makes it difficult—but not impossible—for vendors to integrate a "fat pipe," or higher bandwidth connection, into a matrix switch.

Management is also an issue with matrix switches—you can monitor only one connection at a time. So, monitoring everything that is happening in the switch is out of the question because there is no central point from which you can see all traffic.

Catching the Bus

Bus-architecture switches, such as LANNET Inc.'s MultiNet LET series and ONET Data Communication Technologies Inc.'s LANBooster series, employ a central bus on the backplane, over which all the traffic on the switch travels. See Figure 17-23.

By using time-division multiplexing, either statistical or static, the switch gives each port its own turn to send a packet on the bus. Because the time slot is fixed, known, and predictable, this design provides consistent performance under varying loads.

The bus architecture also makes bus switches a good choice for switching both asynchronous and isochronous protocols. The design handles one-to-many and

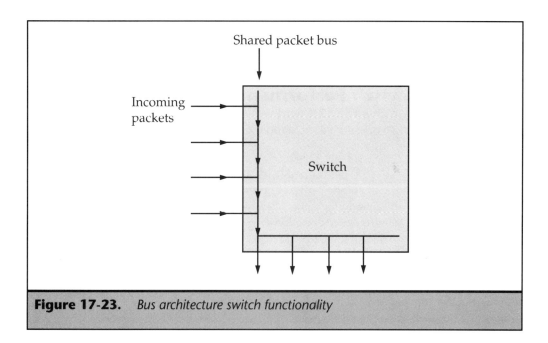

Shared packet bus

Incoming packets

Switch

Figure 17-23. *Bus architecture switch functionality*

many-to-one transmissions more elegantly than the matrix switch's inherent point-to-point orientation. And expanding the switch is relatively easy because inputs don't have to equal outputs. Finally, a central bus provides a somewhat more convenient vehicle for protocol translation than a matrix.

The bus architecture is also quite manageable. Having one central point over which all the traffic must flow lets you monitor all switch traffic simultaneously, and you can control ports with signals on the central bus. So, if being able to see and manage all the traffic on the switch simultaneously is important, the bus architecture is the only way to go.

But bus switches also have a few drawbacks. They tend to be expensive, so brace yourself for sticker shock, especially when you purchase their management packages. And configuring and optimizing them can be overwhelming. By design, the bus architecture lends itself to static switching, in which ports maintain segment assignments until they are manually changed by the network administrator. Allocating the staff time to balancing and reassigning segment assignments can be expensive. On the other hand, it does let you fine-tune your network to peak performance—if you have the time.

Analysis Is Key

Armed with a working knowledge of software and bus and matrix hardware architectures, you can determine which design will be best-suited to your network. Your network's unique traffic patterns and management needs, the expertise and size of your staff, along with your budget, will all play a significant role in your decision. The next thing to consider in evaluating switches is the specific measurements of their performance.

Measures of Switch Performance

Switches have their own criteria for measuring performance. To help you select the right switch for your network, we've included a description of the four major measures of switch performance.

FORWARDING RATE As we mentioned, forwarding rate is the rate at which the switch can transmit traffic from one port to another, expressed in packets per second. Because 10Base-T transmits 64-byte packets at a maximum rate of 14,880 packets per second, this is known as wire-speed for 10Base-T.

Switches have two different measurements for forwarding rate. The first, *port to port forwarding rate*, is the forwarding rate sustainable between two ports. The second is *total forwarding rate*, which is the maximum rate at which packets are transmitted through the network and received by destination ports. Total forwarding bandwidth, expressed in packets per second, is equal to or less than the number of virtual connections multiplied by the wire-speed.

PACKET LOSS Packet loss is the total number of packets transmitted at full wire-speed minus the number of packets received by the destination station. Packet loss is an indication of how a switch handles excessive traffic at wire speeds. If the switch starts discarding packets when its buffers fill, it obviously isn't handling the heavy traffic very well. Therefore, high packet loss means the switch isn't adept at handling heavy traffic, whereas low packet loss means that the switch has implemented mechanisms for accommodating heavy traffic successfully.

Switches that have low packet loss generally have implemented one or a combination of two congestion management techniques. These switches either have huge packet buffers to hold incoming data packets until they can be processed, or they have a mechanism that, when the switch becomes overwhelmed, sends a jamming signal to transmitting ports preventing them from continuing packet transmission until the congestion has cleared.

LATENCY This is the time it takes a packet to travel through the switch from the time it is received on the source port to the time it is transmitted on the destination port. Latency is affected by the forwarding operation of the switch itself.

In *store-and-forward* operation, the switch receives the whole frame before it forwards it to its destination. Once the whole frame has been received, the switch can perform error-checking to ensure that it is not truncated or corrupted before sending it on.

In *cut-through* operation, the switch begins forwarding a packet after it receives the first six bytes of the packet—that is, just as soon as the destination address can be detected. This type of cut-through operation has no error-checking, so some vendors, most notably Grand Junction (now a part of Cisco), have implemented what they call

FragmentFree operation. In FragmentFree mode, the switch begins forwarding a packet after the first 64 bytes have been received. Because most packet errors are resolved within the first 64 bytes—and because the 64 bytes is the smallest supported 10Base-T packet size—FragmentFree operation is a reasonable compromise between store-and-forward and cut-through operations.

Lack of error-checking is not the only weakness of cut-through operation, though. Cut-through can only be used when you're switching data between two networks of the same speed. If you're switching from networks of different speeds, you *cannot start transmitting a frame until you've got a complete frame ready to transmit*. Therefore, any switch that is moving data between a low-speed interface and a high-speed interface must use store-and-forward. Also, cut-through may not necessarily provide a significant performance increase, because some protocols already handle small delays well enough to eliminate the advantage. For example, packet burst protocols are designed to allow for small delays, and therefore some latency within a switch will not decrease performance.

In the last year, many switch vendors have begun offering what they call *adaptive cut-through* operation as a compromise between store-and-forward and cut-through switch operations. In adaptive cut-through operation, the switch functions in cut-through mode, forwarding packets as soon as it receives the first 6 bytes of the packet. However, the switch monitors packet retransmissions, and if packet retransmissions exceed a certain threshold, the switch assumes this is due to packet errors and begins operating in store-and-forward mode. The switch will continue operating in store-and-forward mode, checking all incoming packets for errors before forwarding them, until the packet error rate has dropped below another predefined threshold. The switch then begins functioning in cut-through mode again.

Latency indicates how efficient the switch is handling traffic. The higher the latency, the more likely the switch may become a bottleneck. However, latency numbers are all so low—they're measured in microseconds—that the chances of the switch itself causing traffic jams are very unlikely.

THROUGHPUT   *Throughput* is the maximum number of packets generated and received with no packet loss. To test throughput, we sent Ethernet packets through the switching hubs at wire-speed, then we slowed the transmission rate until the hub forwarded all the data without dropping packets.

This measure will tell you what kind of performance you can expect when your switch is operating at full capacity. The higher the throughput number, the better the switch handles a full load, with fewer dropped packets resulting in retransmissions—and therefore, theoretically, lower response times.

10/100 Switching

Sometimes switching alone isn't enough to speed up your network. Luckily, many switches available today offer a combination of high-speed network segments and switching, as shown in Figure 17-24.

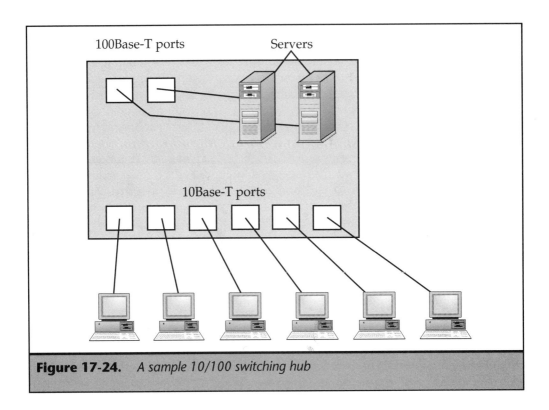

Figure 17-24. *A sample 10/100 switching hub*

Candidates for 10/100 Switching

Backbones and server farms. A single user might be happy with dedicated 10Mbps, but a server simply can't be. High-performance servers quickly saturate 10Mbps networks. Installing switched-10Mbps workgroup switches didn't really eliminate the performance bottleneck—all those users transmitting at the full 10Mbps have simply moved the bottleneck to the backbone.

Power workgroups. Even workstations are demanding a piece of the action. Those fast CPUs sitting on the desktop are processing more data and thus generating more traffic between desktop and server.

The essence of the 10/100 switching strategy is to increase bandwidth from the wiring closet to the server, leaving 10Mbps in place between the desktop and closet. The 10/100 "combination" switching approach has several advantages. Even if you aren't using Category 5 cable throughout your site, you can still take advantage of the 10/100 solution without having to pull new cable everywhere. You don't have to replace the Ethernet adapters in the workstations. You have an easy upgrade path to a total 100Mbps protocol. If you think that 10Mbps is all you will need at the desktop for the time being, 10/100 switching lets you get all the performance you need, where you need it, without having to pay for high bandwidth where you don't need it.

Full-Duplex Protocols

Anyone who is tracking down high-speed network solutions should be aware of Full-Duplex Ethernet. To explain how it works, we first have to look at the architecture of 10Mbps Ethernet.

There are two pairs of wires in star-wired 10Base-T and 100Base-T environments—one for transmitting and one for receiving. However, transmission and receipt cannot take place at the same time. Full-Duplex Ethernet, on the other hand, allows transmission over one pair of wires and receipt over the other pair simultaneously, providing nearly full utilization of both pairs and thus sustainable high data rates. By installing MAC devices that support Full-Duplex Ethernet, you can double the effective bandwidth. Full-Duplex Ethernet can coexist with normal half-duplex Ethernet and make use of the existing 10Base-T wiring.

As attractive as it sounds, Full-Duplex Ethernet has a couple of serious drawbacks. The first is that it requires an investment in NICs, hubs, switches, and firmware and driver upgrades that support Full-Duplex operation. This can be very expensive. The second drawback is that it makes sense only in a few situations. Specifically, this protocol is effective only in point-to-point connections, and then only when there is traffic available to flow in both directions at the same time. Still, in backbone implementations where there is a great deal of traffic among servers, Full-Duplex Ethernet is a technology that may be worth considering to make maximum use of the bandwidth available.

Virtual LANs

Setting up filters or constraints between different groups of users is awkward and time-consuming with conventional bridges and routers. Network managers think in terms of workgroups, not physical location of users. Therefore, they shouldn't have to set up a series of filtering statements based on physical ports. Rather than configuring and reconfiguring routers every time end stations move, network managers can implement *Virtual LANs*. A Virtual LAN is a list of device MAC or network addresses that are independent of a physical port, much like an access list used by some router vendors. However, Virtual LANs have network-wide significance. A device can access any other device on the same Virtual LAN. Virtual LANs can define filters among themselves, just like routers can. Devices on different media can be members of the same Virtual LAN. Furthermore, users can move end stations onto any segment within the virtual subnet without requiring address reconfiguration.

Virtual LANs enable network managers to group devices logically regardless of physical location and provide dedicated bandwidth and services to each, as shown in Figure 17-25.

Users can plug into any port in the network, and the Virtual LAN handles the rest. In addition to address filtering, Virtual LANs also provide

■ Simplified moves, adds, and changes

- Bandwidth allocation
- Security features

Simplified Moves, Adds, and Changes

One of the major problems network managers have in large, routed networks is the big administrative effort required to perform moves, adds, and changes. This is particularly true of Internet Protocol (IP) networks, where each physical LAN is associated with a logical subnet, as shown in Figure 17-26. If a user needs to move from one floor of a building to another, the workstation typically has to be reconfigured with a valid IP address on the new subnet.

To handle such moves, managers of legacy networks have to reconfigure routers manually. Virtual LANs, however, eliminate all of the manual address resolution and reconfiguration. Virtual LANs enable network managers to group devices logically regardless of physical location and provide dedicated bandwidth and services to each, as shown in Figure 17-27.

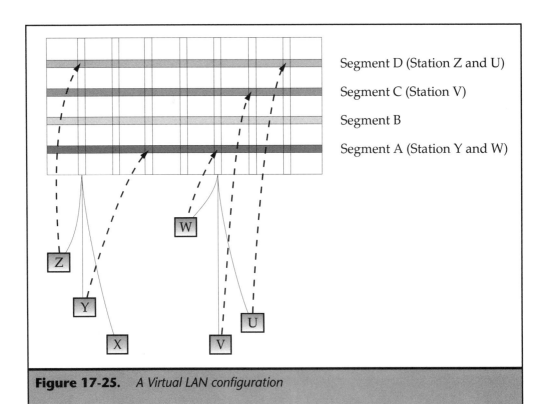

Figure 17-25. *A Virtual LAN configuration*

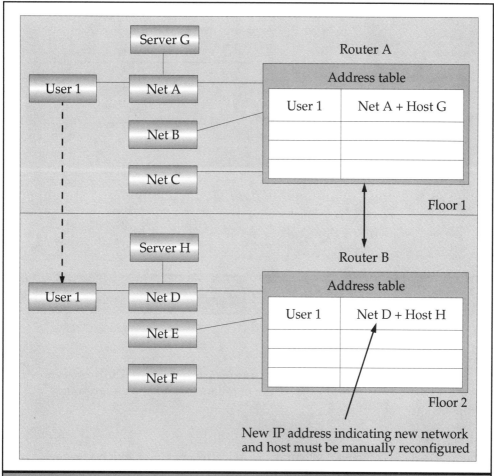

Figure 17-26. *Effect of a physical move on Internet Protocol addressing*

While networks obviously require routing capability, network managers would like to avoid having to manually reconfigure network address assignments every time users move from one network segment to another. Virtual networks let them do just that by identifying the physical address of a new device and associating it with a network layer address based on prior assignment without human intervention to the system or the end station. Users can plug into any port in the network, and the Virtual LAN handles the rest.

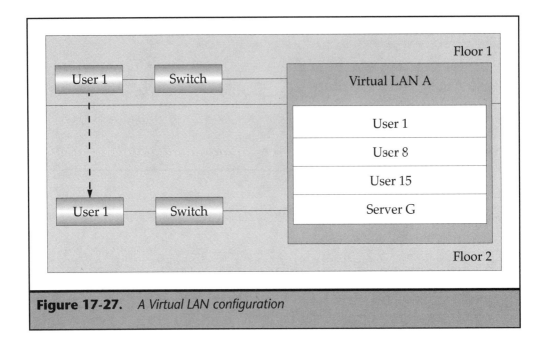

Figure 17-27. *A Virtual LAN configuration*

A Time for Everything

Each of these alternatives to high-speed networking has its place. The trick is knowing how to find that place. Here are a few rules of thumb to help you design your "alternative network."

Bridging

If your network is small and/or centrally located, segmentation with bridges is usually sufficient to improve performance.

Routing

Connecting more than a dozen segments with bridges can introduce excessive internetwork traffic, addressing complexity, and resulting endless looping problems—not to mention network management headaches. In such situations, you're well advised to consider using routers. As well, when your large internetwork includes wide area links—or multiple transport protocols such as 10Base-T, Token Ring, and perhaps even a high-speed backbone—routers are probably your best bet. Furthermore, when efficiency and economy of packet transmission are very important, such as when dealing with high-priority, high-security, and/or time-sensitive traffic, routers are definitely the choice.

Switching

Switching has become so inexpensive over the last few months that it now makes sense to weigh the relative cost of switching any time you are considering bridging. Switches offer more speed, more security, and often more manageability than bridges, so weigh these factors into your "to bridge or to switch" decision.

Switching may also be a reasonable alternative to routing, because switching offers high security and fast performance just like a router. However, if you must support multiple protocols and/or wide area traffic, routing is probably still the best choice—for now.

Virtual LANs

Virtual LANs can really be implemented as a complement to bridging, routing, and switching. While it promises "on the fly" resegmenting, remember that Virtual LAN packages are often expensive and require a great deal of training for network managers to become comfortable with them. Therefore, currently, Virtual LANs may be best deployed in large, widely dispersed networks, where their quick-response reconfiguration and remote access capabilities will offer a quick return on investment.

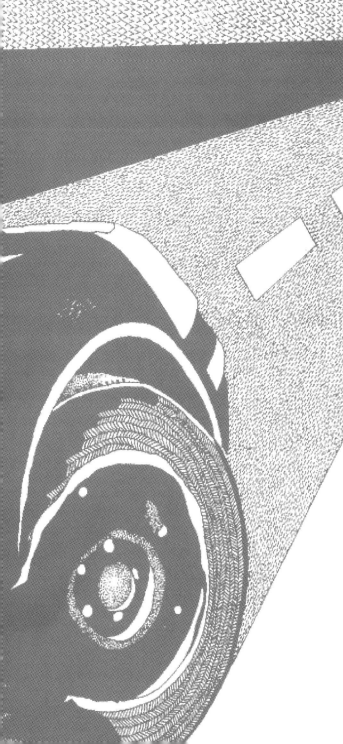

CHAPTER 18

Speed Kills:
Avoiding a
Crash

If this book has met its objectives, you now have a lot to think about. We hope we've given you enough guidance to help you determine where—and whether—you need a high-speed protocol. As well, we hope we've provided enough information about the strengths and weaknesses of each protocol to enable you to choose one, or at least put together a "short list" of suitable high-speed protocols for further investigation. Now the hard part begins: building the high-speed network.

The worksheets in Chapter 6 will help you plan what needs to be done and how much it will cost. They are thorough, so going through them in the context of your organization's network should help you address every detail of the implementation plan. So what do you do after you have created a project work plan and budget?

First: Try Before You Buy

I can't stress this enough. All the vendor promises in the world notwithstanding, before you make your final selection of high-speed networking products, *get the products into your network and test them under real conditions*. I've seen too many products that looked great on the specifications sheets but failed miserably in the real network. Even if the product works out great, you'll probably uncover a detail or two about integrating it into your network that the sales literature didn't mention. For example, you may need to reconfigure the memory of or even add memory to your networked PCs to accommodate the high-speed network adapter. Or you may find that your routers can't be upgraded to be compatible with new protocols, and will have to be replaced altogether. These are things you won't necessarily discover in a vendor's demonstration. In fact, you may never discover them unless you get the products you plan to buy into your shop and put them through real-life testing.

TIP: *In my experience, any vendor who promises that a network product has "seamless integration" and will be "transparent to the rest of the network"—especially if the vendor has never worked on my network—should be shown the door immediately.*

Until you get the network products into your shop and discover all the details of installation, you won't be able to put together a comprehensive budget or schedule. So make this your first priority!

Second: Identify the *Next* Bottleneck

This is something you can do while you're testing equipment. As you probably know, improving network performance is simply a matter of moving the bottlenecks around. Right now, your network's bottleneck is inadequate bandwidth. When that is eased, where will the bottleneck be? Will it be underpowered servers? Decrepit workstations? At the same time you are making your pitch for a high-speed network, you should tell your management where the next slowdown will be and what will cause it. This will add to your credibility, and save you from discussions that begin, "You said if we put in this high-speed network, the network would speed up! What happened?"

Third: Make a Schedule

Using the information from the worksheets in Chapter 6, create a schedule for the project. Determine the order in which the upgrades and installations will have to be done in your organization. Be sure to figure in ordering lead times and delivery delays. Then create a Gantt chart, like the one pictured in Figure 18-1, showing dependencies and which steps have to be completed before others can begin. Assign beginning and ending dates.

TIP: *You'll probably want to schedule network installation one building or one floor at a time.*

Class Time

Consult with training companies or in-house instructors to create a schedule for training staff and network users. Timing is critical here. Training should take place close to the time of network implementation, or everyone will have forgotten what they learned by the time the network is in place. If you have a lot of people to train, you'll probably want to use outside training specialists even if you have in-house trainers, so that everyone can receive training shortly before the new network is put into service.

Fourth: Get Your Budget Approved

Now that you know everything you have to do and buy, how much it will cost, and how long it will take, it's time to get your final budget approved. Frequently it's difficult for a network manager to justify to a non-technical management committee the expense of building a high-speed network. You know it will increase performance, thus saving time and making network users more productive. Productivity, however, is a difficult thing to quantify. Indeed, a high-speed network may be helpful, even vital, to your organization. But given the reluctance of the powers that be to spend money on anything that won't show a tangible economic benefit, how do you convince them to approve the expenditures to build one?

The answer is deceptively simple: Put a price on it. Determine:

- How much the system really costs (you've already done this in Chapter 6)
- How much money it will really save (or make), and
- Figure out if the difference is worth it.

Task	4/1/96	4/15/96	5/1/96	5/15/96	6/1/96
Order test components					
Network adapters	XXXXX				
Switches	XXXXX				
Patch cables	XXXXX				
Hubs	XXXXX				
Router interface cards	XXXXX				
Build test network		XXXXX			
Test protocol			XXXXX		
Final implementation decision				XXXXX	
Notify users of implementation decision					XXXXX
Order components					
Network adapters					
Switches					
Patch cables					
Hubs					
Router interface cards					
Install router interface cards					
Install switches in wiring closets					
Notify users of implementation schedule					
Floor 14					
Floor 15					
Floor 16					
Floor 17					
Floor 18					
Install network adapters					
Floor 14					
Floor 15					
Floor 16					
Floor 17					
Floor 18					
Cut over to new protocol					
Floor 14					
Floor 15					
Floor 16					
Floor 17					
Floor 18					

Figure 18-1. *A Gantt chart for a network implementation project*

6/15/96	7/1/96	7/15/96	8/1/96	8/15/96	9/1/96	9/15/96	10/1/96	10/15/6
XXXXX								
XXXXX								
XXXXX								
XXXXX								
XXXXX								
	XXXXX							
		XXXXX						
			XXXXX					
				XXXXX				
					XXXXX			
						XXXXX		
							XXXXX	
				XXXXX				
					XXXXX			
						XXXXX		
							XXXXX	
								XXXXX

Figure 18-2. *A Gantt chart for a network implementation project*

You'll get a lot more attention when you present a purchase request in terms of money it can make or save your company than when you recommend it for convenience and ease of use. Telling your boss that a high-speed network will improve response time is one thing. Pointing out that having one is like getting an extra workday from each user each year is quite another.

Of course, this answer may be simple, but the means to accomplish it is a little more complicated. The task is to pinpoint the economic benefits of the high-speed network, calculate its exact cost, and determine whether the benefit justifies the cost. This requires not only technical expertise, but also business savvy and creative thinking. Let me give you a few pointers on how to translate benefits and costs into dollars and cents.

It's a Wonderful Life

The first step to putting a price on the benefit of a high-speed network is to take an objective look at life without the product, past, present, and future. Ask yourself what past problems the high-speed network could have eased. For example, did the network in accounting slow to a standstill during year-end closing last January? Are your remote offices unable to start work on time each morning because the nightly data transfers from headquarters are taking too long to complete? Use these as concrete examples for your management of how the high-speed network will be used in your organization.

Next, ask yourself what will—or won't—happen in the future if you *don't* build a high-speed network. Then figure out how that will affect your business. For example, survey your network users to find out how long it takes to complete a print job on a network printer. At the same time, ask them how much they expect their printing to increase over the next few quarters.

As another example, let's say that you manage a network with 2,500 users, and you find through your survey that on the average it takes users ten seconds to save a document. According to your research, the same task on a high-speed network would take two seconds. You also find, through your document management system, that the average network user saves 15 documents a day. "Eight seconds?" You say, "Big deal." A little math will show you that this is a very big deal indeed:

8 seconds x 15 documents x 250 workdays = 8.33 hours per year

This means that saving eight seconds per saved document amounts to saving a day's worth of work each year. Your friendly accounting department can help you put a dollar value on this. Suppose you find that the average salary of a network user is $35,000. A day's salary for an average network user would then be $140. Getting an extra day's work each year from all 2,500 users would mean an annual savings of $350,000. That should certainly get your manager's attention.

Doomsayer

Now that you have a feel for what not having a high-speed network is costing you, take a moment to play Cassandra. Get your known facts together, then conjure up the worst possible scene that could result from this. In our document saving example, for instance, assume that your company is actually paying a day's worth of overtime ($500,000 per year) for work that can't be done during regular business hours.

In another example, determine whether the bandwidth crunch on your network, coupled with increasing network usage, might cause work to slow to the point that important tax or SEC filing deadlines are missed. When you present visions like these to your management, you'll have their attention.

Considering the Alternative

Now it's time to concede that a high-speed network is not the only solution. There may be other ways to solve the problem, as we've pointed out in Chapter 17. To have a persuasive pitch, you will have to acknowledge that there are alternatives and show that you have considered them. Then you have to reveal their inadequacies—if you can.

One of the problems with the alternatives that we have suggested is that most of them require much more maintenance and management than a high-speed network. Network segmentation in particular requires a great deal of configuration and reconfiguration as users are added and moved. As well, virtual networking requires expertise in the software and concepts of virtual networking, as well as time to maintain the virtual segments.

Too Much Is Not Enough

The biggest inadequacy of any of the high-speed networking alternatives is that there is *never, ever* enough bandwidth. Any means of squeezing a little more performance out of 10Mbps is truly a stopgap measure. As more users are added to the network, and PCs gain processing power, and more multimedia applications are put on networks, you will find that even a shared 100Mbps network may not provide sufficient bandwidth for long. One of the driving forces behind this seemingly unstoppable bandwidth drought is user expectations. As users are buying high-powered PCs for home, they will expect their work PCs—despite being networked—to match the response time of their supercharged standalone home PCs.

Therefore, giving your budget committee a short history lesson on the growth of networks, application packet sizes, PC processors, user expectations, and bandwidth requirements over the last three years should bring them around to reality.

The Price Is Right

Now it's time to put a complete price on the high-speed network you want to build. As you are now aware, the cost of a high-speed network is much more than the purchase price. Ask yourself how the new protocol will affect client and server resources. Will additional hardware be required to install and run the system properly? Will you have to purchase annual support contracts? How will implementing the management system affect staffing? Overtime? Training? As we've mentioned, the worksheets in Chapter 6 will help you put together a detailed budget. Be honest with yourself when calculating these costs.

Benefit Analysis

After you evaluate the costs of the high-speed network, you must assess its benefits. If you do build the network, how will it really benefit you? As we mentioned earlier, making your life easier isn't going to satisfy the budget committee. How is it going to save money? A product that cuts staffing and/or overtime, or that solves a significant operational or customer service problem, is going to get the budget dollars.

In my document-saving example, if the total cost of building the high-speed network is $1,000,000 or less, the system will pay for itself in less than three years in time savings alone. After that, the high-speed network will be giving your company $350,000 worth of time each year.

Showtime

Now that you've gathered your facts, found the costs and shortcomings in your own solution, addressed the holes in your own logic, and built a case based on economic need and common sense, it's time to prepare your presentation. Start by telling your management how much the high-speed network will save the company. Then give your example of a past project that would have been done more cost-effectively if the high-speed network had been in place. Next, present the worst-case scenario if the network isn't built, then conclude with a step-by-step explanation of the analysis you used to arrive at these conclusions. Finally, just in case your argument sparks enthusiasm, it's a good idea to have a high-level implementation plan on hand to give your management an idea of what will be involved.

You Can't Always Get What You Want

Your analysis has either produced a sound, justifiable, and hopefully unassailable case for building a high-speed network, *or* a reasonable explanation of why the project just isn't feasible. In either instance, you win. Understanding why a purchase doesn't make business sense will build your credibility with your management just as much as knowing when it does. It also makes you aware of the types of systems and pricing that *will* make sense.

If your analysis shows that building a high-speed network isn't a sound business move, don't give up. Instead, calculate a price at which the network *would* be a good buy. Then present that figure to your vendor (be fair—vendors have to make money, too). You never know, there may be room for negotiation. Even if there isn't, this will give your vendor information to take back to their manufacturers to let them know their products may be overpriced for their market.

This exercise will also give you more than a business case for building a high-speed network. It will help you gain a broad perspective on how your network fits into your organization. It also encourages constant, close communication with other departments and an understanding of how they use the network and information about the network. This is the kind of perspective that will not only make you a better network manager, but also serve you well throughout your career.

Fifth: Set Expectations

As soon as you complete your implementation plan and schedule for your high-speed network, start setting appropriate expectations for your managers, your users, and your staff. Here are some tips:

- **COMMUNICATE.** Write a memo, hold meetings, post notices, and talk with everyone you meet in the hall about what you are doing and why. Explain it in excruciating detail. Tell them why it is necessary. Be a walking, talking seminar on building your high-speed network. Even though some people may not understand everything you're saying, they will have an opportunity to grasp the enormity of the undertaking and perhaps be more sympathetic to any difficulties encountered as a result.

- **Listen to their concerns about "another network project."** Everyone dreads having the network down, and it often seems that every major network upgrade or conversion is followed by a frustrating period of sporadic downtime while working out the "bugs." Some users may be anxious about the network project because they are about to begin demanding projects of their own. You should be aware of these projects and plan the network implementation accordingly. After talking with your users, you may even want to reschedule so that the network won't be "under construction" during a critical work period such as tax season at an accounting firm or a large trial at a law firm.

- **Be very candid about how long the project will take.** You will gain nothing by being overly optimistic. If anything, overestimate the duration of the implementation.

- **Let all concerned know where and when you are likely to encounter problems or delays**. At the same time, share your contingency plans for meeting important deadlines and keeping the work flowing even when the project isn't going as well as planned.

- **Don't oversell the expected performance increases.** Obviously, you wouldn't be undertaking the project if you didn't think it was worthwhile. However, while you should be positive about the benefits of a high-speed network, don't make anyone expect a miracle.

- **Prepare your staff for long hours.** Be sure you have communicated very clearly exactly what this project is going to demand of them. Show them the schedule and the task assignments. Be sure everyone is committed to successful completion of the project. Then help them prepare for it.

TIP: Giving them some time off before the project begins may help ensure that they are fit, well-rested, and in good spirits at the outset. This will help the whole project to go more smoothly, to say the least.

- **Be prepared for cranky users.** No matter how carefully and thoroughly you communicate, there will no doubt be a user or two who becomes frustrated with the progress of the project and lashes out at you and/or your staff. Don't take it personally (no matter how personally it is aimed) and make sure your staff doesn't, either. Tell them that this is likely to happen, and instruct them to listen patiently to angry users, apologize for any inconvenience, tell the users what is being done, and *walk away.*

TIP: It might be wise to offer your staff an incentive—such as a bonus, a victory party, or some time off—or all of the above—when the project is completed.

Surviving Speed

This chapter sounds more like you're preparing for war than for a network upgrade. However, it's not meant to scare you away from building a high-speed network. In fact, it's aim is to ensure that you come away from the project with a high-performance network and an intact career. The secret to a successful implementation is

- Doing your homework and carefully selecting which protocols to implement where
- Carefully planning and scheduling the tasks and expenditures
- Preparing your staff, your users, and your management

Follow the guidelines laid out in this book, and you too can be King—or Queen—of the Network Superhighway!

PART FIVE

Appendixes

APPENDIX A

Open Systems

Open systems, in broad terms, are computer architectures, computer systems, computer software, and communication systems in which the specifications are published and available to everyone. An open system encourages the development of compatible vendor products. Customers benefit from open systems because they can choose from a wide variety of products that work with the system, and most important, are easily interconnected with other vendors' products. An open environment provides standard communication facilities and protocols, or provides a way to use a variety of protocols. The computer community is putting more pressure on vendors for open systems because there is a need to purchase equipment, under open bid, with the guarantee that equipment will work on existing open systems.

Specifying Open Systems

Open systems are defined by vendors, consortiums of vendors, government bodies, and worldwide standards organizations. Typically, the sponsoring vendor, consortium, or standards organization controls the specifications, but works with other vendors and users at public meetings to define the specifications. Recent trends have moved away from striving for complete openness and more towards acceptance of in-place standards. For example, the Transmission Control Protocol/Internet Protocol (TCP/IP) protocols have proved more popular than the Open Systems Interconnection (OSI) protocols because of the momentum gained as the primary protocol in use by the Internet. Most vendors now support TCP/IP while few support the OSI protocols.

Several organizations involved in the standards process are listed next, including those that support the use and integration of in-place standards, such as the Open Software Foundation.

- The *Open Systems Interconnection (OSI)* model was developed by the International Organization for Standardization (ISO) in the early 1980s. It defines protocols and standards for the interconnection of computers and network equipment.

- The *Open Software Foundation (OSF)* is a membership organization that acquires technologies from other vendors to create computing environments. Its environments include the Distributed Computing Environment (DCE), an open platform that simplifies the development of products in heterogeneous environments. It is also involved with OSF/1, a UNIX-like environment, and OSF/Motif, a graphical user interface.

- The *Common Open Software Environment (COSE)* is a consortium of vendors including IBM, Hewlett-Packard, SunSoft, and Novell that are cooperating to deliver a common desktop environment (CDE) to UNIX that can rival Microsoft Windows.

- The *Object Management Group (OMG)* develops a suite of object-oriented languages, interfaces, and protocol standards that vendors can use to create applications that operate in multivendor environments. OMG certifies the compliance of products that are designed to the standard.

■ *SQL Access Group (SAG)* is a group of database management system (DBMS) vendors that have taken on the goal of creating interoperable Structured Query Language (SQL) database standards. SAG consults with the ISO and ANSI (American National Standards Institute) to bring about its goals.

■ *X/Open Ltd.* is a group of vendors that promotes open, multivendor environments for the creation of interoperable applications. It publishes information and provides certification services.

Computer vendors such as IBM, DEC, Hewlett-Packard, and others have recently supplemented or moved away from the proprietary architectures and systems they advocated in the 1970s and 1980s to new open environments. For example, IBM now supports its existing customer needs for Systems Application Architecture (SAA), Advanced Peer-to-Peer Networking (APPN), and other standards, as well as new customer needs for open environments by defining the Networking Blueprint, which has the following features:

■ Hides the underlying networking components so customers can use applications of choice. This is accomplished through the use of the OSF DCE and OSI standards.

■ Allows the use of multiple communication protocols, such as APPN, TCP/IP, and OSI.

■ Uses advanced bandwidth technologies for communication.

Digital Equipment Corporation supports the OSI protocols with DECnet Phase V which was announced in 1987. It provided full compliance with the OSI model and backward compatibility to Phase IV. However, in 1991, DEC announced ADVANTAGE-NETWORKS, a strategy that adds support for other protocols such as TCP/IP. In doing so, DEC backed away from its total commitment to OSI in Phase V. Most important, DEC provides support for TCP/IP and the ability to build multiprotocol backbones that can transport DECnet, TCP/IP, and OSI data. For example, users can transmit data between TCP/IP applications using OSI transport protocols, or between OSI applications using TCP protocols.

Move to Interoperability

The OSI protocols have served as the model for open systems design for the last decade, although general acceptance of the protocols has been slow. IBM and DEC now fully support OSI. Even the Internet community, which uses the TCP/IP protocols, has been working to integrate OSI protocols. However, with generally sluggish acceptance of OSI, vendors continue to design proprietary products and advocate their own networking architectures. Recently, however, TCP/IP has been one of the driving forces toward interoperability, mainly because of its ability to handle internetworking and its widespread use on the Internet.

The open systems movement has shifted from the need to develop one grand protocol model such as OSI to the acceptance of many different protocols. As companies move to integrate their departmental computers into enterprise systems, there is a requirement to integrate IPX, TCP/IP, AppleTalk, NetBIOS, and many other protocols into the emerging network platform that ties everything together. Advances in processing power, multiprotocol routers, and middleware software have made this multiprotocol support feasible.

Middleware in this case is a generic term that refers to software platforms that hide underlying systems from applications and allow applications to interface with one another. For example, a user running a Windows application on a Novell network can access a traditionally incompatible database on a UNIX computer system attached to a TCP/IP network. The middleware product handles all the communication and interfacing requirements.

The acceptance of many different protocols and the availability of equipment to handle them has brought about an expanding market in interoperable products. Network administrators and users now have more choices, and can use many more of the resources available on their networks. In addition, product vendors can concentrate more on designing unique products and concentrate less on compatibility issues.

Open Systems Interconnection (OSI) Model

The OSI model is a standard that was created by the International Organization for Standardization (ISO). It defines a layered model for an open systems environment in which a process running in one computer can communicate with a similar process in another computer if they implement the same OSI layer communication protocols. The OSI model is pictured in Figure A-1. During a communication session, processes running in each layer on each computer communicate with one another. The bottom layer defines the actual physical components such as connectors and cable and the electrical transmission of data bits between systems. The layers immediately above define data packaging and addressing methods. Still further up are methods for keeping communication sessions alive. Finally, the uppermost layers describe how applications use the underlying communication systems to interact with applications on other systems.

The OSI model was designed to help developers create applications that are compatible across multivendor product lines, and to promote open, interoperable networking systems. While OSI hasn't caught on as planned, its model is still used to describe and define how various vendors' products communicate. A comparison of the OSI protocol stack to other protocol stacks is pictured in Figure A-2.

Protocols are loaded into a computer as software drivers. Each layer of the protocol stack defines a specific set of functions. An application at the uppermost layer interacts

Application layer 7
Presentation layer 6
Session layer 5
Transport layer 4
Network layer 3
Data-Link layer 2
Physical layer 1

Figure A-1. *The Open Systems Interconnection model*

with the layer below when it needs to send information to another system on the network. The request is packaged in one layer and passed down to the next layer, which adds information related to functions handled at that layer, creating a new

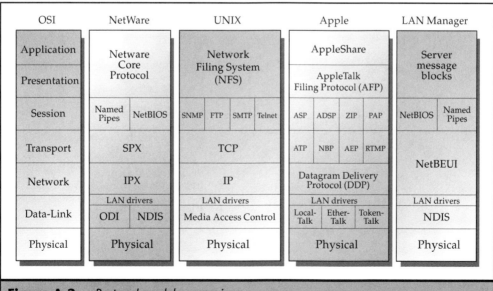

Figure A-2. *Protocol model comparison*

packet within a packet. This package is then passed down to the next layer and the process continues as shown in Figure A-3. Each layer adds information to the message packet and this information is read by the corresponding layer in the receiving system's protocol stack. In this way, each protocol layer communicates with its corresponding protocol layer to facilitate communication.

Each layer defines rules and procedures that communication subsystems must follow in order to communicate with peer processes on other systems. Some example processes handled by communication subsystems are listed next:

- Interaction and exchanges between applications, as well as translations between differences in syntax and data representations

- Data exchange management in either full-duplex or half-duplex modes

- Connection-oriented session management (that is, monitoring and maintenance of a communication channel between two systems)

- Network routing and addressing procedures

- Network drivers (that is, framing of data in preparation for transmission)

- Network interface card functions (that is, the transmission of electrical, optical, or radio signals over the network media)

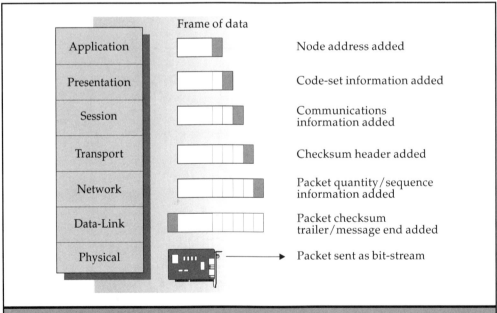

	Frame of data	
Application		Node address added
Presentation		Code-set information added
Session		Communications information added
Transport		Checksum header added
Network		Packet quantity/sequence information added
Data-Link		Packet checksum trailer/message end added
Physical		Packet sent as bit-stream

Figure A-3. *Information related to the functions of each layer are added to a packet as it passes down the protocol stack*

Product developers use protocol standards to create products that interoperate with other vendors' products. For example, the bottom layers define hardware interfacing techniques. A developer working at this level designs network hardware and software drivers following the rules defined in the layer.

In an actual communication session, each layer in the protocol stack communicates with its peer layer in the other system, but it does so by adding the information it needs to communicate to a packet that is passed down to the next lower protocol layer, as mentioned previously.

The following sections describe network protocols. You must have the network hardware—the Physical layer—in place before any of the other layers of communication can take place, so the Physical layer is described first.

THE PHYSICAL LAYER   The Physical layer defines the physical characteristics of the interface, such as mechanical components and connectors, electrical aspects such as voltage levels representing binary values, and functional aspects such as setting up, maintaining, and taking down the physical link. Well-known Physical layer interfaces for data communication include EIA RS-232 and RS-449, the successor to RS-232. RS-449 allows longer cable distances. Well-known local area network (LAN) systems are Ethernet, Token Ring, and Fiber Distributed Data Interface (FDDI).

THE DATALINK LAYER   The Datalink layer defines the rules for sending and receiving information across the physical connection between two systems. This layer encodes and frames data for transmission, in addition to providing error detection and control. Because the Datalink layer can provide error control, higher layers may not need to handle such services. However, when reliable media is used, there is a performance advantage by not handling error control in this layer, but in higher layers. Bridges operate at this level in the protocol stack. Here are common protocols occupying the Datalink layer:

- High-level Data Link Control (HDLC) and related synchronous, bit-oriented protocols
- LAN drivers and access methods, such as Ethernet and Token Ring
- Fast packet wide area networks, such as Frame Relay and Asynchronous Transfer Mode (ATM)
- Microsoft's Network Driver Interface Specification (NDIS)
- Novell's Open Datalink Interface (ODI)

THE NETWORK LAYER   The Network layer defines protocols for opening and maintaining a path on the network between systems. It is concerned with data transmission and switching procedures, and hides such procedures from upper layers. Routers operate at the Network layer. The Network layer can look at packet addresses to determine routing methods. If a packet is addressed to a workstation on the local network, it is sent directly there. If it's addressed to a network on another segment, the packet is sent to a routing device, which forwards it on the network. Here are common protocols occupying the Network layer:

- Internet Protocol (IP)
- X.25 Protocol
- Novell's Internetwork Packet Exchange (IPX)
- Banyan VINES Internet Protocol (VIP)

THE TRANSPORT LAYER   The Transport layer provides a high level of control for moving information between systems, including more sophisticated error handling, prioritization, and security features. The Transport layer provides quality service and accurate delivery by providing connection-oriented services between two end systems. It controls the sequence of packets, regulates traffic flow, and recognizes duplicate packets. The Transport layer assigns packetized information a tracking number that is checked at the destination. If data is missing from the packet, the Transport-layer protocol at the receiving end arranges with the Transport layer of the sending system to have packets retransmitted. This layer ensures that all data is received and in the proper order. A *logical circuit*, which is like a dedicated connection, can be established to provide a reliable transmission between systems. Non-OSI Transport-layer protocols that can provide connection-oriented services include the following:

- Internet Transmission Control Protocol (TCP)
- Internet User Datagram Protocol (UDP)
- Novell's Sequenced Packet Exchange (SPX)
- Banyan VINES Interprocess Communication Protocol (VICP)
- Microsoft NetBIOS/NetBEUI

THE SESSION LAYER   The Session layer coordinates the exchange of information between systems by using conversational techniques, or dialogues. Dialogues are not always required, but some applications may require a way of knowing where to restart the transmission of data if a connection is temporarily lost, or may require a periodic dialog to indicate the end of one data set and the start of a new one.

THE PRESENTATION LAYER   Protocols at the Presentation layer are part of the operating system and application the user runs in a workstation. Information is formatted for display or printing in this layer. Codes within the data, such as tabs or special graphics sequences, are interpreted. Data encryption and the translation of other character sets are also handled in this layer.

THE APPLICATION LAYER Applications access the underlying network services using defined procedures in this layer. The Application layer is used to define a range of applications that handle file transfers, terminal sessions, and message exchange (for example, electronic mail). OSI Application layer protocols are listed here:

- Virtual Terminal
- File Transfer Access and Management (FTAM)
- Distributed Transaction Processing (DTP)
- Message Handling System (X.400)
- Directory Services (X.500)

Figure A-4 shows how data flows through the protocol stack and over the media from one system to another. Data starts at the Application and Presentation layers, where a user works with a network application, such as an electronic mail program.

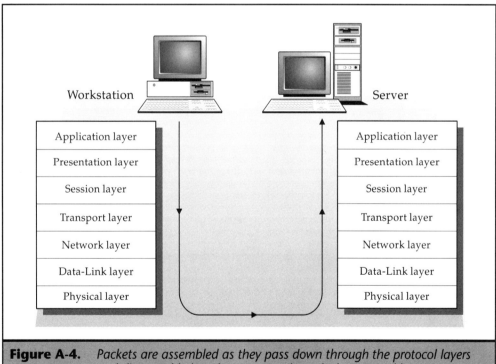

Figure A-4. *Packets are assembled as they pass down through the protocol layers and disassembled as they pass up through the protocol layers*

Requests for services are passed through the Presentation layer to the Session layer, which begins the process of packetizing the information. A connection-oriented communication session may be opened between the two systems to provide reliable transmissions. Once the session is established, protocol layers begin exchanging information as appropriate.

APPENDIX B

The Standards Organizations

Throughout this book I refer to standards and specifications issued by various national and international standards organizations. To help you understand how these organizations interact—as well as to help you make your way through the "alphabet soup" of these organizations' acronyms—I've listed the names and descriptions of the major standards bodies.

American National Standards Institute (ANSI)

This U.S.-based organization defines coding standards and signaling schemes for the entire nation, as well as functioning as the U.S. representative in the International Standards Organization and the International Telecommunications Union's Consultative Committee for Telegraph and Telephone. You can visit their Web site at http://www.ansi.org, or write to them at:

American National Standards Institute
11 West 42nd Street, 13th Floor
New York, NY 10036
212-642-4900

International Consultative Committee for Telegraph and Telephone (CCITT)

The CCITT is a committee of the United Nations organization called the International Telecommunications Union, and is now commonly referred to simply as the ITU. The function of the ITU's CCITT is to study and develop draft technical and procedural standards for international telecommunications. The CCITT forwards its draft standards to the ITU, which votes to adopt or reject the drafts as international standards. The U.S. is involved with the ITU, as it is with all United Nations organizations, through the U.S. Departments of State and Commerce. You can visit their Web site at http://www.itu.ch. You can also get copies of ITU proposals and recommendations by writing:

U.S. Department of Commerce
National Technical Information Service
5285 Port Royal Road
Springfield, VA 22161
703-487-4650

Institute of Electrical and Electronic Engineers (IEEE)

This is a society based in the U.S. that develops standards for the electrical and electronics industries. Networking professionals are particularly interested in the work of the IEEE 802 committees, which develop data communications standards for local area networks. The 802 committees focus their efforts on developing standards protocols for the physical interface of local area network connections, which functions on the Physical and Data-Link layers of the ISO/OSI Reference Model (see Appendix A). These specifications define how data connections among network devices are made, managed, and terminated, as well as specifying physical connections such as cabling and connectors.

After completing draft standards, the IEEE 802 committees forward them to the American National Standards Institute and/or to the International Standards Organization for finalization and adoption.

The IEEE 802 committees are

802.1	Internetworking
802.2	Logical Link Control
802.3	CSMA/CD local area networks
802.4	Token Bus local area networks
802.5	Token Ring local area networks
802.6	Metropolitan Area Networks
802.7	Broadband Technical Advisory Group
802.8	Fiber Optic Technical Advisory Group
802.9	Integrated voice and data networks
802.10	Network security
802.11	Wireless networks
802.12	Demand Priority Access local area networks

You can contact the IEEE at:

Institute of Electrical and Electronics Engineers
445 Hoes Lane
P.O. Box 1331
Piscataway, NJ 08855-1331
908-981-1393
800-678-4333

International Standards Organization (ISO)

The International Standards Organization has representatives from important standards organizations all over the world, including the United Nations' Economic and Social Council. Its goal is to develop and adopt standards of all kinds that will facilitate international trade and intercultural exchange. Therefore, the International Standards Institute is involved in developing standards for everything from weights and measures to business practices to networking protocols. The United States is represented in the International Standards Organization by the American National Standards Institute. You can visit their Web site at http://www.iso.ch, or write to them at:

> International Organization for Standardization
> 1, rue de Varembe
> CH-1211
> Geneva 20
> SWITZERLAND
> 41-22-479-0111

APPENDIX C

The Supporting Organizations

It seems that every protocol we've discussed in this book has its own fan club. These supporting organizations work to develop standards, educate vendors and users, disseminate information, and generally promote the use of the protocol they support. These organizations are a good source of detailed technical and vendor information. Also, don't forget to check your local bulletin boards, Web pages, and even telephone directories for local users' groups for the protocol in which you are interested.

100Base-T: The Fast Ethernet Alliance

The Fast Ethernet Alliance is a multivendor effort committed to providing customers with open, cost-effective, and interoperable 100Mbps Ethernet solutions. The Alliance was formed around common objectives—to extend the existing Ethernet standard in response to industry demand for increased network bandwidth and to address customer need for interoperability among a breadth of Fast Ethernet products. The Fast Ethernet Alliance now has over 75 member companies. You can write to the alliance at:

Fast Ethernet Alliance
C/O Hi Tech Communications
101 Howard Street, Second Floor
San Francisco, CA 94105-1616

or call or fax them at:

415-904-7000
(fax) 415-904-7025

The 100VG-AnyLAN Forum

The 100VG-AnyLAN Forum was formed to promote the IEEE 802.12 (100VG-AnyLAN) standard as the successor to the IEEE 802.3 (10Base-T) protocol. Its membership includes such industry heavyweights as Hewlett-Packard Company. You can write the 100VG-AnyLAN Forum at:

P.O. Box 1378
North Highlands, CA 95660

or call them at:

916-348-0212

Asynchronous Transfer Mode: The ATM Forum

Formed in October 1991, the ATM Forum's worldwide membership currently includes more than 800 organizations, representing all sectors of the computer and communications industries, as well as government agencies, research organizations, and end users. The Forum's charter is to speed the development and deployment of ATM products and services. Activities include the development and recommendation of interoperability specifications and the promotion of industry cooperation and awareness. You can call the ATM Forum at:

415-949-6700

send them an email at:

infoatmforum.com

or visit their website at:

http://www.atmforum.com

To order copies of the organization's proposed specifications, call their Fax on Demand Service at:

415-688-4318

Fibre Channel: The Fibre Channel Association

The American National Standards Institute (ANSI) ANSI X3T9.3 started work on the Fibre Channel standard in 1988. At that time, the main support for the protocol came from its supporting group, the Fibre Channel System Initiative (FCSI), headed by IBM, HP, and Sun Microsystems. The mission of the FCSI was to develop a high-speed open connection standard for Fibre Channel workstations and peripherals. This mission was accomplished early on. During its existence, the FCSI was a major influence in the design of the protocol, developing profiles and specifications that offered interoperability between existing architectures and Fibre Channel.

Since its ratification by ANSI in the early 90s, the Fibre Channel standard has been through many enhancements. For example, in 1991 the standard was modified to include support for copper and multidrop configurations. The most changes came in 1995, when the FCSI and the Fibre Channel Association announced that the ANSI

X3T11 committee overseeing the technology had adopted 2-Gbps and 4-Gbps data rates, a 400 percent increase over the previous 1-Gbps ceiling. The higher speeds are possible using Vertical Cavity Surface Emitting Laser technology. Shortly thereafter, the FCSI pronounced its job complete, and passed its mantel as the standard bearer for Fibre Channel to the Fibre Channel Association (Austin, Texas), which has more than 85 member companies. The Fibre Channel Association will pick up where FCSI left off. For information, contact the Fibre Channel Association, a 100-member consortium of Fibre Channel vendors, in Austin, Texas, at:

(tel.) 800-272-4618
(e-mail) FCA-info@amcc.com

Frame Relay: The Frame Relay Forum

The Frame Relay Forum is an association of Frame Relay users, vendors, and service providers based in Mountain View, California (415-962-2579). The organization is made up of committees that create implementation specifications and agreements for the purpose of developing Frame Relay standards. You can write the Frame Relay Forum at:

303 Vintage Park Drive
Foster City, CA 94404-1138

You can also visit them via the Internet at:

http://cell-relay.indiana.edu

isoEthernet: The isochronous network communication Alliance (incAlliance)

A group of LAN, telecommunications, and compression-product manufacturers has joined together to form the *isochronous network communication Alliance*, or *incAlliance*. As stated in the press release announcing the formation of the group, its five main purposes are

- To demonstrate high-quality, real-time, interactive multimedia and computer-telephony integration products and services, and promote them as key business tools

- To educate the industry on the differences and requirements between voice, video, and data communications for LAN/WAN implementations and how these services can be integrated and synchronized

- To foster industry growth through joint applications development and interoperability testing that ensure robust, yet affordable, total system solutions

- To inform customers of the availability of new isochronous networking technologies such as isochronous Ethernet (isoEthernet) as key enables for delivering interactive communications solutions in the networked enterprise to the desktop

- To provide a vision and roadmap for upgrading networks without causing forklift upgrades and through adherence to and support of open LAN and WAN industry standards

The incAlliance can be contacted at:

2640 Del Mar Heights Road, Suite 134
Del Mar, CA 92014
(tel.) 619-792-7964
(fax) 619-792-7967

Integrated Services Digital Network (ISDN)

Almost a quasi-standards body, the North American ISDN Users' Forum (NIUF) actively proposes standards and works diligently for their adoption. You can visit their Web site at:

http://www.ocn.com/ocn/niuf/niuf_top.html

Switched Multimegabit Data Service (SMDS)

The SMDS Interest Group (SIG) is the biggest promoter of Switched Multimegabit Data Service. It is an association of SMDS product vendors, service providers, carriers, and end users. The SIG has not only user groups, but also working groups that promote SMDS and work on specifications. The *technical working group* works on improvements to the IEEE 802.6 standard, while the *intercarrier working group* suggests enhancements to the standards that dictate the interconnection and management of intercarrier SMDS. They also sponsor a user group and, of course, have a public relations group that organizes seminars and disseminates information about SMDS available.

For additional information contact SIG at:

SMDS Interest Group Incorporated
303 Vintage Park Drive
Foster City, CA 94404-1138
(tel.) 415-578-6979
(fax) 415-525-0182
http://www.sbexpos.com *and* http://www.cerf.net/smds.html

APPENDIX D

Bibliography

Technical knowledge obviously comes from many places. Mine has come from a variety of sources: testing and working with products, talking to analysts, debating with vendors, pouring through standards documents, and reading everything I can on the subject of high-speed protocols. Although there is no substitute for the knowledge I've gained from my experience working with these technologies and the people who develop and work with them, reading has been an invaluable source of reference material and ideas. The following is a selective bibliography of the works that I have found especially helpful.

Black, Uyless, *ATM: Foundation for Broadband Networks*, Prentice Hall PTR, Englewood Cliffs, NJ, 1995.

Black, Uyless, *Data Link Protocols*, Prentice Hall PTR, Englewood Cliffs, NJ, 1993.

Bryce, James Y., *Using ISDN*, Que Corporation, Indianapolis, IN, 1995.

Handel, R., and Huber, M. N., *Integrated Broadband Networks: An Introduction to ATM-Based Networks*, Addison-Wesley Publishing Company, Reading, MA, 1991.

Held, Gilbert, *Ethernet Networks*, John Wiley & Sons, Inc., New York, NY, 1994.

Hopkins, Gerald L., *The ISDN Literacy Book*, Addison-Wesley Publishing Company, Reading, MA, 1995.

Miller, Mark A., *Managing Internetworks with SNMP*, M&T Books, a subsidiary of Henry Holt and Company, Inc., New York, NY, 1993.

Motorola University Press, *The Basics Book of ISDN*, 2nd edition, Addison-Wesley Publishing Company, Reading, MA, 1992.

Shah, Amit, and Ramakrishnan, G., *FDDI: A High Speed Network*, Prentice Hall PTR, Englewood Cliffs, NJ, 1994.

Sheldon, Tom, *LAN Times Encyclopedia of Networking*, Osborne/McGraw-Hill, Berkeley, CA, 1994.

Sheldon, Tom, *LAN Times Guide to Interoperability*, Osborne/McGraw-Hill, Berkeley, CA, 1994.

Smith, Philip, *Frame Relay: Principles and Applications*, Addison-Wesley Publishing Company, Reading, MA, 1993.

Index

K

L

LAN TIMES Free Subscription Form

○ **Yes,** I want to receive (continue to receive) LAN TIMES free of charge. ○ No.

I am ○ a new subscriber ○ renewing my subscription ○ changing my address

Signature required _____ Date _____

Name_____

Title _____ Telephone _____

Company _____

Address _____

City _____

State/County _____ Zip/Postal Code _____

Free in the United States to qualified subscribers only

International Prices (Airmail Delivery)

Canada: $65 Elsewhere: $150

○ Payment enclosed ○ Bill me later

Charge my: ○ Visa ○ Mastercard ○ Amer. Exp

Card number _____

Exp. Date _____

All questions must be completed to qualify for a subscription to LAN TIMES. Publisher reserves the right to serve only those individuals who meet publication criteria.

1. Which of the following best describe your organization?
(Check only one)
- ○ A. Agriculture/Mining/Construction/Oil/Petrochemical/Environmental
- ○ B. Manufacturer (non-computer)
- ○ C. Government/Military/Public Adm.
- ○ D. Education
- ○ E. Research/Development
- ○ F. Engineering/Architecture
- ○ G. Finance/Banking/Accounting/Insurance/Real Estate
- ○ H. Health/Medical/Legal
- ○ I. VAR/VAD Systems House
- ○ J. Manufacturer Computer Hardware/Software
- ○ K. Aerospace
- ○ L. Retailer/Distributor/Wholesaler (non-computer)
- ○ M. Computer Retailer/Distributor/Sales
- ○ N. Transportation
- ○ O. Media/Marketing/Advertising/Publishing/Broadcasting
- ○ P. Utilities/Telecommunications/VAN
- ○ Q. Entertainment/Recreation/Hospitality/Non-profit/Trade Association
- ○ R. Consultant
- ○ S. Systems Integrator
- ○ T. Computer/LAN Leasing/Training
- ○ U. Information/Data Services
- ○ V. Computer/Communications Services: Outsourcing/3rd Party
- ○ W. All Other Business Services
- ○ X. Other _____

- ○ K. Office Automation
- ○ L. Manufacturing/Operations/Production
- ○ M. Personnel
- ○ N. Technology Assessment
- ○ O. Other

4. How many employees work in your entire ORGANIZATION?
(Check only one)
- ○ A. Under 25
- ○ B. 25-100
- ○ C. 101-500
- ○ D. 501-1,000
- ○ E. 1,001-5,000
- ○ F. 5,001-9,999
- ○ G. 10,000 and over

2. Which best describes your title? (Check only one)
- ○ A. Network/LAN Manager
- ○ B. MIS/DP/IS Manager
- ○ C. Owner/President/CEO/Partner
- ○ D. Data Communications Manager
- ○ E. Engineer/CNE/Technician
- ○ F. Consultant/Analyst
- ○ G. Micro Manager/Specialist/Coordinator
- ○ H. Vice President
- ○ I. All other Dept. Heads, Directors and Managers
- ○ J. Educator
- ○ K. Programmer/Systems Analyst
- ○ L. Professional
- ○ M. Other _____

3. Which of the following best describes your job function?
(Check only one)
- ○ A. Network/LAN Management
- ○ B. MIS/DP/IS Management
- ○ C. Systems Engineering/Integration
- ○ D. Administration/Management
- ○ E. Technical Services
- ○ F. Consulting
- ○ G. Research/Development
- ○ H. Sales/Marketing
- ○ I. Accounting/Finance
- ○ J. Education/Training

5. Which of the following are you or your clients currently using, or planning to purchase in the next 12 months? (1–Own; 2–Plan to purchase in next 12 months) (Check all that apply)

Topologies	1	2
A. Ethernet	○	○
B. Token Ring	○	○
C. Arcnet	○	○
D. LocalTalk	○	○
E. FDDI	○	○
F. Starlan	○	○
G. Other	○	○

Network Operating System	1	2
A. Novell Netware	○	○
B. Novell Netware Lite	○	○
C. Banyan VINES	○	○
D. Digital Pathworks	○	○
E. IBM LAN Server	○	○
F. Microsoft LAN Manager	○	○
G. Microsoft Windows for Workgroups	○	○
H. Artisoft LANtastic	○	○
I. Sitka TOPS	○	○
J. 10NET	○	○
K. AppleTalk	○	○

Client/Workstation Operating Sys.	1	2
A. DOS	○	○
B. DR-DOS	○	○
C. Windows	○	○
D. Windows NT	○	○
E. UNIX	○	○
F. UnixWare	○	○
G. OS/2	○	○
H. Mac System 6	○	○
I. Mac System 7	○	○

Protocols/Standards	1	2
A. IPX	○	○
B. TCP/IP	○	○
C. X.25	○	○
D. XNS	○	○
E. OSI	○	○
F. SAA/SNA	○	○
G. NFS	○	○
H. MHS	○	○

6. Is your Organization/Clients network... (Check all that apply)
- ○ A. International
- ○ B. National
- ○ C. Regional
- ○ D. Metropolitan
- ○ E. Local
- ○ F. Other _____

7. What hardware does your department/client base own/plan to purchase. (Check all that apply)

	Owns	Plan to purchase in next 12 months
A. Bridges	○	○
B. Diskless Workstations	○	○
C. Cabling System	○	○
D. Printers	○	○
E. Disk Drive	○	○
F. Optical Storage	○	○
G. Tape Backup System	○	○
H. Optical Storage	○	○
I. Application Servers	○	○
J. Communication Servers	○	○
K. Fax Servers	○	○
L. Mainframe	○	○
M. Network Adapter Cards	○	○
N. Wireless Adapters/Bridges	○	○
O. Power Conditioners/UPSs	○	○
P. Hubs/Concentrators	○	○
Q. Minicomputers	○	○
R. Modems	○	○
S. 386-based computers	○	○
T. 486-based computers	○	○
U. Pentium-based computers	○	○
V. Macintosh computers	○	○
W. RISC-based workstations	○	○
X. Routers	○	○
Y. Multimedia Cards	○	○
Z. Network Test/Diagnostic Equipment	○	○
1. Notebooks/Laptops	○	○
2. DSU/CSU	○	○
99. None of the Above	○	○

8. What network software/applications do you/your clients own/plan to purchase in the next 12 months? (Check all that apply)
- ○ A. Network Management
- ○ B. Software Metering
- ○ C. Network Inventory
- ○ D. Virus Protection
- ○ E. Menuing
- ○ F. E-mail
- ○ G. Word Processing
- ○ H. Spreadsheet
- ○ I. Database
- ○ J. Accounting
- ○ K. Document Management
- ○ L. Graphics
- ○ M. Communications
- ○ N. Application Development Tools
- ○ O. Desktop Publishing
- ○ P. Integrated Business Applications
- ○ Q. Multimedia
- ○ R. Document Imaging
- ○ S. Groupware
- ○ Z. None of the above

9. What is the annual revenue of your entire organization or budget if non-profit (Check only one)
- ○ A. Under $10 million
- ○ B. $10-$50 million
- ○ C. $50-$100 million
- ○ D. $100-$500 million
- ○ E. $500 million-$1 billion
- ○ F. Over $1 billion

10. How much does your organization (if reseller, your largest client's company) plan to spend on computer products in the next 12 months? (Check only one)
- ○ A. Under $25,000
- ○ B. $25,000-$99,999
- ○ C. $100,000-$499,999
- ○ D. $500,000-$999,999
- ○ E. $1 billion

11. Where do you purchase computer products? (Check all that apply)
- ○ A. Manufacturer
- ○ B. Distributor
- ○ C. Reseller
- ○ D. VAR
- ○ E. System Integrator
- ○ F. Consultant
- ○ G. Other _____

12. In which ways are you involved in acquiring computer products and services? (Check all that apply)
- ○ A. Determine the need
- ○ B. Define product specifications/features
- ○ C. Select brand
- ○ D. Evaluate the supplier
- ○ E. Select vendor/source
- ○ F. Approve the acquisition
- ○ G. None of the above

ICS1639

---

fold here

Place
Stamp
Here

LAN TIMES

McGraw–Hill, INC.

P.O. Box 652

Hightstown NJ 08520-0652